hotels • lodges • restaurants • shops • spas

For regular updates on our special offers, register at

hotels • lodges • restaurants • shops • spas

ecochic

text pascal languillon • foo mei zee • kate o'brien

thechiccollection

about this book

Welcome to the long-awaited *Eco Chic*. Just a decade ago, most of the hotels and establishments featured in this book did not exist. Eco consciousness was seen as the latest eccentric fad to sweep the world, and 'recycling' was seen as an unappealing way of rehashing old knick knacks.

How times have changed. Eco awareness today has pervaded our collective consciousness to the extent that our attitudes and world views have undergone a paradigm shift. Green objectives are on every agenda, from individual and household levels to government and international arenas. No longer do we buy even the smallest item from a supermarket without considering the need for a carrier bag. Many enlightened countries today give environmental concerns the same importance as economic ones.

Eco Chic is a statement of how far we have come. Eco awareness is no longer a fringe consideration—it is a part of our modern lifestyle. Gone are the days when going green was synonymous with rusticity. Top designers and style mavens are bringing eco consciousness to the forefront of fashion, luxurious eco hotels and ecologically sustainable tours are flourishing, while an increasing number of shops are carrying products that cater to consumers who want to maintain high standards of living without compromising the planet.

This book will be a useful reference for both neophytes and fervent advocates of the green revolution. Providing extensive coverage of earth-friendly shops, brands, restaurants, hotels and other establishments, *Eco Chic* proves that it's possible to live in style and be mindful of your ecological footprint at the same time. To demonstrate that point, this book has been printed on paper certified by the Forestry Stewardship Council (FSC), an independent, non-governmental, and not-for-profit organisation which promotes responsible management of the world's forests.

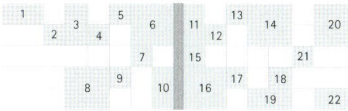

COVER CAPTIONS:

1, 3 AND PAGE 2: *Southern Ocean Lodge, the epitome of eco-consciousness in the luxury travel industry.*
2: *Day-trips come with sumptuous picnics at Six Senses Hideaway Zighy Bay.*
4: *Palm trees are incorporated into haute couture.*
5 AND 8: *Nature features heavily at Six Senses Hideaway Yao Noi, inside and out.*
6: *Pool villas at Six Senses Hideaway Ninh Van Bay.*
7: *Boris Bally's chairs are made from recycled signs.*
9: *Organic soaps made by Bird Textiles.*
10: *Dining al fresco in an African eco-lodge.*
11: *The magnificent aurora borealis.*
12: *Hedgehog foot brushes are found throughout Six Senses resorts.*
13: *Baobab trees are known for their moisturising and anti-aging properties.*
14: *Overwater suites at Anantara Dhigu Resort + Spa, Maldives bring guests close to nature.*
15: *Jimbaran Puri Bali suites feature local accents.*
16: *Detail of the Grand Canyon.*
17: *Tea is brewed traditionally at Vila Naiá.*
18: *Have an indulgent soak at Banyan Tree Ringha.*
19: *Offset your carbon footprint by investing in renewable energy sites.*
20: *Design-savvy Hi Hotel combines cutting-edge style with green technology.*
21: *Embark on a blissful spa journey in the Maldives.*
22: *A bathtub has been refashioned into a sofa.*
OPPOSITE: *The iconic mud huts of Earth Spa.*
THIS PAGE: *Indulge in gourmet eco-cuisine.*
PAGE 8 AND 9: *Ice boulders remain after a flood caused by melting snow caps.*

managing editor
francis dorai

executive editor
melisa teo

editors
li yuemin • suzanne wong

designer
chan hui yee

production manager
sin kam cheong

sales and marketing director
antoine monod

sales and marketing manager
rohana ariffin

sales and marketing consultants
**alejandra crespo barnetche •
françoise kuijper • isabelle du plessix •
james mcleod • pascal languillon**

first published 2009 by
editions didier millet pte ltd
121 telok ayer street, #03-01
singapore 068590
telephone : +65.6324 9260
facsimile : +65.6324 9261
enquiries : edm@edmbooks.com.sg
website   : www.edmbooks.com

©2009 editions didier millet pte ltd

Printed by Tien Wah Press (Pte) Ltd, Singapore

All rights reserved. No part of this publication may be reproduced, stored in a retrieval system, or transmitted in any form or by any means, electronic, electrostatic, magnetic tape, mechanical, photocopying, recording or otherwise, without prior written permission from the publisher.

isbn: 978-981-4217-53-8

FSC
Mixed Sources
Product group from well-managed forests and other controlled sources
Cert no. DNV-COC-000025
www.fsc.org
© 1996 Forest Stewardship Council

contents

map 10 • introduction 12 • green living 20 • green is the new black 24 • eco beauty: more than skin deep 28 • eating green: living on the veg 32 • on the go 36 • eco travel 40 • more than a lifestyle 42

europe 46

map of europe 48 • introduction 49 • europe: restaurants 54 • europe: shopping 62

Swinton Park 66 • L'Auberge Basque 68 • Hôtel Les Orangeries 70 • Le Domaine de Saint-Géry 72 • Hôtel Le Morgane 74 • Hi Hotel 76 • Domaine de Murtoli 78

africa+themiddleeast 80

map of africa + the middle east 82 • introduction 83 • africa + the middle east: restaurants 88 •

Kasbah Du Toubkal 90 • Origins Dar Itrane 92 • La Sultana Oualidia 94 • Borana Lodge 96 • Campi ya Kanzi 98 • Tsara Komba Lodge 100 • Lazuli Lodge 102 • Six Senses Hideaway Zighy Bay 104

106 asia+thepacific

map of asia + the pacific 108 • introduction 109 •
asia + the pacific: shopping 114 • asia + the pacific: spas 118

Anantara Dhigu Resort + Spa, Maldives 124 • Soneva Fushi by Six Senses 126 • Soneva Gili by Six Senses 128 •
The Dune Eco Beach Hotel 130 • Banyan Tree Ringha 132 • Evason Ana Mandara + Six Senses Spa—Nha Trang 134 •
Six Senses Hideaway Ninh Van Bay 136 • Hotel Majestic Saigon 138 • Four Seasons Tented Camp Golden Triangle 140 •
Evason Hua Hin + Six Senses Spa 142 • Six Senses Hideaway Hua Hin 144 • Six Senses Hideaway Samui—A Sala Property 146 •
Anantara Phuket Resort + Spa 148 • Evason Phuket + Six Senses Spa 150 • Six Senses Destination Spa Phuket 152 •
Six Senses Hideaway Yao Noi 154 • El Nido Resorts 156 • Jimbaran Puri Bali 158 • Ubud Hanging Gardens 160 • Nukubati Island 162 •
Bamurru Plains 164 • Paperbark Camp 166 • Southern Ocean Lodge 168 • Treetops Lodge + Wilderness Experience 170

172 theamericas

map of the americas 174 • introduction 175 •
the americas: restaurants 180 • the americas: shopping 186

Clayoquot Wilderness Resort 190 • Trout Point lodge 192 • Hotelito Desconocido 194 • Azúcar 196 •
Hotel Eco Paraiso Xixim 198 • Laguna Lodge Eco-Resort + Nature Reserve 200 • Maca Bana 202 • Hamadryade Lodge 204 •
Pousada Vila Kalango 206 • Pousada Rancho Do Peixe 208 • Cristalino Jungle Lodge 210 • Vila Naiá 212

index 214 • picture credits 217 • directory 218

introduction

tourism + heritage

All too many seasoned travellers have experienced the disappointment of returning to one of their favourite beaches only to find it completely ruined by large development projects: big roads, large hotels and department stores have replaced dirt tracks, small boutique properties and traditional stores. Unfortunately, tourist development can have a substantial negative impact on the paradises of this world—many have been literally loved to death.

Over 900 million people travelled internationally in 2007. By 2020 this number is expected to reach 1.6 billion. As one of the world's largest industries, tourism can have dire consequences for destinations, triggering the destruction of habitats, the extinction of species and the loss of traditional cultures. Tourism need not be so destructive. When done right, it can be a powerful tool to not only conserve natural and cultural heritage, but to also alleviate poverty and construct sustainable communities.

Numerous landscapes have been designated as World Heritage sites, and are therefore protected and promoted by UNESCO. As a result, local populations have come to realise the multi-faceted benefits of preserving the surrounding environment. Costa Rica has been at the forefront of this concerted worldwide effort, safeguarding rainforests with the help of eco tourism dollars and reaping long-term economic benefits instead of exploiting their forests for timber and agriculture and short-term gains. This approach is being applied around the world. In Kenya, for instance, elephants are being protected from poachers, and game reserves generate large tourist revenue streams each year. Artisans near Venice, Italy are reviving traditional lacework and glassmaking, protecting a cultural heritage that would otherwise gradually fade from existence. Many other such examples abound—people everywhere are awakening to the importance of preserving vulnerable environments.

A healthy social and natural environment is the first and most important resource of the tourism industry. It makes business sense for tourism stakeholders to tread lightly on the planet, and as a result, many hotels no longer contend with simple measures such as giving guests the option of not having their sheets and towels changed daily. Today, enlightened hoteliers understand that many travellers are more interested in having an enriching travel experience than merely staying at a posh resort.

ecochic: the new luxury

Eco-chic luxury, where travellers enjoy small-scale properties located in unspoiled environments and experience the finest architecture and service indigenous and local communities have to offer, is here. Green city hotels, safari camps and eco lodges are booming all around the world,

THIS PAGE: *The travel industry is expanding, and with it comes the increasingly pressing need for eco-conscious travel. Lazuli Lodge for instance, is built entirely from natural materials.*

OPPOSITE: *The magnificence of these elephants on the plains is a sight that may be enjoyed for a long time if responsible tourism measures take hold.*

introduction 13

offering a holistic experience for travellers in search of relaxation, fulfilment, discovery, adventure and, most of all, a deep connection with the planet and its people. Eco-chic travellers value authenticity and privacy, and understand that smaller groups make cultures more accessible. They want to minimise their impact while maximising the benefits of their visits to local people and the environment—and they want to have the time of their lives while doing it.

Today, being a green traveller is not just limited to taking environmentally conscious holidays. It can involve luxurious rooms, indulgent spas, and exquisite food. All the eco-chic properties profiled in this book understand this. They offer the highest standards to ensure a luxurious travel experience and also take into consideration the three bottom-lines of sustainability. Firstly, eco-chic establishments need not only be financially viable businesses, they also must provide financial benefits for the local community. Secondly, they respect and highlight the culture and traditions of the local community. Thirdly, they minimise negative environmental impacts and, where possible, make positive contributions to the conservation of local biodiversity and natural heritage.

green hotels + eco resorts

There are as many ways to be a green hotel as there are leaves on a tree, and a responsible tourism policy always needs to be tailored to its particular local environment. Energy, waste and water-saving measures, fauna and flora conservation programmes and involvement of the local population are the basics, which all the properties profiled in this book meet.

Reduce, reuse and recycle is the new mantra. Some properties even have recycling bins in their rooms. They also limit the use of water with low-flow showerheads that don't impact comfort but save large quantities of this precious resource. Solar panels and wind generators are now economically viable—they enable hotels to limit their dependence on fossil fuels and are widely used by eco-chic properties, especially in tropical countries. Natural ventilation is more hip than air-conditioning, and new systems of ionised or natural swimming pools mean fewer chemicals in the water—which is also better for your skin. Some properties go even further. Six Senses Resorts & Spas has announced that Soneva Fushi in the Maldives will become totally carbon neutral by 2010. It recently installed a biodiesel plant to convert used cooking oil from the resort into fuel that can power the resort's two generators.

green authenticity

When being green is in and every multinational wants to jump on the bandwagon, how can you tell the difference between greenwashing—talking green but not delivering—and authentically green hotels? Here are some questions you can ask your hotel before you book your stay to make sure they are truly concerned about the environment and their host community.

'Do you have an environmental and social responsibility policy?' If not, question their commitment to being green. 'How are you protecting the environment?' Green hotels will always be proud to tell you about their solar panels or their contribution to a local environmental fund. 'Do you hire local workers and provide training?' If so, such measures will have a positive economic impact on their host community.

'What percentage of your revenue is redirected to the local community?' Responsible hotels give back more to the local community than they take away, through donations to schools, clinics, and other areas of life. 'Are you certified by a sustainable tourism organisation?' Accreditation schemes like Green Globe or the European Ecolabel ensure the hotel meets a minimum standard of green practices.

The United Nations recently teamed up with several leading Non Governmental Organisations (NGOs), including the Rainforest Alliance, to create a common understanding of what sustainable tourism really means—and the best practices for achieving it. They developed a comprehensive set of standardised global criteria to evaluate sustainable hotels and tour operators, and launched this under the name, The Global Baseline for Sustainable Tourism Criteria, in October 2008. This programme aims to enable consumers, the travel industry, the media, and even governments to recognise and support sustainable tourism (see www.sustainabletourismcriteria.org)

THIS PAGE: *Reducing water usage through the installation of low-flow showerheads is one way that hotels such as Anantara Phuket Resort + Spa can give back to the earth*

OPPOSITE: *Getting in touch with nature at Four Seasons Tented Camp Golden Triangle in Chiang Rai, Thailand.*

THIS PAGE: *Flying can greatly increase your carbon footprint.*

OPPOSITE: *Metropolises such as Paris have turned to alternative methods to ease traffic congestion and pollution.*

flying and global warming

The sky has never been so busy. More and more commercial flights link all the different parts of the world, and low-cost airlines have made an impressive entrance into the market. This is fantastic on one hand, as this opens new economic opportunities for many people, but it is also a threat, as commercial aircraft account for 3.5 percent of the total human impact on climate change—and air travel is expected to double in 15 years.

Global warming is caused by the build-up of greenhouse gases in the atmosphere, among them Carbon Dioxide (CO_2), which are by-products of all kind of human activities. Planes are among the worst offenders, as they release these gases at high altitudes into the atmosphere. Two people taking a return flight between Europe and Asia will contribute as much to climate change as an average European household's gas and electricity consumption over a year.

Melting glaciers, coral bleaching, and rising sea levels are all matters of concern for the tourism industry and travellers alike. Low-lying destinations like the Maldives are already forced to build protective dikes to prevent the tiny islands from being washed away. Ski resorts are relying more and more on summer activities as diminishing snow cover threatens winter operations. These threats have convinced the travel industry that something needs to be done to try to mitigate the impacts of climate change. Airlines and other transport companies are now embracing environmentally responsible practices, including what is called 'carbon-offsetting'.

The basic idea behind carbon-offsetting is that it is possible to release CO_2 into the atmosphere and still be carbon-neutral, so long as it is offset by a reduction of CO_2 emissions elsewhere. This is achieved by supporting programmes such as renewable energy, energy efficiency and reforestation projects. Nature Air is a domestic airline in Costa Rica which has pledged to become the first carbon-neutral airline—it offsets all of its emissions by protecting vast reserves of rainforest.

Another interesting initiative is the Leading Hotels of the World Green carbon offset scheme paid for by the brand on behalf of its guests, and operated in conjunction with the non-profit Sustainable Travel International (STI). Leading Hotels of the World pays USD$0.50 to STI for every night's stay booked on www.lhwgreen.com. Other hotel groups are taking this issue very seriously—Six Senses wants all of its resorts to become carbon-neutral by 2010.

This works for the traveller, too. You can visit websites such as www.climatecare.org, www.nativeenergy.com or www.futureforests.com to calculate the amount of greenhouse gas emissions your trip creates, and offset them by giving a small amount of money—it would cost you about USD$30, for example, to offset your New York-to-London round trip. Carbon offsets are only part of the solution to fight global warming. Another solution is to take it slow—travel

16 ecochic

as much as possible by bike, by foot, and by train. Trains do not emit as much CO_2 and enables travellers to actually see the countries they are passing through. Check the excellent website resource www.seat61.com for comfortable train trips all around the world.

before you travel

Do as much research as possible about your destination in order to understand something about the place you are going to. For instance, consider if the local conditions will suit you. There is nothing worse, for you and your hosts, than to go on the wrong trip.

Try to minimise your carbon emissions: could you take a train rather than fly? If you have to fly, try to minimise stopovers, as the worst carbon emissions are emitted during take off and landing, and look at offsetting your carbon emissions to have a carbon-neutral journey. Remove all excess packaging from your suitcase—waste disposal is difficult in remote places and in developing countries.

While on holiday, respect and understand the culture of your hosts: the concepts of personal space, time, and socially acceptable behaviour might be very different from home—strive to embrace these differences. Learn as much of the local language as you can, as your hosts will appreciate your effort. Dress appropriately, especially in conservative cultures, and be especially careful when you are in sacred places. Remember that travelling with respect earns you respect.

Buy local produce in preference to imported goods, as this means your money goes directly to the community. Have fun with bargaining but keep things in perspective. One dollar does not mean the same thing to you as it does to the seller. Do not buy souvenirs made from wild animal products. Be aware of suggested distances and other recommendations for observing wildlife.

When you return home, write to your tour operator or hotel with any comments or feedback about your holiday, and include suggestions on reducing the environmental impact of tourism and increasing benefits to local communities. If you have promised to send pictures or gifts to local people, remember to do so.

THIS PAGE: *The philosophy of 'Leave only footprints, take only memories' encapsulates the essence of eco travel.*

OPPOSITE: *Staying at any of the Six Senses hotels allows you to relax in the knowledge that your holiday is making minimal impact on the environment.*

glossary of terms + resources

- **Carbon offsetting:** A carbon offset is a process to offset carbon emissions from one activity with a corresponding reduction in carbon emissions somewhere else.
- **Carbon footprint:** A measure in carbon dioxide (CO_2) of the impact of activities on levels of greenhouse gases. It calculates the amount of greenhouse gases produced in our day-to-day lives or activities through burning fossil fuels for electricity, heating, transportation, and so on.
- **Sustainable tourism = responsible tourism:** Travel that has a minimal impact on the environment benefits the local community and supports conservation.
- **Fair trade:** A worldwide marketplace standard that provides an opportunity for suppliers and consumers to trade goods and services based on social and environmental standards that reflect sustainable practices. It focuses, in particular, on exports from developing countries to developed countries, notably handicrafts, coffee and sugar.
- **Eco lodge:** A small hotel that is well-integrated into its environment and provides direct benefits for the conservation of local biodiversity. It also provides tangible financial benefits and contributes to the empowerment of the local community.
- **Tourism for tomorrow awards (www.tourismfortomorrow.com):** These are international awards that recognise excellence in responsible tourism development. Six Senses Resorts & Spas won the Global Tourism Business Award in 2008.
- **The international ecotourism society (www.ecotourism.org):** This is the largest and oldest organisation dedicated to generating and disseminating information on eco tourism.
- **Green globe 21 (www.greenglobe21.com):** This is the largest worldwide certification scheme for responsible tourism operators and communities
- **responsibletravel.com:** A web travel agency based in the United Kingdom that specialises in trips that tread lightly on earth.
- **Responsible tourism awards (www.responsibletourismawards.com):** These awards have the widest worldwide consultation as winners are nominated by tourists.
- **Sustainable tourism criteria (www.sustainabletourismcriteria.org):** The new internationally recognised standard criteria for sustainable tourism, which are organised around four main themes: sustainability planning; social and economic benefits for the local community; enhancing cultural heritage; and reducing negative impacts on the environment.
- **Sustainable Travel International:** This is a non-profit organisation specialising in the promotion of responsible practices within the travel industry. It also provides a carbon offset programme.
- **Sustainable development:** Meeting the needs of the present without compromising the ability of future generations to meet their own needs.

...people everywhere are awakening to the importance of preserving vulnerable environments...

green living

To be conscionably green does not just involve wearing natural fibres, eating organic, buying fair trade goods and cycling to work. It should involve your home too—especially when constructing, maintaining and living in homes account for some 30 percent of a developed nation's carbon dioxide emissions. Experts at organisations such as the **Town and Country Planning Association** (www.tcpa.org.uk) in the UK say sustainable homes should be built with materials selected from natural, renewable or recycled sources; have energy-efficient designs; include water-saving appliances and water-recycling systems; accommodate recycling bins; and, by their location and design, reduce car dependency.

That said, how does one go about looking for an eco home? Especially if you are not much of an eco pioneer and don't really want to sort out the solar panels and energy insulation by yourself.

Unfortunately, if you look in the classified advertisements for homes to purchase, you will not see a list of eco homes for sale, yet. But while there are no eco estate agents, there are some property sites that specialise in listing eco homes for sale. Green consultant Julian Brooks set up **www.greenmoves.com** which lists about a hundred properties around the UK. There is also **www.whatgreenhome.com** that was established by journalist Gordon Miller. It lists eco developments around the world with a very easy-to-use tick system for grading the eco credentials of the developments, including carbon efficiency, materials and water usage.

The fact that such websites exist, even if the range of homes is still quite limited, shows that the market is taking the first tentative steps forward in pioneering the eco home to the wider mass market. For the rest of us who would like to start transforming our current energy-guzzling home into a zero-carbon triumph, these are a few baby steps we can take.

from the ground up

While eco homes might not be readily available on the market yet, there are a slew of green architects who will soon set that right. Helping people make the transition to a new eco-friendly world, these architects are eschewing energy-guzzling, carbon-spewing homes and offices for modern structures that run on very little energy, are made from natural materials, and are at the same time extremely stylish.

Traci Rose Rider is one of the founders of **Emerging Green Builders** (www.egbny.com), a coalition of professionals and students who promote green living, with members in 45 cities throughout the US. Rider (www.traciroserider.com) designs spaces not just to be inhabited, but to positively influence the well-being of its users and the surrounding environment as well.

KieranTimberlake is an American architectural firm dedicated to pushing the boundaries of sustainable design (www.kierantimberlake.com). Its innovative concepts go beyond having eco-friendly features added on—instead, these features are inseparable from the buildings themselves.

One example is Loblolly House on Chesapeake Bay in the US. Constructed off-site and assembled in less than six weeks, the 204-sq-m (2,200-sq-ft) pre-fab structure exists in harmony with the forest, to the point of having its foundations laid on timber piles. Viewed from the east, its uneven rain screen siding acts as camouflage amid the loblolly pines. Natural daylight, ventilation and glazing also minimise its impact on the environment.

William McDonough of William McDonough & Partners, Architecture and Design (www.mcdonough.com), designs environmentally friendly

THIS PAGE (FROM TOP): *Conserve water the fuss-free way by installing rain harvesters at home; Soaring ceilings and an open concept reduces the need for energy-guzzling air-conditioning in countries with a warmer climate.*

OPPOSITE: *The best examples of eco architecture maintain a close affinity with natural elements inside and out, such as the Loblolly House.*

greenliving 21

green living

THIS PAGE (FROM TOP): *Nani Marquina's rugs will spruce up any living space; an old bathtub becomes a stylish conversation piece with some judicious upholstering.*
OPPOSITE: *Solar power and natural ventilation are some green features that are increasingly integrated into modern homes.*

offices, factories and corporate campuses for Nike, Gap and IBM. Currently, he is planning an ambitious series of green communities in China, the UK and the US.

Architects **Alex Michaelis** and **Tim Boyd** (www.michaelisboyd.com) create structures that can heat themselves—a particularly useful advantage in damp and chilly England, where they operate.

Down in warmer climes, **Guz Wilkinson** (www.guzarchitects.com), voted by *Wallpaper* magazine as one of the top 10 architects in the world, creates naturally cool homes in tropical Singapore. He accomplishes this with 'open' buildings that include breezy atriums and cantilevered roofs which maximise air circulation and protect against tropical downpours. In addition, Green technology is also employed in the form of photovoltics, water-recycling systems and tools that minimise energy usage.

interiors + furnishing

'Eco' has become the hippest prefix to almost any activity, However, as with anything that is embraced with such enthusiasm, will there eventually be a backlash? There is an army of eco-savvy and inventive product designers who think not. Converting old baths into comfortable armchairs and expelled grenades into funky oil lamps, these designers are considering the past as well as the future life of their materials. By reusing existing resources, they hoping to make a dent in the world's expanding waste mountain.

The eclectic rugs at **Nani Marquina** (www.nanimarquina.com) are beautifully and responsibly handmade in North India. The company itself began over two decades ago in Barcelona, with a range of designer rugs by founder Marquina. Its product line has since expanded to include pieces of all shapes and sizes alongside complementary accessories such as pillows and small furnishings. Only biodegradable materials are used, and each rug carries a 'Care & Fair' guarantee that no child labour was employed in its production.

On **www.vivavi.com** are some brilliant examples of repurposed furniture. One of them is a sofa woven together with automotive seatbelts, which not only makes for a great-looking texture, but also provides very strong and functional support. Who would have thought that bicycles could be reincarnated into a designer table or chair? One of the best websites for repurposed furniture, **www.screwhead.org**, features a range of highly original furniture created out of twisted bicycle parts. The Metra Cocktail Table is especially funky—made from handlebars and a green window from a commuter train. There is also some extraordinary art work, such as the Millenium Chandelier by **Stuart Haygarth** (www.stuarthaygarth.com), fashioned from party poppers collected from streets and dance floors.

There are also companies that specialise in eco-smart furniture made from materials that are environmentally friendly. For example, **www.el-furniture.com** has some truly elegant pieces that are 'designed with integrity', meaning they are completely biodegradable and feature non-toxic finishes and veneers.

Of course, the most eco-friendly new sofa is either a refurbished or reused one. And finding an eco sofa is easy. If you have money to spend, there are antique markets. Sofas at rock-bottom prices can be found on **eBay** (www.ebay.com) or the neighbourhood supermarket home-clearance board. There are websites that even offer free furniture, such as **www.freecycle.org**. Contrary to popular belief, going green can mean serious savings.

investing in eco technology

One of the easiest ways to keep your green conscience clean without changing your lifestyle is by installing water-conserving, energy-reducing appliances at home. A rain harvester is one of the simplest to install—the water collected can be used in washing machines and bathrooms. Installing energy-efficient lighting is another easy step. Making the switch is convenient too—these bulbs can be found in most DIY shops now.

Solar panels are the way to go: either solar photovoltaic systems, which generate electricity, or the simpler solar hot-water system that just provides hot water for home use. Visit **www.lowcarbonbuildings.org** as well as **www.altestore.com** for ideas and products.

Kitchen appliances are known to consume a lot of electricity and have long been the focus of energy efficiency campaigns. The familiar A to G labels have been successfully driving improvements in design, so that there are now plenty of A-rated models on the market. Visit **www.energystar.gov** for a list of energy-efficient appliances.

greenliving 23

green is the new black

To talk about being green and fashionable would have been a bewildering oxymoron just a few years back. Today, thankfully, it is possible to lead an ecologically conscious life without literally wearing it on your burlap sleeve. As more and more designers, companies and consumers become increasingly sophisticated and knowledgeable about environmental issues, there is a lot more on offer these days for the savvy dresser with an eco conscience. International designers and brands from **Diane von Furstenberg** to **Banana Republic** have been participating actively in the conservation of the environment by making eco-friendly dressing accessible and creative—going way beyond the green standard of organic cotton tees and jeans.

While there is an enormous range of dazzling fashion wear accessible to the stylish tree-hugger today, it is also helpful to know more about the huge impact the fashion industry has on the environment. The process is a complex one. Considerations range from the material used (whether it is synthetic or natural, organic or non-organic cotton) to how the clothing was assembled (in sweatshops or by local craftsmen), how it affects global warming through the usage of Earth's resources, the ecosystems exposed to the production chemicals, and the impact on local communities in the most far-flung countries.

What is commonly classified as 'eco fashion' most often refers to the category of clothing and accessories that have been manufactured using environmentally friendly processes, with a minimum use of chemicals. The term encompasses organic clothing, recycled clothing, clothing that is produced from recycled items, as well as fashion and jewellery that have been sourced through fair trade practices. Materials commonly used in eco fashion are organic cotton (which is grown without the use of chemicals), as well as hemp and linen, which is made from flax. The latter two crops are seen as being 'greener', as they are less damaging to land and soil, and do not require as many chemical fertilisers.

Taking a step beyond the issue of sustainability, the **World Fair Trade Organization** (WFTO), a global network of organisations, ensures that artists and craftspeople are paid decent wages for their work. It also sources for speciality artisanal crafts such as weaving and intricate metal- or beadwork that can command good prices in cosmopolitan cities. The association ensures that the money earned goes towards steady incomes for the craftspeople as well as resources for their communities.

look smart + do your part
When **Calvin Klein**, **Jil Sander**, **Marni** and **Yves Saint Laurent** start creating looks that are eco-friendly yet high fashion, you know it's time to change your mindset about hemp and linen. No longer are such 'clothes-with-a-conscience' limited to unflattering designs in uninspiring fabrics. They now take centre stage in international fashion fiestas such as **New York Fashion Week**, and involve designers whose boutiques line Fifth Avenue.

Sustainable couture had its first taste of the limelight in 2005 when non-profit organisation **Earth Pledge** kicked off New York Fashion Week with high fashion green creations from designers such as **Oscar de la Renta** and **Diane von Furstenberg**.

The show generated such interest that the **FutureFashion** initiative was launched, ensuring a green presence in the subsequent seasons. In its latest showing, the designers that went the eco-friendly route included **Ralph Lauren**, **Versace** and **Donna Karan**.

Other fashion-oriented events include **EcoChic**, most recently held in Shanghai at the beginning of 2009. Organised by Hong Kong-based non-profit organisation **Green2greener**, the Shanghai event was part of a touring eco fashion platform for the promotion of sustainable fashion. Previous stops were made in Jakarta and Hong Kong, with future events planned for Sydney, in line with the EcoChic aim of raising environmental awareness in the region.

Stella McCartney has always maintained a design philosophy that is in harmony with the environment. This is evident from her initial plug for cruelty-free clothing to her recently developed capsule collection of organic clothing that had a long waiting list even before it hit the stores. **Phillip Lim**, a New York-based designer whose clothes are carried in cutting-edge fashion boutiques from Barney's in New York to Club 21 in Singapore, is also launching a range of eco clothing, **Go Green Go**, that features natural materials, such as silk and natural cottons.

THIS PAGE (FROM TOP): *Phillip Lim's clean-lined, fuss-free range of eco clothing is displayed in his appropriately minimalist shops; evening gowns made from the spathe of palm trees; haute couture goes green at EarthPledge's FutureFashion show.*
OPPOSITE: *A Diane von Furstenberg creation on the catwalk.*

greenisthenewblack 25

green is the new black

THIS PAGE (FROM TOP): Ecoist produces unique bags and accessories made out of repurposed waste material; Anya Hindmarch's tote bag helped meld eco-awareness and fashion.

OPPOSITE: Edun designs eco fashion with a distinctive edge.

Putting design first seems to be the way forward for fashion brands that are going the environmentally friendly route—they hope to target the mass market, not just green hippies. Most, like **Banana Republic**, which recently initiated a green campaign in its designs and store management around the world, create eco-friendly clothes that will appeal to the average customer who puts fashion first. High street brand **Zara** has a range of baby clothing made from organic cotton that will appeal for its supreme softness and attractive designs at the outset, with the added bonus of material purity and environmental conscience.

green first, style later

In 2007, British designer **Anya Hindmarch** caused a bit of a stir with her canvas 'I'm Not A Plastic Bag' tote. In London, 80,000 people stood in line when it made its grand debut in a Sainsbury's grocery store. When Hindmarch launched her bag in a mall in Hong Kong, a stampede of eager shoppers resulted and police officers had to close down the shopping complex for the day. As further proof of the bag's huge popularity, fakes soon lined almost every street bazaar, from Portobello Road in London to Phuket's night markets.

Being green is—now more than ever—all the rage, and there are fashion creations that are being designed and sold with the primary marketing feature of being environmentally conscious. One of these products is the **Monterey** bag, co-created by accessories designer Rebecca Minkoff and actress/model

Bijou Philips. The bag can be found on popular Internet shopping site **shopbop.com**, and is made with non-toxic, metal-free dye and recycled scraps of eco-friendly leather that are leftover skins bought from meat factories. Another eco bag label is **Ecoist** (www.ecoist.com) which merges fashion, functionality and environmental awareness with its handmade clutches and totes. They are created from recycled candy wrappers, food packages and soda labels, and make funky accessories as well as conversation pieces.

There are also green inventions that are pure genius, such as the **Kemplar Voltaic Solar Backpack** (www.kemplar.com) that comes with a solar power pack to keep your MP3 player, mobile phone, PDA and laptop fully charged. Added bonuses are the handy spaces, pockets and wire channels for your multiple electronic devices. Its sturdy design is built for the grind of school and work, as well as tough weekend hikes when you still want to feel connected.

Yvon Chouinard, founder of rugged-wear apparel **Patagonia**, demonstrates that fashion can also be a compassionate business. He runs his organisation with the zeal of an eco revolutionary. His motto is 'Build the best product, cause no unnecessary harm, and use business to inspire and implement solutions to the environmental crisis'. Patagonia uses environmentally sensitive materials such as organic cotton, recycled and recyclable polyester, and hemp, and both sponsors and participates in environmental initiatives that range from promoting wildlife corridors to combating genetic engineering. And yet, by maintaining the high quality of its products, Patagonia has stayed highly profitable without losing any of its soul.

Setting a good example as the head honcho of a profit- as well as ecologically driven company, Chouinard donates 30 percent of his annual salary to activist environment groups. He has also founded **1% For The Planet** (www.onepercentfortheplanet.org), an alliance of companies now numbering more than 200,,committed to paying an 'earth tax' of at least 1 percent of annual sales to environmental groups.

Unabashedly created for the greater good is casual wear brand **Edun**, founded by Ali Hewson (her husband is U2 bombastier Bono). Hewson applies her philosophy of wholesomeness by using organic products and paying workers fair wages to create Edun's range of chemises, jeans and dresses. The eco clothing line goes a step beyond the aid and debt-relief campaigns for which Hewson's husband is known; Edun also creates jobs in developing nations and promotes environmental awareness to boot.

The clothes, which are made in Africa, India and South America according to fair trade practices, are available in the US in Saks and Barneys department stores. That they are designed by jeans designer Rogan Gregoryof boutique jeans label, **Rogan**, gives the collection some street cred too. With great, environmentally savvy creations such as these in the stores, there is no reason for your wardrobe not to catch up with the green revolution.

eco beauty: more than skin deep

Although standards of beauty vary across the world, what remains consistent wherever you are is the collective pursuit and appreciation of natural beauty in all its diversity.

Achieving and maintaining a glowing complexion naturally while holding back the hands of time is possible, as long as the skin is adequately nourished from the inside out. In addition to a fresh, seasonal diet brimming with super-nutrient essentials, a natural regime working in harmony with the skin to enhance healing and cellular regeneration is the prescription for healthy radiant skin at every age.

Now that it is medically accepted that the body absorbs significant amounts of what is used on the skin, consumers are fast becoming more aware of what they are applying on their skin and hair, giving the natural and organic sector a significant boost. This greener, cleaner and more sustainable mindset is here to stay, with a myriad of deliciously scented, all-natural, botanical ingredients packed with the best of nature's very own healing treats.

What's more, as the extraction of active properties from natural ingredients becomes increasingly refined, the results and benefits of natural products may soon match the performance of technologically advanced synthetic alternatives.

While all products need preservatives to maintain their shelf life, safety and efficacy, this is even more important with natural and organic products that are more prone to oxidation and damage from harmful bacteria and fungi.

Vitamin E and certain plant oils are widely used to preserve and safeguard natural products. Additionally, by ensuring a protective barrier is generated through effective airtight packaging, the safety and shelf life of natural products can be extended and improved.

As we strive to clean up our world, keep in mind that the packaging is as important as the product ingredients. Whether it is plastic, glass or paper, it too must be entirely sustainable and leave no footprint.

natural + organic certification

The organic label tells you how an ingredient has been grown. It does not tell you how beneficial the ingredient or product is for the body.

The main benefit of organic systems is that they work in harmony with nature by creating a healthy environment. At the same time, greater emphasis is placed on building and maintaining healthy soil, nutritious crops and animal welfare.

When it comes to defining cosmetics there are no hard and fast rules. The United States Department of Agriculture (USDA), for example, only permits its seal on products that are 95 percent or more organic and the remaining 5 percent of ingredients must come from approved natural sources. The British Soil Association allows a product to be certified if it contains up to 5 percent non-organic ingredients, but only if there is no organic alternative available. There are a number of certifiers in Australia, each with their own specific criteria for certification, while in other countries, a product needs only have a minuscule organic content to receive the organic seal of approval.

Organic skincare does not necessarily mean it is chemical-free. Every ingredient is a chemical, regardless of its origin. Water, for example, is technically a chemical and is uncertifiable. As many skincare products contain water, none of these can be labelled 100 percent organic.

When purchasing skin and body products, always check the labels. If a product claims to be natural, read what it contains and, more importantly, observe what is left out (such as synthetic preservatives, fragrances, petrochemical and other suspect chemical derivatives).

Check where the ingredients are produced, their carbon footprint and if the packaging is biodegradable or recyclable. Always look for certification (natural or organic) from a credible certifying body.

The product ranges featured here have been meticulously chosen for their integrity, transparency and respect for the earth. They contain only the purest of indigenous ingredients cultivated by skilled artisans who hail from the Himalayas, the Amazon rainforest and Morocco.

Some are organic (and certified), others contain the best of ethical, sustainable and natural ingredients, but all are free from harsh and suspect chemicals and share an ethical commitment to protect the planet and nourish the skin in the most delicious way.

The Damascan rose otto in the **Ila** (www.ila-spa.com) range comes from Pawan, a spiritual cooperative farmer in the Himalayas. Pawan is a true adherent to his cause, respecting the planet and supporting other Indian farmers in maintaining ancient farming methods. His rose oil is amongst the purest and sweetest on the planet. His fields are irrigated using solar power, and the delicate roses are shaded and protected by jasmine and marigolds instead of artificial structures. The blooms are harvested at dawn when they are at their most fragrant and are distilled on site in a process powered by biofuel.

Japan may be the most futuristic country in many ways, but when it comes to beauty, tradition reigns, and many of nature's tried and tested ingredients remain at the cutting-edge of today's skincare prescriptions.

Camellia oil has long been used by the Japanese for radiant skin and hair. The wild camellia seed oil from **Chidoriya** (www.chidoriyaworld.com) is manufactured using the traditional cold press technique in a family-operated factory in Kyushu, Japan.

'Safe enough to eat' is the tagline of Australian-based **Mukti**'s certified organic range of botanicals (www.muktibotanicals.com.au). Products are made in small batches to preserve quality and freshness, while plant-based ingredients are grown to the highest degree of purity to ensure each product is gentle on the skin and kind to the environment.

Origins (www.origins.com) may be one of the biggest names in skincare to have all its products derived from all-natural sources such as organic herbs and pure essential oils, while also harnessing environmentally friendly methods in the process.

THIS PAGE (CLOCKWISE FROM TOP): a collection of fresh flowers and plants forms the basis of Mukti's eco beauty products; Origins' line of skincare emphasises an affinity with the earth; Damascan roses are highly sought after for their divine fragrance.
OPPOSITE: It is commonly accepted that the body absorbs large amounts of what is applied on the skin.

ecobeauty:morethanskindeep 29

eco beauty: more than skin deep

THIS PAGE (FROM TOP): With David Babaii 4 Wildaid's natural products, one can acquire American actress Kate Hudson's silky tresses and help save endangered species too; from organic ingredients to recyclable packaging, every care has been taken to ensure that Nude cosmetics gives back to the earth.
OPPOSITE: The baobab has many properties that make it an ideal ingredient for beauty products.

Origins' luxurious plant resources are renewable, and the company offsets its energy footprint by purchasing wind and hydroelectric power. The stylish packaging may not look it, but it is almost entirely recycled. Going beyond its products, Origins also organises community action such as the Origins Earth Initiative, which promotes reforestation in many countries.

The range of ethically conscious **Bamford** (www.bamford.co.uk) body products offers contemporary luxury. Full of pure ingredients, they are suitable for even delicate baby skin.

The rarest of African herbs and fynbos plants such as rooibos (redbush) extract and cyclopia (honeybush)—both overflowing with protective antioxidants—Cape Chamomile and essential oil-rich mongongo nut oil can be found in the organic and sustainable **Maruwa Range** from South Africa.

'Out of the box and into your garden' is the promise of **Pangea Organics'** (www.pangeaorganics.com) award-winning packaging, which is compostable, biodegradable and plantable. Manufactured with zero waste from post-consumer newsprint, the American-based company's boxes are embedded with seeds such as sweet basil and flowering amaranth. Simply soak a box, plant it and the medicinal herbs will start to sprout.

By choosing the **David Babaii 4 Wildaid** (www.db4wildaid.com) range of natural hair care products, you are helping to preserve endangered wildlife. Created by Los Angeles hair stylist David Babaii in collaboration with actress Kate Hudson, the brand is at the forefront of Wildaid, a non-profit organisation that aims to reverse the devastation of the planet's wildlife.

The wild, oil-rich nuts at the heart of **Nude**'s skincare products (www.nudeskincare.com) are collected by hand from the forest floor or from the banks of the Amazon. Nude is carbon-neutral, its packaging is entirely recyclable, and its eco projects include wind power operations in China and forest protection in Brazil.

In Somalia, eco-centric **Aromatherapy Associates** (www.aromatherapyassociates.com) sources frankincense for its heavenly Rose and Frankincense Facial Oil. The organically grown frankincense is gathered by hand from native trees.

Skincare products should be kept away from direct heat and light. Once purchased, a product normally has a shelf life of one year (slightly less for active botanical and natural/organic products), after which it loses some of its therapeutic benefits. Always check the label for expiry dates.

exotic ingredient selector

Argan (*Argania spinosa*): Extracted from the leaves of Morocco's Argan tree, Argan oil is rich in essential fatty acids and anti-oxidants, protecting the skin against environmental damage and premature ageing.

Baobab (*Adansonia digitata*): Oil from the African Baobab tree is moisturising and anti-ageing, with emollient and soothing properties.

Buriti (*Mauritia flexuosa*): Native to Brazil and Amazonia, oil from the Buriti palm tree contains the largest natural reserve of provitamin A and is a powerful free-radical scavenger. Buriti oil is usually found in creams that protect against sunburn.

Cape Chamomile (*Eriocephalus punctulatus*): Native to remote mountain areas in South Africa, this rare and aromatic shrub is packed with azulenic compounds that can help treat depression, stress-related complaints and inflammation.

Cupuacu (*Theobroma grandiflorum*): The seeds of this Brazillian tree are cold-pressed to produce a creamy butter that provides long-lasting moisturisation.

Cyclopia (Honeybush): A shrub indigenous to the coastal districts of the cape of South Africa, cyclopia extract is rich in antioxidants. The herb protects skin from sun damage.

Juazeiro (*Zizyphus joazeiro*): This native South American tree contains natural foaming saponins which are used in gentle skin cleansers.

Marula oil (*Sclerocarya birrea*): Extracted from the nuts of the Marula tree, it is rich in antioxidants and moisturises and rehydrates the skin.

Manketti (*Ricinodendron rautanenii*): The Manketti tree is native to Africa. Rich in vitamin E, it is a powerful antioxidant that protects the skin from environmental stress and sun damage.

Moringa (*Moringa oleiflora*): Prior to alcohol, all perfumes were diluted in moringa oil, one of the oldest oils known to man. Found in Africa, Egypt and the Himalayas, it is rich in antioxidants and excellent for dry skin.

Rooibos (*Aspalathus linearis*): Rooibos or redbush is exclusive to South Africa's Western Cape and has soothing and healing powers.

eating green: living on the veg

clean plate, clean conscience

Until recently, it was considered fairly radical to buy organic produce; in fact, the phrase 'ethical food' was almost unheard of. Today, millions across the world are trying to improve their health (and the planet) by eating only organic, healthy, additive-free food that has been produced responsibly.

However, with farmers, food manufacturers, politicians, retailers, and the media providing us with all kinds of (frequently conflicting) information, it can sometimes be confusing when you are at the supermarket. Do you reach out for the certified, organically grown, sustainably cultivated coffee beans that have been shipped from across the world, or is it 'greener' to pick the locally grown and packaged ones?

There doesn't seem to be one way to calculate how eco-sensitive one edible product is over the other. Even the definition of organic food is far from simple. Conventionally, all organic food must be completely free of chemical pesticides and artificial fertilisers and should be processed with a minimum of artificial methods, materials and conditions. Livestock are reared without the routine use of antibiotics and growth hormones.

Thankfully for the end consumer, organic food production has become more legally regulated. Currently, the European Union, the United States, Australia, Japan and many other countries require producers to obtain organic certification before they can market their food as organic.

Traditionally, organic farms have been relatively small and family-run, which is why organic food was once only available in small stores or farmers' markets. Early consumers who were keen on organic food would buy directly from growers: 'know your farmer, know your food' was the motto then. Farmers grew vegetables and raised livestock using organic practices, with or without certification, and it was the individual, having had first-hand contact with them, who decided on how organic the produce was.

The 1990s heralded the start of the worldwide demand for organic food—and the market for organic food grew at the rate of around 20 percent a year. Which is why it has become viable for large supermarket chains such as **Tesco**, **Asda**, **Marks & Spencer**, **Wal-Mart** in the US and UK, **Dewsons** and **Coles** in Australia and **NTUC Fairprice** in Singapore to start their own organic production lines. This has made organic food more mainstream, replacing the direct farmer connection. Though organic food has thus become more easily accessible, its production has become more obscure, and product labels are all that the consumer has to rely on.

Besides production, there are other elements that contribute to the 'greenness' of a food product, such as the packaging used—whether it's recyclable or biodegradable—and whether energy-saving technologies were used in its production. 'Buying locally' is an aspect of the organic food movement that advocates conserving transport energy by cutting out long distances.

Food is also better tasting and, to some degree, more nutritious by dint of its freshness. What's more, the act of buying produce that have been locally cultivated benefits native farmers, and is seen as a direct investment into the community. There is also the Fairtrade Movement that is related to the all-encompassing wholesomeness of organic food. After all, environmental sustainability and social responsibility are inextricably interdependent.

high-profile advocates
H.R.H. Prince Charles, Prince of Wales started talking about sustainable farming and organic production some years ago. He is unstintingly pro-green, supporting campaigns that encourage school children to visit farms so that they will know where their food comes from.

The prince is also a patron of the **Year of Food and Farming** (www.yearoffoodandfarming.org.uk), which aims to provide opportunities for children to grow vegetables in school: 'even a window box is enough, but just think what a difference it would make if some of that ubiquitous black Tarmac around schools was turned into productive growing areas.'

Other personalities with an eco agenda include **Nell Newman**, who uses her celebrity inheritance not to get into the latest nightclubs but for bringing organic foods to the all-American-family table. With a little investment from her father, Oscar-winning actor Paul Newman, Nell established her own organic brand in 1993. She now stocks supermarkets with **Newman's Own Organics** chocolate bars, vinegars, cookies, popcorn, coffees, and even dog food.

In keeping with the family's philanthropic approach, Nell's line of organic goodies has generated

THIS PAGE: *From fair trade coffee to heirloom vegetables, the range of organic produce is growing and made increasingly available to the eco-conscious shopper.*
OPPOSITE: *Cattle, too, can be reared organically, without use of chemical feeds or hormone boosters.*

eatinggreen:livingontheveg 33

eating green: living on the veg

THIS PAGE (FROM TOP): *The green team behind hip green boutique Eco includes British actor Colin Firth (third from right); UK celebrity chef Jamie Oliver is trying to oust bad eating habits from the country.*

OPPOSITE: *Your choice of supermarket can make a difference, as some will plough customer dollars back into green initiatives like reforestation.*

millions for organic-agriculture research and wildlife preservation, among other causes.

Colin Firth, who set up two fair trade coffee shops in London's Notting Hill and Covent Garden areas (www.progreso.org.uk) has also decided to lend his celebrity status to the Green movement. Firth's newest foray into the field is an eco boutique in Chiswick. The shelves at **Eco** are stocked high with green goodies such as Poppy Organic face cream and biodegradable wallpaper.

pro-vegan hero

People should have one meat-free day a week if they want to make a personal and effective sacrifice that will help tackle climate change, advocates **Dr Rajendra Pachauri**, chairman of the United Nations Intergovernmental Panel on Climate Change. Although coming from the head of the panel that won a joint share of the Nobel Peace Prize in 2007, this statement on how the individual can tackle global warming has since proved controversial and unpopular.

Apparently, diet change matters because of the huge greenhouse gas emissions and other environmental problems (including habitat depletion) associated with rearing cattle and other animals. The UN's Food and Agriculture Organisation has estimated that meat production accounts for nearly a fifth of global greenhouse gas emissions. Methane, a harmful gas emitted by livestock during digestion—this is especially so for cows—is known to be 23 times more potent as a global warming agent than carbon dioxide. The agency has also warned that meat consumption is set to double by the middle of the century. Cut out the meat, is what Dr Pachauri is saying. It's easier for most than switching from car to bike.

saving the world— one bite at a time

When Craig Sams and Josephine Fairley founded the organic chocolate company **Green and Black's** in 1991, they were the first people to bring organic, and then fair trade chocolate, to the mass markets. The brand's Maya Gold chocolate bar is the main livelihood for a whole district of Belize—it doesn't hurt either that it tastes incredibly good.

doing it for the kids

Jamie Oliver is on a crusade against mass-produced school food that contains the nutritional value of the packaging it came in. His television programmes have made the world sit up and pay attention to his efforts in providing school kids with healthy, affordable, ethically sourced meals.

Oliver collaborates with the RSPCA to increase awareness of the appalling conditions chickens endure in battery farms—the largest source of low-cost meat on the market. The TV show **Jamie's Fowl Dinners** hopes to persuade consumers to change their poultry-buying habits and to seek out happier, better tasting chickens.

the march of the supermarket titans

Tesco, with its far-reaching arm in almost every developed and developing country in the world, is playing its part to save the planet by unrolling a 'go green' programme that makes it easier for the consumer to take the eco-friendly route.

Terry Leahy, Tesco's CEO, says that his supermarket empire wants to 'create a mass movement in green consumption' by making environmentally friendly products more affordable and accessible.

Besides sourcing for organic produce from local farms and reducing the use of plastic bags, Tesco is also implementing green programmes for its production stations around the world, such as water-conservation efforts in China, and reforestation efforts in Thailand.

Leahy said at a press conference, 'We are achieving this while Tesco grows. That's the critical point: the choice is not "green or grow". That is a false choice. You can do both—and you must do both. Reducing emissions does not merely fight climate change, it also cuts costs.'

Over at **Marks & Spencer**, CEO Stuart Rose is spearheading a move to be a part of **Together**—a campaign that aims to provide consumers with compelling products and services while reducing their CO_2 emissions.

Recognising that many of Marks & Spencer's customers are aware of the need for environmental action, Rose ensures that the consumer can trust the British supermarket chain to do some of the hard work for them 'by offering eco-friendly products, fair trade products, sustainable and healthy products, in energy efficient stores.' This move will help green consumers make more informed decisions.

on the go

There are so many issues involved in taking the environmentally friendly road that it is easy to get them all muddled up. Are we hoping to save the planet by cutting down on CO_2 emissions; are we more interested in saving money with the escalating cost of fuel; or does energy security play a role here when there are conflicts involving oil-rich countries? These may be related but are quite distinct subjects.

You'll also find that trying to unearth the overall environmental impact of transport is not easy. You may be done calculating your carbon footprint in terms of the fuel emissions on a single journey, but what about the manufacture and disposal of the vehicle itself? You may have an electric or hybrid car, but what happens to all those batteries when it is scrapped? One has to start somewhere, though. Here are some of the latest trends in transport habits that can help save the planet.

two wheels, not four

And why not? Scooters are sexy, fashionable and environmentally friendly. Like anything else that's powered on two wheels, they use less fuel than a car. There are also the latest electrically powered scooters that are even more energy-efficient than traditional models that use the air-polluting two-stroke petrol engines. In 2007, a lightweight version was designed by an MIT professor and several of his students, which has the added bonus of foldability—it halves its size by folding over, a huge plus point for storage in urban environments. In its folded state, the scooter can be wheeled along like a trolley suitcase and be taken along on trains or even indoors. Called RoboScooter—it is currently under production by major Taiwanese scooter manufacturer **SYM**, and **ITRI**, Taiwan's Industrial Technology Research Institute (visit www.itri.org.tw/eng/).

Though the world of bikes traditionally doesn't bother much with alternative fuels, US firm **Hayes Diversfied Technologies** (www.hdtusa.com) produces multi-fuel motorcycles that can run on diesel and aviation kerosene. These bikes were initially designed for the military, which is trying to simplify its supply lines of fuels. In addition, **Honda** and the US firm **eCycle** (www.ecycle.com/hybrid.html) have also developed experimental hybrid and hydrogen fuel-cell bikes.

Or you could opt for some leg power over conventional fuel with a bike, like the Parisians do with **Vélib'**, their superb urban bike-sharing programme. Launched in the summer of 2007, there are now 20,000 bikes scattered over a thousand stations at various stops around the city—which works out to approximately one station every 229 m (250 yards). It is not the first time the French are taking to the two-wheel system: Lyon, France's third-largest city, launched a similar system two years before. It is said to be so successful that Lyon's urban landscape has changed since then—unlike in other cities, you see more people than vehicles now.

There is also a practical side to using two wheels besides reducing air pollution and carbon emissions: in a recent study that compared modes of transport in a city, among cars, bikes, taxis and walking, bikes were always the fastest!

The bike programme, which is run by **Cyclocity**, a subsidiary of outdoor advertising behemoth JCDecaux, is also found on a much smaller scale in Brussels, Vienna and the Spanish cities of Cordoba and Girona. London, Dublin, Sydney and Melbourne are said to be considering similar rental programmes.

You could get started pedalling right away in your own city with your very own bike. Consider the latest two-wheeled beauties on offer, such as the **Azor Opa** (www.dutchbikeseattle.com), a Dutch-made, hand-crafted two-wheeled classic bike with every amenity the metropolitan rider could wish for: fenders, a mud flap and an enclosed chain case to keep your clothes clean; a built-in lock, and, of course, a chirpy bell that can still be heard above cacophonous traffic. There's also the **Brompton M3L** (www.nycewheels.com), which collapses into a handy suitcase size in less than 15 seconds. Best thing is, the latest bikes ride and look as great as anything with a gas pedal. And no more petrol fill-ups means you get to go easy on your wallet, and on the environment to boot.

buy carbon offsets

This doesn't mean you should go out and buy a petrol-guzzling six-litre Hummer, but buying carbon

THIS PAGE (FROM TOP): *Paris' successful bicycle rental system has a network of bikes available for rent all over the city as an alternative to driving; eco-friendly fuels are rapidly gaining favour in today's oil-frantic markets.*
OPPOSITE: *The problem of high vehicle emissions in urban settings is an immediate concern for anyone with a vested interest in the environment—i.e., all of us.*

onthego 37

on the go

offsets helps you to alleviate some of the guilt of adding to the carbon footprint each time you chug along and release more noxious pollutants into the environment.

Climate Care (visit their site at www.climatecare.org) helps you to calculate the impact of activities in terms of CO_2 emissions and provides a mechanism for offsetting them. Payments made via the site are spent on renewable energy, energy-efficiency measures and reforestation. **The CarbonNeutral Company** (www.carbonneutral.com) manages an offset scheme for Honda that applies for the first three months of ownership.

take the train, not the plane

How you choose to travel on your holiday has a dramatic impact on your carbon footprint. Choosing to leave the car at home is step one for a carbon-neutral holiday.

A train journey of 150 km (93 miles) will produce 19 kg (42 lb) of CO_2 per person but a flight will produce 330 kg (728 lb) of CO_2 per person, while a car on the same journey produces 73 kg (161 lb) of CO_2. What's more, taking a train also means that you can sit back and enjoy some of the scenery and dispense with the long airport security queues, surely a major plus point these days.

electric or hybrid?

Electric and hybrid cars help address local pollution problems—there are no local emissions when running on electric power. Some electric vehicles, such as Piaggio's

38 ecochic

Porter Electric (www.vtl.piaggio.com) and Reva's **G-Wiz** (www.revaindia.com), need to be plugged into the mains overnight, while hybrids such as Toyota's **Prius** (www.toyota.com/prius-hybrid/) and Honda's **Civic Hybrid** (www.automobiles.honda.com/civic-hybrid/), and the luxurious **Lexus hybrid** (check out these models at www.lexus.com/hybriddrive) have both electric and petrol power.

using alternative fuels

The latest fuel getting attention is **E-85**: which is made from 85 percent bioethanol, a renewable fuel that is made from rapeseed, wheat or sugarbeet, and just 15 percent petrol. Car models with E-85 capable versions are the **Ford Focus** and the **Saab 9-5**. Another option is **LPG** (liquefied petroleum gas), which has lower CO_2 emissions than petrol; and **CNG** (compressed natural gas) technologies that are compatible with diesels. There are alternatives that we can anticipate: hydrogen fuel-cell technology, which has been demonstrated by **Honda's FCX** and **Mercedes-Benz's F600 Hygenius**, among others.

Sir Richard Branson, magnate of the skies, recently made history when a VA747, powered by a blend of oil of babassu nut, coconut oil and conventional jet fuel, flew from London to Amsterdam. Branson has pledged to spend US$3 billion in the next 10 years to find viable, renewable energy alternatives. Hopefully by then, we will have made enough strides in eco technology to be able to take to the skies (relatively) guilt-free.

THIS PAGE (FROM TOP): *Carbon offsetting schemes invest the money you pledge in efforts such as constructing renewable energy sites; Ronn Motor Company's Scorpion doesn't sacrifice aesthetics in pursuit of being eco—the car's engine burns hydrogen, with minimal emissions.*
OPPOSITE: *Taking the train is much friendlier to the environment than aeroplane journeys—and are often more scenic and enjoyable.*

eco travel

'Ecotourism' may be the latest fad, but do we actually know what it means? According to The International Ecotourism Society, it goes beyond retrofitting hotel rooms to conserving energy or planting an organic herb garden on its grounds. Ecotourism is described by the association as 'responsible travel to natural areas which conserves the environment and improves the welfare of the local people'.

So before you plan your holiday around the greener good, you might want to do some research on your tour company or hotel to see whether it deserves the ecotourism badge. There are companies that are devoted to eco-friendly travel planning, such as **My Green Travels** (www.mygreentravels.com), with useful tools that help you track your personal CO_2 emissions and a comprehensive list of endangered seafood, among other features. Once you've made your decision, check **www.ecotourism.org** and **www.responsibletravel.com** to see whether the tours or lodges that you've logged on to are actually vetted.

Here are some other terms that you might find useful to know as they are freely bandied around in the industry of green travel. Hopefully, they will help you navigate through the haze of sustainable vacations—and enable you to make decisions that will make a difference to the environment and to local communities around the world.

Alternative energy: Energy sources that cause considerably less environmental damage than traditional fossil fuels. Some forms of alternative energy are solar, wind, flowing water and biomass, the latter being derived from organic matter that has been photosynthesised.

Biodegradable: Materials that can be broken down by Mother Nature via decomposition into harmless compounds. This is the old-fashioned way of getting rid of the world's junk.

Biofuels: These are kind-to-the-earth substitutes to petrol, diesel and LPG, and are made from plants or animals, or manure.

Buying green: This means being an environmentally savvy shopper and looking out for labels and buying things that are organic, eco-friendly, fair trade protected and recycled.

Carbon footprint: A calculation of the amount of carbon dioxide we release into the atmosphere by living our everyday lives. It includes everything from turning on the lights to taking a plane. There are companies that can help you calculate how large your carbon footprint is, such as San Francisco-based organisation, **Terrapass** (www.terrapass.com).

Carbon neutral: This describes what environmentally concerned consumers can do to theoretically remove an amount of carbon equal to that which they release. This could mean planting a tree to absorb the CO_2 a trip has generated, or paying for **carbon offsets**, a financial unit used to reduce greenhouse gas emissions.

If you purchase carbon credits, make sure that they are from a reputable vendor and audited by third parties. These are some of the companies you might want to look at: www.conservationfund.org, www.atmosfair.com, www.climatefriendly.com, and www.carbonneutral.com.

Desalination: This is about removing salt—either from water for drinking or from soil for better farming. It helps open up sources of water, another scarce resource on earth, that we can use.

Ecologically sustainable development: This describes activities that will not only benefit the existing environment, but also preserve the environment for future generations.

Energy-efficient: This refers to a process or device that uses as little energy as possible to perform a function. This can refer to energy-efficient lighting, as well as energy-efficient transport—as when you use your legs to pedal a bike as opposed to using fuel to power up a car.

Environmental footprint: Somewhat like a carbon footprint but in a broader sense; it includes your personal impact on the world around you. Everyone has it—it's the amount of resources we use and the waste we generate.

Fair trade: A movement that promotes independence for small farmers and producers, as well as provides more equality for them in the global market.

There is also the environmental focus in fair trade which means that products featuring the label use techniques such as shade cultivation (which is better for soil) and composting instead of pesticides. All fair trade products must meet standards set by the **Fairtrade Labelling Organisations International**.

Fossil fuels: The organic remains of plants and animals, like natural gas, oil and coal, which can be burned to be turned into energy.

Global warming: This describes the increase in the average temperature of the earth's atmosphere and oceans in recent decades. This is due to the build-up of greenhouse gases that trap the sun's heat in the atmosphere. These gases include CO_2, methane, ozone and nitrous oxide.

Green certification: What consumers should look out for if they don't want lip-service from a company that professes to be environmentally sound. Some organisations you can seek advice from are **Greenleaf Foundation** (www.greenleaffoundation.org), a Bangkok-based non-profit unit that has developed a certification system for environmentally friendly hotels. There are other certification systems around the world such as **Green Globe** (www.greenglobe.org) in Australia and the US-based **Sustainable Tourism Initiative**.

Hybrid car: A car that does not cause as much damage to the environment due to its lower fuel consumption and carbon emission.

Hybrid cars usually combine a petrol or diesel engine with a propulsion system that is powered by a rechargeable energy source.

Organic food: Crops grown without the use of chemical pesticides, artificial fertilisers or genetic modification. Cattle, pigs, sheep and fowl that are considered organic feed on non-pesticide grains and grass and are not given antibiotics or growth hormones.

THIS PAGE: Lots of places such as the Anantara Dhigu Resort & Spa, Maldives (below) offer eco-friendly cuisine and lodging—do your travel research beforehand to make sure your holiday stays green.

OPPOSITE: More and more people are taking time out from their busy lives in the city to get back in touch with nature.

more than a lifestyle

going green: a reality check

Although saying that you would like to turn over a new green leaf and look after the environment may be easy enough, the reality of implementing this programme may be something else entirely.

Accommodating your new mantra in your daily life takes commitment and persistence. For example, everyone knows it is far more conscionable to take a train to get to holiday destinations, but it is just easier and faster to do it the energy-guzzling way—by plane. You would like to buy Fairtrade-certified goods and buy produce from local sources, but with prices of groceries rapidly shooting up, it is tempting to just pick out the cheapest basket of goods from the supermarket.

For the most part, we make bold statements about how we love the environment, but many of us are just not willing to make the changes in our lifestyle that will dramatically contribute towards saving our planet.

where there's a will...

That said, there are ways to soothe your eco conscience without drastically changing your lifestyle. Where there's demand, there's supply—there are huge industries out there catering to consumers who want to buy into the green movement without changing their living habits too much. And one thing consumers know how to do is buy— into green investments, with green credit cards, using green loans and insurance. Most of these financial products operate by giving a cut of your premium or interest to an environmental charity or to buy carbon offsets. Thus you can go about quite happily in your everyday life knowing that your money is 'greening up' the world for you.

There is this to be said about the economics of global warming: consumers are so keen on improving the environment that a whole new financial sector has sprung up to serve this growing market. This poses somewhat of a caveat for investors and funds. Even in the best of times, choosing a financial product of good value is dicey enough, much less one that is green, with good returns.

With the increased awareness surrounding Al Gore's much-publicised eco documentary, *An Inconvenient Truth*, and strengthening evidence of man-made global warming, the certainty that something needs to be done is convincing enough for investors to believe that there is money to be made from anything that can combat climate change.

banking on eco power

One of the many funds formed in the last few years that specialise in clean energy is **Clean and Green Resources Asia** (www.clsa.com) by CLSA, a brokerage and investment group banking on green technology. Says Andrew Pidden, managing director of the fund, 'Companies are realising there is great profit to be made in supplying non-carbon energy solutions to the marketplace. The idea of going green is no longer altruistic alone; it is good business.'

Financial experts specialising in global warming see the biggest potential in the water conservation sector, with water being seen as a rapidly diminishing resource with an increasing demand and no substitute. Also by CLSA is **Clean Water Asia**, the region's first water and waste fund that looks into developing water infrastructure, pollution abatement and waste management. Its high-growth areas are in the supply and treatment of water. The fund's analysts estimate the market for such water treatment to be worth US$132billion in China alone from 2006 to 2010.

There are a slew of other funds that promise investors a greener environment and good returns. Stop by **www.greenchipstocks.com** for some updates on the latest green funds, or go to **www.trustnet.com** for a source of ethical funds. And there's always **www.nrdc.org** (**Natural Resources Defense Council**), where you can find out more about where to put your money where it counts.

bringing the message home

The green campaign extends to home mortgages too. Bank of Ireland's **Giraffe** (www.giraffemoney.co.uk) is a specialist mortgage lender that offers a mortgage scheme that buys carbon credits to offset the carbon emissions from your home during the first three years of your mortgage. There is also the **Ecology Building Society** (www.ecology.co.uk), where you'll only be eligible for a mortgage if you're willing to invest money in making your home energy-efficient, or if you're living in an eco-friendly property. What's more, customers who meet certain energy efficiency benchmarks can receive discounts on their

THIS PAGE (FROM BOTTOM): Environmental activists stage a demonstration to raise awareness of climate change; research into water conservation and infrastructure is gaining in importance at the confluence of increasing water scarcity and a burgeoning global population.

OPPOSITE: Fairtrade certification ensures that everyday products you buy, such as tea, are compliant with labour guidelines and ethically responsible towards the producers.

morethanalifestyle 43

more than a lifestyle

THIS PAGE (FROM TOP): For eco-conscious homeowners, there are various green mortgages available in the market; your money could be going towards a wildlife fund via your mortgage.
OPPOSITE: The high density of traffic in modern cities is a problem that is being tackled by motor insurance schemes that offer incentives for ecologically-aware driving habits.

mortgages. There are also banks such as the **Co-operative Bank** (www.co-operativebank.co.uk), which gives money to the environmental charity **Climate Care** each year for every mortgage on its books. The money collected has helped fund environmental education projects in Madagascar and wind turbines in India, as well as conservation projects in Uganda. Like the other financial institutions sensitive to the environment, their rates may not necessarily be the best in the market, but their green agenda is still a draw for the eco-minded.

eco-friendly plastic?

Who would have thought that plastic could be green? But it's true. There are a number of 'green' credit cards in the market that make donations for every dollar you spend, or who hand a share of their profits out to worthy environmental causes. Credit card companies offer 'affinity cards' such as the **RED American Express** (www.americanexpress.com) card, which provides donations to non-profit organisations whose logo or image feature on the card.

Donations usually involve half a percentage point from every purchase, balance transfer or cash advance made with the card. The credit card company **MBNA** offers the most affinity cards, and even has a PVC-free **WWF** (www.wwf.org.uk) card available in Europe.

Considered one of the 'greenest' affinity cards, **Working Assets Visa Card** (www.workingassets.com), donates 10 cents with every purchase to your choice of one of 40 non-profit organisations. Another option, the **Salmon Nation Visa Card** (www.salmonnation.com), provided by eco-friendly lending institution, **Shorebank Pacific**, offers the biggest eco bang for your buck. Half of the income generated from the card goes to Salmon Nation—an economic, cultural and ecological collective in the region that contains Pacific salmon spawning grounds.

There is also **Barclaycard**'s **Breathe** card (www.barclaycardbreathe.com), which gives half its profits to tackling climate change. Alternatively, opt for a card such as the **Greenpeace Visa** (www.greenpeace.org.uk) which donates to an environmental charity.

on the (eco) road

The green fad is creeping into almost every part of our lives, and the latest green wagon to hop onto is a green insurance plan. **The Co-operative Bank** in the UK led the way in this market with a motor insurance policy that promises to offset 20 percent of all customers' car emissions. It also makes other green commitments such as using mechanics who pledge to always try and repair a vehicle before scrapping it.

Another approach to the motor insurance market is **More Than Green Wheels** (www.morethan.com. Drivers can now analyse their driving habits and get pointers on reducing carbon emissions through a device installed in the car. This is assessed through one's speed; the more one accelerates, the more pollution is generated.

By examining your behaviour behind the wheel, you could cut your emissions, and your petrol bill to boot. Two big insurers in the US are offering pay-as-you-drive discounts via the **MyRate** programme (www.myrateplan.com) and the **Low Mileage Discount** programme (www.lowmileagediscount.com). Such programmes are launched in the hope that with their widespread adoption, driving (and CO_2 emissions) will be reduced nationwide.

Insurance companies are also reaching out to hybrid car owners who can get discounts on their plans. For example, **Travelers Insurance** (www.travelers.com) offers the scheme in most states in the US. The discounts seem to be enticing enough: new hybrid car business for the company more than doubled since its launch of the programme.

To raise awareness about the discount and hybrid cars, Travelers created **www.hybridtravelers.com** to provide information on federal and state tax benefits alongside other perks for hybrid car odrivers.

There is also green insurance in the travel market, such as **climatesure** (www.climatesure.co.uk), backed by AXA, which will pay for carbon offsets for any trip you make.

In the UK domestic market, the **Environmental Transport Association** (www.eta.co.uk) is finding popularity with its pledge to offset emissions caused by heating and electricity in the home for all policy holders.

These eco-friendly developments are fabulous for closet 'greenies' who are suffering from ethical apathy—if they can't make the changes in their lifestyle for a better environment, perhaps their money will go the green mile for them.

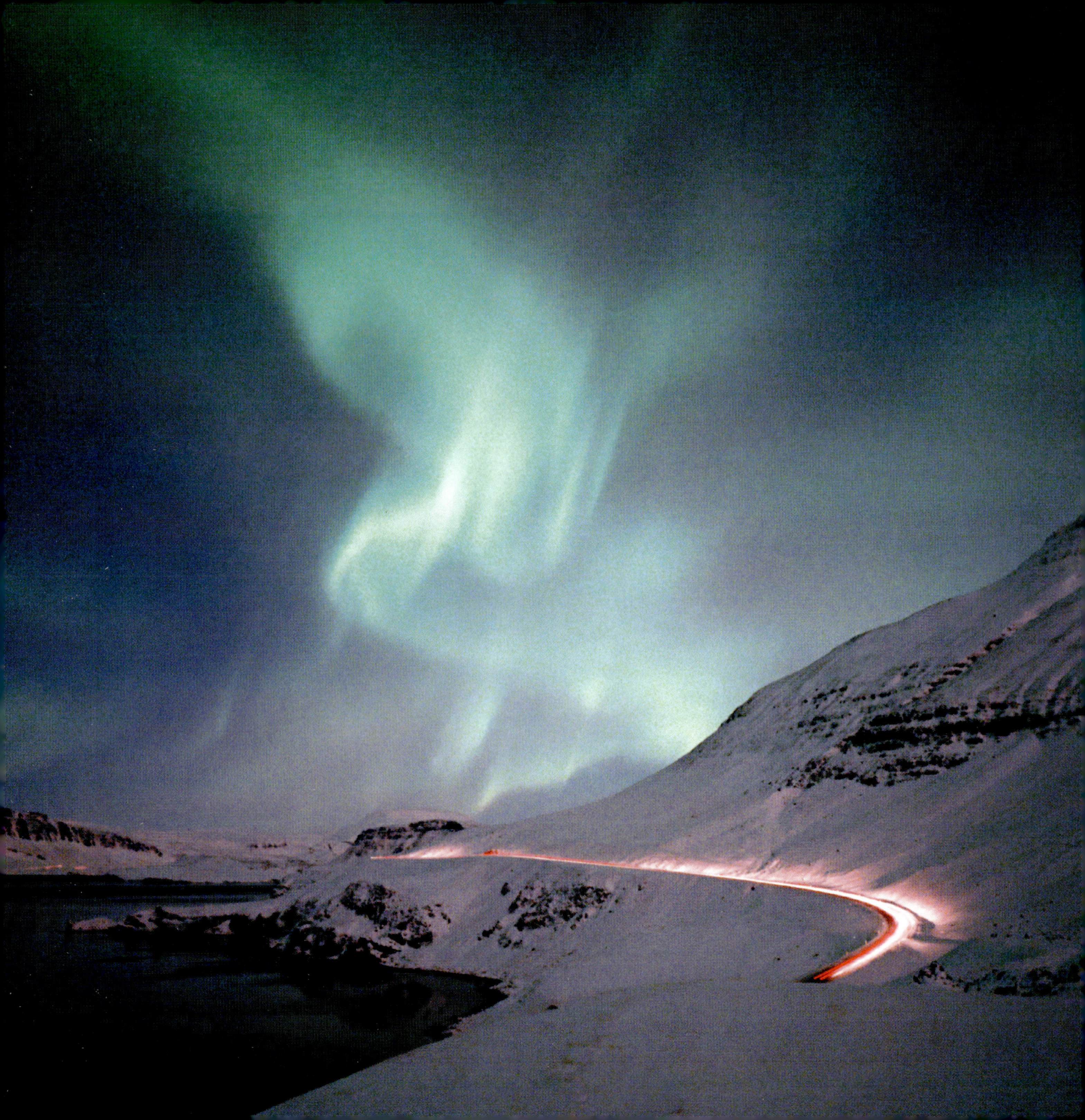

europe

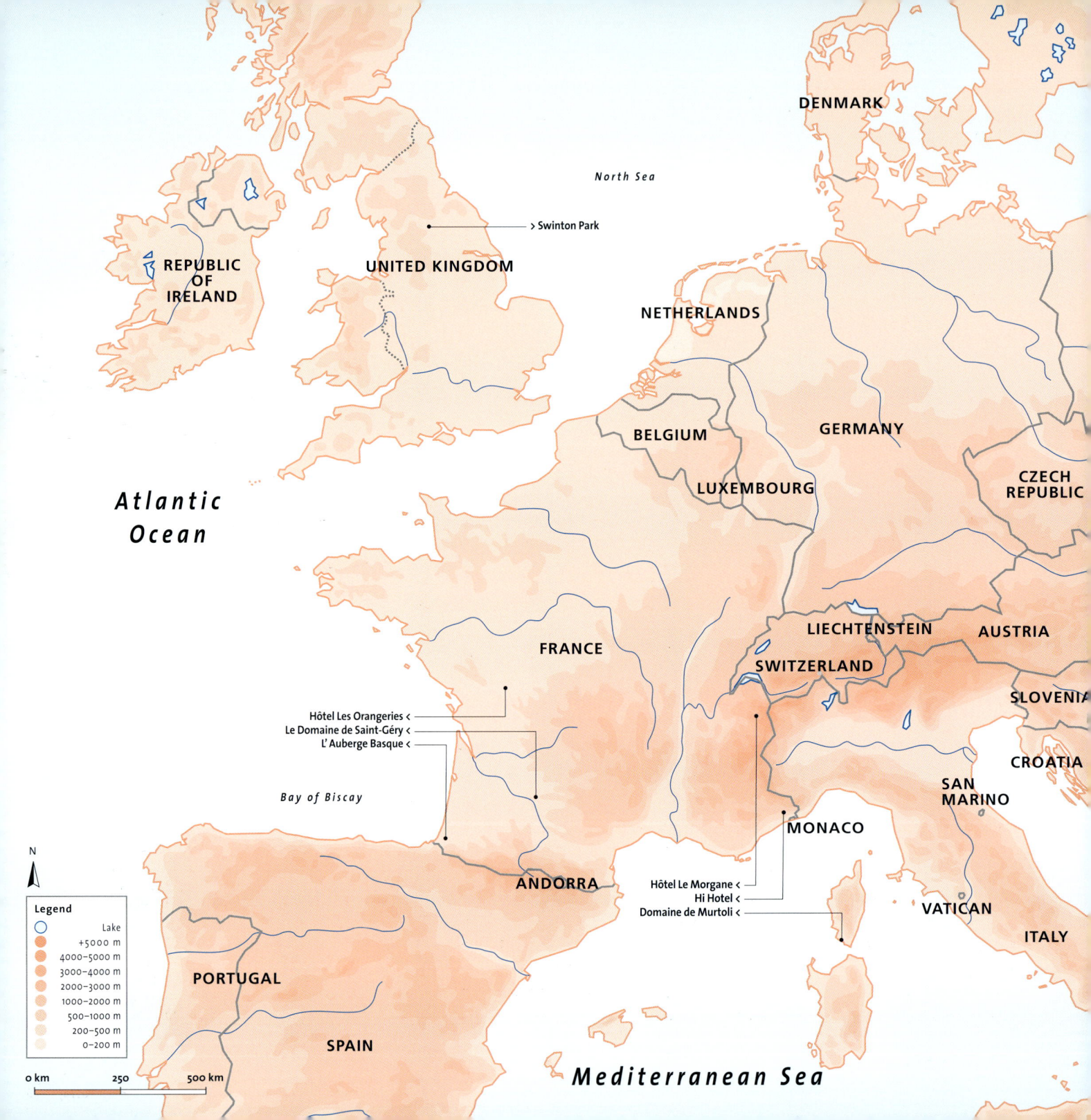

Europe

Atlantic Ocean

North Sea

- Swinton Park

REPUBLIC OF IRELAND

UNITED KINGDOM

DENMARK

NETHERLANDS

BELGIUM

LUXEMBOURG

GERMANY

CZECH REPUBLIC

FRANCE

- Hôtel Les Orangeries
- Le Domaine de Saint-Géry
- L'Auberge Basque

Bay of Biscay

ANDORRA

PORTUGAL

SPAIN

LIECHTENSTEIN

SWITZERLAND

AUSTRIA

SLOVENIA

CROATIA

SAN MARINO

MONACO

- Hôtel Le Morgane
- Hi Hotel
- Domaine de Murtoli

VATICAN

ITALY

Mediterranean Sea

Legend
- Lake
- +5000 m
- 4000–5000 m
- 3000–4000 m
- 2000–3000 m
- 1000–2000 m
- 500–1000 m
- 200–500 m
- 0–200 m

0 km — 250 — 500 km

europe

a land of wonder

Europe is a land of wonder, with its patchwork of languages, cultures and landscapes packed side by side. Europe is so rich in history and traditions that it is often dubbed a living museum. Call it 'dolce vita' or 'savoir-vivre', the old world has invented gastronomy and most of the finest things in life, from Chanel and Gucci, to Mozart and Picasso. Its global influence in the past and present is undeniable. Europe is crammed with old monuments and renowned landmarks, but it is also craving for novelty.

Ecotourism is developing faster there than anywhere else. Spotting a bear while hiking on the slopes of Romania's mountains is every bit as exciting as seeing a leopard in the African bush. Europe has more to offer than fairy-tale castles, Roman churches and beautifully preserved medieval towns. Today, Europeans are rediscovering their own natural treasures, and beautiful wilderness sites such as Finland's Oulanka National Park or Iceland's rugged interior are increasingly becoming popular destinations. This new demand has forced countries such as Bulgaria to establish and implement a national ecotourism strategy and help tourism businesses develop green products.

rapid changes

While Europe has so much to be proud of, it has its share of problems. Due to its high population density and its long industrial history, the continent's ecosystems have deteriorated over the centuries. This is why its inhabitants are now paying a lot of attention to environmental problems, and why its governments are currently leading the race against global warming. As Europe faces increasingly rapid global changes, the need to address unsustainable trends and change the behaviour and attitudes of its citizens is more pressing than ever.

The European Union's goal of reducing greenhouse gas emissions to 8 percent below 1990 levels by 2012 has ensured a focus on the environment by all businesses, including hotel developers and operators. Europe's need for new and alternative sources of energy has made Germany the world leader in renewable energies: the country has more wind turbines and solar panels than any other country in the world. The industry intends to grow by 10 percent each year and to reach a turnover of around 120 billion euros by 2010.

THIS PAGE: Northern Ireland's Giant's Causeway is both a UNESCO World Heritage site and a sanctuary for many rare plants and animals.
PAGE 46: The Northern Lights—an awe-inspiring natural phenomenon otherwise known as the Aurora Borealis.

Germany has long been perceived as Europe's Green Knight, but northern Europe's Scandinavian countries are equally green. They use geothermal energy, have a mostly sustainable timber industry, and boast excellent national parks. Some of the most prominent ecotourism labels originate from Scandinavia, and the national ecotourism associations of Sweden and Norway are among Europe's most vibrant.

Despite their efforts to protect the environment, Scandinavians are worried about the effects of global warming on their glaciers and Arctic ecosystems, and they frequently lobby governments of rich and emerging nations to act against climate change.

In southern Europe, people are also getting concerned about the state of the environment. The Mediterranean has become one of the most polluted seas in the world, with 150 million people inhabiting its glorious coastline, and another 200 million holidaying there every summer. This problem has urged governments and environmental organisations to launch awareness campaigns and take action against polluters. The devastation of other natural areas of Europe is raising concern, forcing local people to review their traditional use of the land and implement drastic water-saving measures in periods of severe drought.

Being green is now part of the political life in Europe, and most environmental organisations have switched from protests and demonstrations to more traditional tactics such as lobbying political leaders and companies to embrace the cause.

carbon-free travel made easy

As the Green Movement becomes more mainstream all around Europe, travel operators are realising the potential purchasing power of this sector and are eager to appeal to this market. The focus of these operators is usually on carbon-free transport. The continent's train network is very efficient and reaches even the most far-flung corners, considerably reducing the need to use airplanes for domestic travel. High-speed trains run from London to Paris by going under the Channel. Take the time to savour the varying landscapes from the comfort of a train seat or as you dine at its onboard restaurant.

Plan a guilt-free holiday—opt for a cycling tour around Holland or France. This mode of travel is becoming very popular, especially when it is combined with stays at locally run bed and breakfast inns. The United Kingdom and the Republic of Ireland also provide many opportunities for cycling and eco travel, with their beautiful countrysides dotted with castles and old churches, waterways for canal boats and barges, and easy to-find natural retreats.

urban eco-chic

The green building revolution is a worldwide movement for energy-efficient, environmentally aware architecture and design, and Europe is at the forefront of it. For example, since 2009, German legislature has required the use of renewable energy in the building sector. This is also a trend in the hospitality industry. The UK firm Travelodge recently constructed a 'recyclable hotel' in London made entirely from modified steel shipping containers—it can be dismantled and moved to another location when there is a need for more rooms!

Europe is the birthplace of some of the eco-friendliest urban hotels, which have introduced initiatives such as flow regulators on showerheads, the use of eco-friendly detergents and the installation of energy-efficient appliances on their properties. They also use ecological paints, wooden furniture made from sustainable forests and organic cotton sheets. The best ecological hotels also heat water using solar panels, use rainwater collectors to water the plants and serve organic food at their restaurants.

Being green does not mean fewer luxuries—these urban eco hotels are regarded as the epitome of hip design. On the French Riviera, Nice's Hi Hotel is the perfect 21st-century hotel: beautiful, practical and green. Hotel Le Morgane in Chamonix is another sustainable hotel praised for its sensational design. And the trend is not just in boutique properties: large hotel chains are also jumping on the green bandwagon. The Scandinavian chain, Scandic Hotels, has refurbished more than 10,000 'eco rooms' throughout its European franchise with almost 100 percent recyclable material. It is also committed to eliminating all its fossil CO_2 emissions by 2025.

rural beauties + organic gastronomy

Green travel has now entered the mindset of European cities, but its true essence originates in the small rural boutique properties which have long led the way, and have integrated environmentally friendly practices and preached organic farming for decades. Echoing sustainable living movements such as the Slow Food movement (www.slowfood.com), these hotels combat fast food and strive to preserve their regional cuisines and their associated

THIS PAGE: *Eco awareness in Europe is at unprecedented levels.*

OPPOSITE (FROM TOP): *Many European governments are turning to alternative energy sources to power up their countries; carbon-free travel is making a comeback, with people eschewing cars for bicycles.*

produce. Slow Food promotes local farmers and local flavours through regional events such as wine tastings and Taste Workshops. The European network, Bio Hotels, which was created in Austria in 2001 and is now expanding to Germany, France and England, promotes the use of 100 percent organic food at its gourmet restaurants.

France and Italy are renowned for their fine food and exquisite wines—and offer fantastic rural experiences where visitors can stay in beautiful wine estates and dine on locally grown produce. They can even learn to cook in a great chef's own kitchen, using only the finest local ingredients. The Domaine de Saint-Géry is one such gem hidden in the South of France. This eco-friendly intimate hotel and restaurant serves exquisite food and wine and leads guests to discover the wonders of aromatic organic truffles grown on the estate. Such examples of wonderful rural experiences are far from being limited to these two countries—every European country has something special from its rural heritage to share.

endless opportunities for adventure

Fancy an eco holiday in Europe, but don't know where to go? With its towering peaks and glittering lakes, Switzerland is an outdoors paradise, summer and winter. France has much more to offer beyond its famed capital: take a train to the Bordeaux region to visit the wineries and then book a sustainable hotel in the Alps.

High-rise buildings might overshadow most of Spain's Mediterranean coast, but eco travellers can still find peaceful villages and untouched landscapes inland. Italy is the country that practically invented agritourism and culinary-centred trips, but if you would rather have an active holiday, go hiking in Majella National Park where bears and wolves still roam free. Then, there are the azure waters off the Dalmatian coast of Croatia, which are dotted with hundreds of little islands and inlets that can only be discovered by boat. This hot destination also boasts picturesque medieval villages, towns and castles.

If you are looking for great open spaces, then head up north to Sweden or Finland for their beautiful lakes and forests. Try dog sledding and witness the beauty of the legendary Northern Lights. Or if you want a close encounter with fjords, Norway's are the world's most beautiful. In the market for some drama? Discover Nature's forceful side in the volcanoes and icebergs of Iceland. And for sun-kissed beaches and splendid classical architecture, explore the myriad wonderful islands just off the coast of Greece.

The list goes on and on—Europe has an incredible wealth of places to find adventure. Dozens of lifetimes would not suffice to explore them all. So why not start now, staying at luxurious and earth-friendly accommodation along the way?

THIS PAGE (FROM TOP): *With many shops championing eco agendas, European consumers have become more environmentally conscious; Europe still has pockets of nature where wildlife roam.*

OPPOSITE: *The coast of Dalmatia is dotted with islands that offer visitors a wealth of nature-centric exploration.*

The azure waters off the Dalmatian coast of Croatia...

europe: restaurants

london, england

London is perhaps the only city in the world where you can enjoy gourmet pub food that is organic as well. Welcome to the **Duke of Cambridge** (30 St Peter's Street, Islington, N18JT, +44.20.7359 3066), one of the country's most famous gastropubs that has earned its popularity not only for its hearty, close-to-the-heart English fare, but for its green aspirations as well.

The all-organic menu here includes everything on its beer list as well as dishes for lunch and dinner. Meat dishes such as steak, and the beef and gorgonzola pie are all from happy, free-roaming English cows. There are other fave English pub hits such as fish and chips, cauliflower and bacon soup, roasted trout and confit of duck leg.

Acorn House (69 Swinton Street, King's Cross, WC1X 9NT, +44.20.7812 1842) not only offers environmentally friendly, sustainable cuisine, it also runs an eco-friendly training course (limited to 10 local young adults a year) for aspiring chefs. The modern interior hints at its green soul with lots of natural wood and bright splashes of apple green.

Food is an all-day roster of sandwiches, paninis, power shakes and pastries, as well as an array of mouth-watering wholesome cooked foods such as roast pork chop with soy honey and thyme, chargrilled sea bream, pea and broad bean soup, and pastas and risottos. Desserts in an English restaurant wouldn't be the same without rice pudding; here it is given a sweet douse of strawberry jam. Don't miss out on the chocolate puds too.

Water House (10 Orsman Road, Dalston, N15QJ, +44.20.7033 0123) strives to be a responsible restaurant in every way. The food offered is low on carbon usage and highly seasonal; the wines stocked are organic and biodynamic; fish is bought from sustainable stocks and produce is transported by car, as opposed to the fuel-guzzling airplane.

Diners can expect plenty of simply prepared dishes here that highlight the freshness of the food such as roasted cod, meats and salads. The lemon polenta cake is a must-have.

The Clerkenwell Kitchen (31 Clerkenwell Close, Clerkenwell, EC1R 0AT, +44.20.7101 9959) serves delicious, seasonal food that avoids intensive agriculture. Dishes are homely, with bacon and free-range eggs for breakfast, and pastries and lemon tarts for tea.

Cooked meals for lunch and dinner include courgette and parmesan tart, honey-roasted gammon and seafood stew. The design of the place is modern, simple and sleek, attracting the arty crowd from the nearby architectural workshops.

Saf (152–154 Curtain Road, EC2A 3AT, +44.20. 7613 0007) comes out top of the list for eco-conscious dining as it is a vegan restaurant. Concerns about animal welfare, factory farming and fish supplies are dealt with in one fell swoop. Much of the food on the menu isn't even cooked—served either raw or having been heated to low temperatures—so energy usage is a fraction of what it might have been.

Surprisingly, despite all its worthy causes, a dining experience here is far from dull—the food here is colourful, imaginative and beautifully presented with plenty of flavour and texture. It doesn't hurt that the restaurant décor is a stunner too.

VitaOrganic (74 Wardour Street, Soho, W1F 0TE, +44.20.7435 2188) serves up organic vegan food and plenty of raw foods. Salads are served on a buffet bar, while cooked foods, such as *moussaka* and Thai green curry are ladled out of pots. A cabinet displays cakes and desserts such as vegan chocolate almond cake, and there are enough permutations of healthy juices on offer here to fill up a large board.

Another organic restaurant with a cafeteria pick-your-own-food style is **Beatroot** (92 Berwick Street, W1F 0QD, +44.20.7437 8591) where you can choose your size of meal box and fill it up with hot and cold food from the counter. You can choose from coleslaw, potato salad, shepherd's pie, vegetable curries and rice. There are also, soups, juices and smoothies. The food served is good and hearty, and easy on the pocket too.

Red Veg (95 Dean Street, W1V 5RB +44.20.7437 3109) is fast food for vegans with a taste for comfort 'junk food'. Choose from red veg burgers, hot dogs, breaded baby corn and fries—it proves that vegan food doesn't have to be limited to salads, *falafel* and *tempeh*.

First Out Café-Bar (52 St Giles High Street, WC2H 8LH, +44.20.7240 8042) is London's first gay-lesbian café which offers delicious, organic vegan-friendly fare. During the day, dine on casual café-style food such as soups, sandwiches and salads; the cakes are delicious here. Come evenings, and the place transforms

THIS PAGE (FROM TOP): The Clerkenwell Kitchen serves up wholesome eco cuisine in modern interiors; vegan dishes are available at Saf.
OPPOSITE: Acorn House is big on eco consciousness, and also scores high marks on the chic design front.

europe: restaurants

THIS PAGE (FROM TOP): Manchester has declared its admirable aim to become Britain's greenest city; L'Auberge Basque proffers an organic take on the Basque countryside.
OPPOSITE: The David Bann Restaurant is convincing proof that you don't have to be shabby to be green.

into a lively bar. The staff are friendly and the atmosphere is laid-back. Whatever your inclination, you are bound to have a good time here.

manchester, england
Who would have thought that Manchester, the factory hub of England, would possess a green heart? The city recently declared its intent to become Britain's greenest, and is now an official fair trade city. Manchester has a large number of organic, sustainable eateries, which range from hippy cafes to surburban delis and high-end eateries.

Greens (43 Lapwing Lane, Didsbury, M20 2NT, +44.0161.434 4259) is an award-winning vegetarian restaurant run by a meat-loving chef. Although meals are vegetable-based, the tastes still appeal to carnivores.

Isinglass (46 Flixton Road, Urmston, M41 5AB, +44.0161.749 8400) is one of the city's best restaurants and sources its produce from around the area. Chef Lisa Walker gets her salad leaves from Chat Moss, courgettes from Cheshire, and ice-cream from Dunham Massey, proving that with the freshest ingredients, people will be willing to travel far and wide, in this case to Urmston, for a taste of it.

Fetish for Food (Deli, 430 Bury New Road, Prestwich, M25 1BD, +44.0161.798 5558; Bistro, 2 Church Lane, Prestwich, M25 1AJ, +44.0161.773 3366) is a deli and separate bistro that specialises in organic and regional food. Here, you can find organic meat—bought direct from farms in Cheshire and Wales—and independently produced cheese. In the bistro down the road, diners will have the chance to taste some of the oh-so-fresh produce.

Earth Café (16–20 Turner St, M4 1DZ, +44.0161.834 1996), in the basement of the Buddhist Centre, serves up delicious organic, vegan or fair trade cuisine. Consume tasty soups, savouries, veggie burgers, quiches and salads—all delicious fare to keep the green conscience happy.

devon, england

Riverford Farm (Wash Barn, Buckfastleigh, +44.0845.600 2311) offers visitors an introduction to the finer details of organic farming. After getting your wellies muddy, gather around the communal tables in the farm's **Field Kitchen** restaurant for a hearty lunch of braised lamb shoulder and plenty of vegetables.

edinburgh, scotland

David Bann Restaurant (56–58 Street Mary's St EH1 1SX, off the Royal Mile and the Cowgate, +44.0131.556 5888), one of the most famous restaurants in the pretty town of Edinburgh, serves healthy meals with 'world influence'. This translates to Thai fritters, spiced noodles, vegetarian haggis and Jerusalem artichoke bake. Most of the menu is vegetarian with a few vegan items, but even the most hardened meat-eaters head to David Bann for its wholesome cuisine.

Engine Shed (19 St Leonard's Lane, near the University of Edinburgh, +44.0131.662 0040) is one of those establishments that combines altruism with business. It offers training programmes for adults with learning disabilities, applying their skills to its outdoor catering business, bakery, and organic tofu making operation. The café, situated at the historical engine shed of the Innocent Railway (so called because no one died working for it) serves vegan food within a cosy environment that is child- and family-friendly.

Henderson's Bistro (94 Hanover Street, ED2 1DR, +44.0131.225 2605) serves vegan-friendly juices and snacks, while adjacent **Henderson's Shop and Salad Table** (+44.0131.225 2131) is an all-day salad bar as well as a store selling local fruits and vegetables, baked goods, organic wines and teas among other foodstuffs. You can find vegan haggis in filo pastry served with gravy, as well as other vegetarian pies and sandwiches. Desserts one the menu feature fruit pies and tarts. Soya lattes are also available.

france

Vegetarian and vegan food in the country of the world's finickiest gourmands has a finesse not found anywhere else—many are worthy of Michelin stars. And even the most incorrigible carnivores head for some of these world-famous restaurants for a taste of a finely grilled portobello, or a supremely stuffed courgette.

L' Auberge Basque (Vieille Route de Saint-Jean de Luz, 64310 Saint-Pée sur Nivelle, +33.05.5951 7000) offers an eating experience directly connected to the beautiful Basque Country, far from the trends of modern city dining.

Chef Cédric Béchade serves traditional recipes made from fresh local ingredients, presented with artful simplicity. The seasonal fare is complemented by a large wine list of

europe: restaurants

over 160 varieties selected by 2005 Sommelier of the Year (Gault Millau), Samuel Ingeraere. The dining room is ideally situated to take advantage of the pastoral view, which includes the La Rhune Mountains.

Eating at the modern **Hi Hotel** (3 Avenue des fleurs, 06000 Nice, +33.49.707 2626) is every bit the design revolution one might expect. The property's HI Food project is not so much a restaurant as it is an expression of freedom. Guests can build their own meals from organic choices displayed in refrigerated cases, and dine at their leisure in relaxed surroundings. Meals are enjoyed off an exclusive porcelain tableware collection created by the hotel's wunderkind designer, Matali Crasset.

Le Potager du Marais (22 Rue Rambuteau, 75003 Paris, +33.1.42 74 24 66), one of Paris' world-famous vegetarian restaurants, incorporates vegetables into seductive pates, tarts, tartines, gratins and *moussakas*. A cosy setting decorated with an abundance of blooms, Le Potager is where you get traditional French cuisine—a purist's French onion soup, or an asparagus terrine—in vegetable mode. Desserts, such as the mousse, are outstanding. Vegans have plenty of choices as well.

Those who like Le Potager head to **La Victoire Suprême du Cœur** (27–31 Rue du Bourg Tibourg, 75004 Paris, +33.1.40 41 95 03) as well. The restaurant makes it a point to buy its vegetables from non-GM sources around the country. The international and French menu features dishes such as mushroom terrine, vegetarian lasagna, seitan steak with mushroom sauce. Unlike most French restaurants, the portions here are generous. Note that no alcohol is served here.

Tien Hiang (92 Rue du Chemin Vert, 75011 Paris, +33.1.43 55 83 88) is a small Buddhist restaurant that serves vegan-friendly food, and is very popular among the Parisien vegetarian crowd. There are mock meat options, but if you don't fancy them, choose from other healthy vegetable choices on the menu. The fried dumplings are excellent, as are the stuffed tofu and curried 'chicken'. The restaurant's close proximity to the Père Lachaise cemetery gives it a calming atmosphere as well.

Grand Appetit (9 Rue la Cerisaie, 75004 Paris, +33.1.40 27 04 95) is a casual macrobiotic café with a health food shop next door. Its menu serves vegetable sushi, vegetable platters and healthy soups. Great for those looking for a quick and healthy meal, the café offers both a buffet-style salad bar and à la carte hot food. Its casual dining experience, quality ingredients and well-executed dishes keep the regular customers coming back for more.

Au Grain de Folie (24 Rue la Vieuville, 75018 Paris, +33.1.42 58 15 57) is an organic restaurant that is run by the owner who happens to be the chef and waiter as well. Don't expect a large menu—there will most likely be only two items to choose from.

However, its cosy, intimate ambience and freshly prepared dishes are very popular among gourmands—the owner's pets even come in and out of the kitchen to greet customers. Be prepared to wait when the place gets crowded.

frankfurt, germany
Naturbar (Oder Weg 26, +49.69.554 486) is a predominantly organic restaurant that serves fish from responsible sources, and offers vegans some options on its menu as well. Expect spa-like food such as avocado salad, as well as pita bread with melted cheese and curried lentil dishes. It has a fairly central location in the city and has an outdoor terrace for al fresco dining.

hamburg, germany
Cafe Koppel (Lange Reihe 75 / Koppel 66, +49. 40.249 235) offers vegan-friendly German food and a variable menu; the main course changes every day—which should please fickle palates. It also stocks a range of German beers, including the famous Pinkus organic beer, and wine.

Piccolo Paradiso (Bruderstr. 27, +49.40.3571 5358) is a family-style restaurant that serves organic food with a small selection for vegetarians and vegans. It is on a quiet street and has a peaceful atmosphere.

Hin and Veg (Schulterblatt 16, West Schanzenviertel, +49.40.5945 3402) is a small vegan-friendly vegetarian restaurant which serves organic fast foods such as veggie bratwurst, veggie curry-wurst and veggie burgers. It also offers a selection of beers and wines.

rome, italy
Il Margutta Vegetariano (Via Margutta 118, +39.6.3265 0577), ideally situated near the Spanish Steps, serves Italian food with an emphasis on fresh vegetables. There is even a vegan-friendly four-course set menu daily. Il Margutta's dishes are refined Italian choices of pastas, soups and terrines. There is also an antipasto buffet spread with dozens of succulent sides.

At **Bibliothe** (Via Celsa 4, near the Pantheon, +39.06.678 1427), you can dine on Ayurvedic-inspired, mainly Indian, dishes that use organic wheat, flour and rice for their pastas and *dosa*. Try the Indian rolls as well as the fragrant ginger tea—said to ease travel sickness.

milan, italy
Joia (Via p. Castaldi, 18, +39.02.204 9244, and Corso di Porta Tichinese, 106, +39.2.8940 4134) receives rave reviews for its haute cuisine. Offering seafood as well as an extensive array of vegetarian and vegan creations, dishes are meticulously prepared with an finesse worthy of its one-Michelin star rating.

Vegetarians and vegans will be glad to know that the preparation of vegetarian food here is as much a priority as meat and fish dishes. Here, vegetables are coaxed into elaborate creations on the plate—asparagus bread, cheese-filled zucchini flowers and delicate courgette foam.

Girasole (Via Vincenzo Monti, 32, +39.2.8969 7459) serves up organic, vegan-friendly buffet lunches and à la carte dinners. Expect rich, hearty dishes, not 'skinny' meals associated with vegetarian or vegan cuisine.

THIS PAGE (FROM TOP): Il Margutta Vegetariano's quirky interior; this edible flower salad looks almost too good to eat; Organic cuisine is not limited to restaurants—many speciality shops throughout Europe offer ethically grown artisanal produce as well.

OPPOSITE: Hi Hotel serves up custom-made organic creations any time of day or night.

europe: restaurants

Alla Vecchia Latteria Di Via Unione (Via Dell'Unione 6, near Cathedral Square, +39.2.874 401) is a small restaurant which has been run by the Notari family for many generations. It offers Italian cuisine that is friendly to both vegetarians and non-vegetarians, with a good selection of healthy grilled seafood as well as vegetarian fare.

zürich, switzerland

Hiltl (Sihlstrassse 28, at Bahnhofstrasse, +41.44.227 7000) is said to be the first vegetarian restaurant in Europe, and its European and Indian vegetarian creations are compiled in a cookbook that diners can bring home with them. The restaurant may be large but it is always busy, so reservations are highly recommended.

Some of the dishes that are firm favourites are the mille feuille with wild mushrooms, Casamir rice and vegetable curries. There is a good selection for vegans as well.

The funky, buffet-style cousin to the elegant Hitl, **Tibits** (Seefeldstrasse 2, at Falkenstrasse, +41.44.260 3222) caters to busy vegetarains on the go. It serves the same high-quality vegetarian food with a hot and cold buffet, and meals are charged by weight. The restaurant is also very prettily situated next to a lake.

Restaurant Bona Dea (Bahnhofplatz 15, +41.44.217 1515) dishes up a vegan-friendly buffet with an emphasis on Indian cuisine. The fixed-price buffet offered often tempts diners to pile their plates with spicy and exotic dishes, as well as delicate sweets in pretty colours.

Samses (Langstrasse 231, +41.44.440 1313) offers vegan-friendly options in its buffet. There are salads, tofus and pastas on offer, as well as many Italian dishes on its à la carte menu.

geneva, switzerland

Eveil Café Epicerie Bio (80 route de Chêne, +41.22.700 0530) is a vegetarian café with a grocery that sells organic food. **Le Kid** (Boulevard, Carl-Vogt 99, +41.22.320 4496) has vegetarian options as well as seafood. Its menu includes tofu, *tempeh* and veggie burgers.

barcelona, spain

Vegetalia (Escudellers 54, +34.93.317 3331) is actually a producer of organic and natural vegetarian food. Its café is a casual self-serviced outfit for diners to taste the wide range of seitan, tofu and meat substitutes it produces.

Juicy Jones (C/Cardenal Casanas 7, Ciutat Vella, +34.93.302 4330) is a young and hip restaurant which offers organic vegan food. Standard soups and salads are available here —the soups are mostly served cold— in addition to the more exciting fare of Spanish tapas, *thalis*, Indian curries, and tofu with *satay* sauce. There are plenty of desserts to choose from, including Indian sweets.

Maoz Falafel (Carrer de Ferran 13, off La Rambla, +34.65.384 7653, Calle de Jaume) is a vegan-friendly, fast-food joint that serves Middle-Eastern cuisine. Perfect for vegans on a budget, diners can stuff their pita breads with a selection of vegetables, hummus, guacamole, falafel balls and various other *mezzes*.

Organic (Junta de Comerç, 11, +34.93.301 0902) is a self-service, vegan-friendly restaurant that serves an extensive organic whole-foods buffet during lunch and à la carte meals in the evening. Diners can also have a massage on its grounds before or after meals.

madrid, spain

Yerbabuena (Bordadores 3, +34.91.548 0811) is a vegan-friendly restaurant that has received good reviews. It serves up veggie burgers, salads and pastas. Pizzas have wholemeal bases and fresh organic toppings. A selection of Spanish tapas are also available, as well as Asian-inspired dishes such as spring rolls and tofu.

El Septimo (Diego de Leon 7, +34.91. 562 2940) sells interesting vegetarian dishes, though the menu is far from being just vegetarian. Stylishly decorated and in the expensive neighbourhood of Serrano, it offers homely Spanish fare such as vegetable couscous, puff pastry stuffed with vegetables and stuffed peppers alongside a variety of rice and pasta dishes. Wine aficionados will also be delighted to sample from the extensive selection of Spanish wines available here.

Isla del Tesoro (Manuela Malasana 3, +34.91.593 1440) is another popular restaurant which serves haute vegetarian cuisine. Expect out-of-this-world croquettes with dashes of olive, sesame and beet, as well as fusion dishes such as Tan Tan de Seitan sprinkled with Japanese mock-fish flakes, and an oriental combo of spring rolls, dumplings and sushi rolls. Organic wines and beers are available.

THIS PAGE : *Tibits' extensive range of delectable vegetarian fare ensure that fickle palates never get bored.*
OPPOSITE: *Tuck into vegetarian fine-dining amid Hitl's elegant interior; today's organic cuisines are netiher bland nor boring.*

europe: shopping

london, england

Most of us know that today's hottest environmental issues centre around carbon footprints, fossil fuels, climate change and global warming. However, a lack of practical knowledge makes it difficult for us to implement a change in our lifestyle that will be good for the earth.

Eco (213 Chiswick High Road, London W4 2DW, +44.20.8995 7611)— a new retail concept in London— makes it easier for consumers to inculcate good green habits at home and the workplace by offering inspiration, ideas and specific solutions. The store, showroom and consultancy business bring together a range of household products, appliances and building solutions that are stylish and ecologically sound. For a green home inside and out, consumers can get tips on improving insulation and lessening energy usage, as well as pick up eco-friendly furniture, paints and wallpaper while they are at it.

Eco was founded by Nicola Giuggioli, together with sister Livia Firth whose husband, English actor Colin Firth, has also lent his fame to the store. Since its inception, Eco has received a lot of press coverage and has brought eco living to the forefront of consumers' consciousness.

The store itself is an ecological destination of sort. Energy-wise, it is completely self-sufficient through its use of solar panels, wind turbines and power-saving appliances. The shop has also been installed with the latest water recycling systems so that all water—except drinking water— is recycled and collected in different ways. The grounds of Eco are stylish as well with a spare, modern appeal that will definitely strike a chord with today's green urbanites.

Eco sells a wide range of products for the home. Beginning with solar chargers, vases, lamps and bulbs, the store extends it accessories for the home to toys, books, cardboard furniture, wind-up radios, paints and wallpaper. Eco-friendly kitchen appliances such as washing machines, kettles, dishwashers, toasters, fridges and oven can also be found, while groovy items such as a bamboo computer and hangers recycled from old chairs will add character to any green living space.

Fair Share (Soho London, 102 Berwick Street, London W1F 0QP, +44.20.7287 8827) sells a range of handmade gifts and cards as well as a selection of foodstuffs from certified fair-trade suppliers. The eco establishment supports fair trade groups—organised primarily for the benefit of the local community. These groups ensure that local workers are paid fair wages, provided good working conditions, and most importantly, are able to participate in the ownership of the business.

Our Eco Shop (303 Westbourne Grove, Notting Hill, London, W11 2QA) is a 'pop up' affair of sorts. A collaboration between UK designers and small green companies, the makeshift boutique— it is open only for a few months every year—brings together a quirky selection of fair trade, ethical, organic and eco-friendly products.

The range includes mattresses made with all natural materials, unique eco-friendly home furnishings such as organic upholstery, organic fashion and green office stationery. Check back on www.ourecoshop.co.uk for the latest 'pop up' shop location and its vendors.

Karavan (167 Lordship Lane, London SE22 8HX, +44.20.8299 2542) has been selling fair trade products since the 1980s. It has opened its first major eco-friendly retail outlet—the shop sports a coat of natural paint and has an renewable energy supply—and stocks up on fair trade, organic and natural products. There are also items that help consumers make their lives more eco-friendly, such as green home-cleaning products, energy-saving lights and portable solar chargers.

Karavan also strives to inculcate eco awareness at an early age with toys for the toddler such as adorable mini homes and castles made of recycled cardboard. Home accessories such as bamboo fibre towels, organic cotton linen and a range of green-themed books can be found as well.

Red Door Gallery (10 Turnpin Lane, Greenwich London SE10 9 JA, +44.20.8858 2131) showcases ceramics, jewellery and crafts made by designers from Southeast London. Acting as an outlet for the little cottage industry of artists in the area, the pieces displayed in the gallery are all unique, original and entirely handmade.

Local british brand **Enamore** (www.enamore.co.uk) is leading a revival of pin-up model style with its sassy lingerie collection, remixed for a new generation with modern pizazz. Highlighting the label's irreverent dresses and inventive separates, these unique undergarments are made from ultra-soft sustainable fabrics which include organic cotton, hemp, bamboo, soy and silk.

Founder Jenny Ambrose started the brand in 2004, toying with vintage prints and styles as a means of countering the many excesses of the modern fashion industry. The company is based in the spa town of Bath and supports local suppliers for all its needs, while hiring graduates from across the UK. Enamore can also be found in ethical high street fashion boutique **Equa** (28 Camden Passage, Islington, N1 8ED, +44.20.7359 0955).

So Organic (Eagle House, 7 Turnpin Lane, Greenwich, SE10 9JA, +44.20.8465 5600) stocks up on a limitless range of skincare, bath products and cosmetics that are good for you, the environment and the people who make them. Advocating the benefits of organic skincare, So Organic's owners and staff personally test all the products before they hit the shelves, so that items come with personal recommendations.

The shop's range of makeup is also natural and completely free from parabens, petroleum, synthetic fragrance and other hidden chemicals commonly found in commercial brands. Its pure baby products—soaps, shampoos, creams and reusable nappies—make green-hearted mums go absolutely ga-ga.

Nelsons Homeopathic Pharmacy (73 Duke Street, London W1K 5BY, +44.20.7629 3118) has been an advocate of homeopathic medicine since the 1860s. Homeopath Edward Bach begun selling his famous Bach Original Flower Remedies here in the 1930s and the store has many evocative artefacts reflecting its history.

THIS PAGE (FROM TOP): Eco offers an itinerant selection of organic, ethical and fair trade merchandise for sale; an organic camisole set from Enamore's lingerie line.

OPPOSITE: In addition to its green products, Eco's consultation services help novice green-consumers tog their home out in style.

europe: shopping

THIS PAGE (FROM TOP): TRAID highlights the second 'R' in the green mantra 'Reduce, Reuse and Recycle'; Luma's exquisite collection of bedlinen is worth buying even if you are not eco-conscious.
OPPOSITE: Stock up on eco clothing and homeware at Altermundi.

The pharmacy has an enormous 'potency bank' which holds more than 2,000 homeopathic remedies—there is a steady demand for them over the counter, online and by mail order. During spring, its Pollenna hay fever remedy flies out the store.

Howies (42 Carnaby Street, London W1F 7DY, +44.20.7287 2345) is a sporty ethical brand with its first stand-alone store in London. Ethically kitted out in sustainable wood furniture and eco paints, the store issues e-receipts too.

It also sells a range of weird and wonderful recycled gifts such as belts made from bicycle tyres, and clothes for men and women.

Luma (98 Church Road, London SW14 0DQ, +44.20.8748 2264) offers luxurious organic home bedding such as superfine cotton bedlinen, merino wool blankets, handmade organic mattresses and baby layettes. Children's bedlinen are charmingly adorned with embroidery and are made from organic cotton percale with a 200 thread count.

All products in the shop are officially Fairtrade-certified and organic. Linens, too are certified by independent agency Skal, which inspects every stage of production to ensure that neither the environment nor anyone's health has been damaged during the manufacturing process. Good for you too are the in-house bath and skin products that are stringently pure and organic.

The most environmentally friendly clothes are old clothes—thus vintage outlets offer the fashionable an alternative that is super stylish, one-of-a-kind and eco-friendly to boot.

Beyond Retro (112 Cheshire Street, London E2 6EJ, +44.20.7613 3636) is a vast warehouse that is packed with over 10,000 items, and is considered somewhat of an East End institution with its own following of hip fashion students, stylists, musicians and artists.

There are classics such as jeans, shirts, leather jackets and cowboy boots, as well as plenty of off-beat items to appeal to those who like to push the fashion limits.

Jumping on the vintage bandwagon is **Palette London** (21 Canonbury Lane, London N1 2AS, +44.20.7288 7428). The boutique specialises in collectible designer vintage and avant-garde labels such as Pucci, Courreges and Ossie Clark.

TRAID (2 Acre Lane, London SW2 5SG, +44.20.7326 4330) which stands for Textile Recycling for Aid and International Development, has nine thrift shops across London, with each specialising in specific stock ranging from clothes fashioned from reclaimed fabrics, to second-hand designer clothes. These wares have been lovingly donated by the British public through TRAID's Clothes Recycling Banks, scattered throughout London.

For books, head to the Shepherd's Bush branch, while designer bargains can be found at the Westbourne Park store. The Brixton outlet stocks the best range of quirky vintage fashion. Look out for 1980s frocks—which are, alarmingly, coming back to fashion—and get them for a song.

paris, france

In Paris, all savvy fashionistas, green-hearted or otherwise, head for **Come On Eileen** (16–18 Rue des Taillandiers,

75011 Paris, +33.1.4338 1211) which has been described as an 'orgasmic fashion venue'. Vintage pieces from Lanvin, Gucci, Yves Saint Laurent, Azzedine Alaia and Valentino line the racks. Prices are high, but with Kylie Minogue as a regular, there is real competition to be had in grabbing the best of these one-off pieces.

Sobosibio (82 Avenue de Peygros, 06530 Peymeinade, +33.4.9340 2294) is a fashion and gifts business that works towards 'protecting the environment and ensuring good working conditions for those who work with them'.

What you can find in its quaint little boutique are comfy clothes to lounge in at home, sleepwear and Asian-inspired ladies' fashion. The handmade crafts make unique gifts.

Paris-based **Ethos** (showroom at 12 Rue Marius Delcher, 94220 Charenton-le-Pont, +33.1.4378 8325) has become famous in the world of green fashion for its ethically created range of casual wear that includes jeans, tees and jersey dresses. All garments are made from organically grown cotton from India and certified by Skal. Clothing styles are designed in Paris and produced in India by a unit that promotes fair labour practices.

Sexy eco warriors stock up on **g=9.8** (21 Rue de la Gaité, 75014 Paris, +33.1.4631 2261) lingerie when they are in Paris. Created out of white pine trees, the range of slips, knickers, bras and bedwear are heaven to wear, and are modern and stylish to boot. Founder Sophie Young, an architect by training, believes in recycling, re-using and reducing consumption, which is why each piece of g=9.8 lingerie is made from recycled pine wood fibre, is made to last, and is packed in a recycled cardboard box.

Monsieur Poulet is a designer of ethical tee-shirts—wear a message on your chest in witty, humorous designs. Choose your slogan and your cause from one of the many boutiques that carry the brand, such as **Alter Mundi Paris** (41 Rue du Chermin vert, 75011 Paris, +33.1.4021 0891), **Alter Mundi Rivoli** (9 Rue de Rivoli, 75001 Paris, +33.1.4459 8166) and **Alter Mundi Beaurepaire** (25 Rue Beaurepaire, 75010 Paris, +33.1.4200 1573).

The fastest way to introduce a piece of eco clothing in your wardrobe is to get a pair of 'green' jeans. **Nu jeans** (8 Rue Taylor, 75010 Paris, +33.1. 8081 5030) sells an excellent range of fair trade, ethically produced denims in the most modern cuts and colours. Fancy a pair of low-slung ones in faded blue, or the most-up-to-date high waisted indigos with button fly? They are all here—which makes it tempting to throw 'reduced consumption' out the window and get more than one pair.

Como No (www.como-no.fr) has great boots not just because they are exceedingly environmentally friendly and ethical: only transitional cotton is used, and the brand works with cooperatives in Buenos Aires to promote fair trade.

Como No's footwear also displays plenty of street cred, with durable rubber soles and cotton high tops. Designs range from grafitti prints and whimsical polka dots to eye-catching neon shades. Leftover material from making the boots is used to make tote bags, wallets and cuddly soft toys.

swinton park

A historic North Yorkshire castle dating back to 1695, and home to the Earl of Swinton's family for generations, Swinton Park is a distinctive luxury resort with much to offer. Owned today by the family of Mark Cunliffe-Lister, great-grandson of the first Countess to reside at Swinton Park, and his wife Felicity, the entire property has been rejuvenated and transformed into a five-star establishment without losing an ounce of its charm.

The complex has seen many additions over the years—including an impressive tower and turreted battlements—but wandering through the perfectly restored rooms within leaves one only with a sense of English design's timelessness. Surrounding the hotel is the family's 81-hectare (200-acre) estate of meticulously tended gardens and wide expanses of open parkland. The landscape is ideally suited to long walks, and a number of established routes will take visitors past lakes, rivers, and moorlands that exemplify the calm and serenity of Yorkshire's countryside.

The almost prelapsarian beauty of the views all around was no doubt sufficient inspiration for the couple's eco-friendly approach to running Swinton Park. A carbon-neutral woodchip boiler handles all of the property's heating and hot water needs without relying on oil products. Laundry is also cleaned on-site with sophisticated ozone technology, cutting down on transport and the use of cleansing agents, while also wasting less water. Energy-efficient lighting, recycled pencils, and reusable water bottles in rooms also ensure that guests leave only the tiniest of footprints.

Each of the castle's 30 guest rooms and suites is individually designed and located on either the first or second floor, with lifts and accessibility features making most wheelchair-friendly. In addition to such modern amenities as WiFi internet access, flat-screen televisions, and trouser presses, all rooms enjoy superb views out over the gardens. As a further indulgence, Suites and 'Dukes' rooms are stocked with luxury bath products from the renowned English boutique brand, Jo Malone.

THIS PAGE: *A pleasant getaway awaits in the countryside.*

OPPOSITE (FROM LEFT): *Elegantly designed rooms invite guests to step back in time ; The standalone vintage bathtub makes bath time an indulgent experience.*

north yorkshire **united kingdom**

One of Swinton Park's most notable green achievements is also its most appetizing. A walled garden measuring some 2 hectares (4 acres) was created by Susan Cunliffe-Lister in 2004 to provide the restaurant with fresh produce. Susan, an award-winning gardener of national renown, worked closely with the head chef to plant a mix of fruit and vegetables not commonly associated with kitchen gardens. Artichokes, asparagus, autumn-fruiting raspberries and blueberries form the bulk of the harvest, but over 60 species of herbs and vegetables are produced all year round. The garden is presently the largest hotel kitchen garden in the United Kingdom—a fact made even more remarkable by its caretakers' refusal to use pesticides or weed-killers.

Under the direction of chef Simon Crannage, Swinton Park's restaurant elicits the finest results from the garden's ingredients, as well as fresh game, fish, and poultry from the fields and streams of the 8,094-hectare (20,000-acre) estate beyond. In recognition of its excellent food and service, Samuel's has been awarded 3 AA rosettes and is a member of the Chaine de Rotisseurs association and the Tea Guild. It is also listed in the Michelin Guide, and its instructional courses earned it a spot on the *Sunday Times*' 'Top Ten list of Cookery Schools' in 2008.

For its commitment to environmentally responsible tourism, Swinton Park has also received prestigious awards such as the Green Tourism Business Scheme award.

rooms
25 rooms • 5 suites

food
Samuel's: fresh seasonal fare from the hotel kitchen garden

drink
Bar and lounge

features
spa with jacuzzi and sauna • WiFi Internet access • library • meeting rooms • cookery school • golf • fishing • clay shooting • horse riding • trekking • children's play area

green features
woodchip burner provides carbon-neutral heating • ozone laundry service saves water and energy • recycled materials • energy-saving bulbs • largest hotel kitchen garden in the UK provides fresh ingredients to restaurant

nearby
Swinton • art galleries • museums • caves • churches • estate tours • falconry • gardens

contact
Masham, Ripon, North Yorks HG4 4JH, United Kingdom •
telephone: +44.1765.680 900 •
facsimile: +44.1765.680 901 •
email: reservations@swintonpark.com •
website: www.swintonpark.com

l'auberge basque

THIS PAGE: *The farm manor's rustic charm has been updated with a few contemporary touches.*

OPPOSITE (FROM LEFT): *The interiors' warm wood tones tastefully blend with the lush exterior; guests can savour sumptuous cuisine in tranquil surrounds.*

A beautiful gastronomic retreat in the Northern Basque Country, L'Auberge Basque is the culmination of three individual stories woven together as one by will of fate and mutual passion. The first story is that of its chef and owner, Cédric Béchade, a man who has spent over a decade in some of France's finest kitchens, many of them at the side of Alain Ducasse at Le Plaza Athénée's La Cour Jardin, and yet is only in his early thirties.

Béchade's professional career began at the Hotel du Palais in Biarritz, a Basque Country town just miles from the Spanish border, where he spent a year and a half practising his craft before accepting an offer from Paris. His sudden departure from the beautiful coastal town was bittersweet, but altogether necessary in the pursuit of greater heights. Years later, already an accomplished talent with a dream of establishing his own restaurant, he would meet the sommelier Samuel Ingelaere through his friendship with the Michelin chef Marc Veyrat.

Like Béchade, Ingelaere was a young man of great talent whose name was becoming known on the French culinary scene through his five-year tour at La Ferme de Mon Père. In 2005, he was named 'Sommelier of the Year' by the respected *Gault Millau* guide. The two men formed an immediate bond, with Béchade sharing his vision for a restaurant-inn, and the other man pledging to follow his lead.

All that remained was to find the right location, which is where the story of an old farm manor near St Jean de Luz comes in. Originally built in 1672, the house would need 11 months of intensive refurbishment before it was ready to receive guests. This was accomplished with the help of the architect Christian Larroque and interior designer Isabelle Juy, from Flamant Home Interiors. Using a team of local artisans and workers, they restored the rundown building into the contemporary inn that it is today. Facing the La Rhune Mountains and surrounded on all sides by greenery, with a faint hint of the

st pée sur nivelle france

sea air wafting in from the nearby beach, it is a spectacular complement to Béchade's cuisine and Ingelaere's handpicked wine lists.

The chef's deep-seated love for the Basque Country is evident on every plate that comes out of his humble yet world-class kitchen. Based exclusively on locally available ingredients, the imaginative and colourful presentations taste as lively and fresh as they look. All this, and a wine list of over 160 varieties, is enjoyed in a spacious dining room with a full view of the rolling parklands and mountains for an experience as close to nature as it gets.

In every one of the 11 smartly appointed rooms and suites, heating and cooling services are naturally provided throughout the year through underground geothermal systems. Water-wasting baths are replaced by 'rain dance' showers which blend every litre of water with three of air for a unique sensation. Béchade's sense of responsibility towards his beloved Basque landscape extends to almost all of L'Auberge's practices. Biodegradable materials and eco-friendly products are used everywhere, and the kitchen manages to find a use for every last bit of waste, even if it ends up as compost.

With two culinary independents at the helm, and some of the most beautiful countryside in France, L'Auberge Basque offers visitors a deeply luxurious opportunity to taste something new with every last one of their senses combined.

rooms
9 rooms • 2 suites

food
contemporary European

drink
extensive wine list

features
refurbished farm manor • wireless Internet access • landscaped gardens • meeting room

green features
geothermal heating • combination water/air shower systems • selective waste disposal • use of biodegradable products • thermal and acoustic insulation

nearby
Biarritz • Spanish border • San Sebastian • Bilbao Guggenheim Museum

contact
D 307, Vieille Route de St Jean de Luz 64310 St Pée sur Nivelle, France •
telephone: +33.05.5951 7000 •
facsimile: +33.05.5951 7017 •
email: contact@aubergebasque.com •
website: www.aubergebasque.com

hôtel les orangeries

THIS PAGE (FROM LEFT): *Take a cooling dip as temperatures hit a high; relax in the hotel's lush gardens.*

OPPOSITE (FROM LEFT): *Guests at the games room can enjoy a range of traditional boardgames; buttery crossaints, fairtrade coffee and organic jams await guests in the morning.*

Nothing is more romantic than the languid French countryside, with its historic castles, untouched landscape, and quaint villages. Lussac-les-Châteaux in Poitou is one such place, popular with visitors as a charming stopover to Ile de Ré or the southwest corner of France.

Set within the village centre, just a two-hour train ride from Paris, Hôtel Les Orangeries occupies a country house dating back to the 18th century. The building has been carefully renovated to modern standards without losing any of its traditional charm. Parquet floors have been given back their original lustre, while stone fireplaces, oak panelling and wrought iron ornamentation have been refurbished to bring out the hotel's old world charm.

In spite of its downtown location, the boutique hotel's grounds maintain privacy with high stone walls surrounding the compound. Offering 15 impeccably appointed rooms and suites, guests' desires are seen to with personal attention and efficacy. Interiors are individually decorated and add to the encompassing rustic charm. Each room offers sumptuous beds, in addition to satellite television, wireless Internet and en-suite bathrooms complete with mahogany panelling and a sizeable bathtub.

Guests can enjoy meals in the grand dining room. Hôtel Les Orangeries' fragrant orchards provide for the organic jams and fruit that accompany the daily breakfast spread, while a seasonal menu—featuring organic produce and locally-sourced ingredients—can be savoured in the evening. Post-dinner drinks in the lounge are a cosy affair, with organic herb teas and local liqueurs to choose from. Guests can also head to the games room, where they can engage in a game of billiards or a number of traditional board games.

lussac-les-châteaux **france**

Such an air of intimacy is also evident in the captivating gardens outside. Landscape artist Patsy Boughton lends her talent here, crafting a 'jardin l'anglaise' where guests can stroll along sculpted flowerbeds and explore the fruit orchards. The 35-m (115-ft) -long pool is ensconced within this picturesque setting, and is an ideal place for one to sunbathe in the summer. The Poitou countryside offers more than 800 km (497 miles) of nature walks, and one can view these idyllic landscapes via foot or electro-powered bike.

Hôtel les Orangeries was the first in France to receive the European Commission's Ecolabel for its commitment in environmental preservation. Throughout the renovation process, natural materials such as hemp were used for insulation, while paints were made from natural pigments and lime milk. Using only renewable energy sources, electricity consumption is kept low through the use of energy-saving light bulbs and green petrol. Due to an ongoing water shortage in the region, a rainwater harvesting system has been installed while taps, showers and toilets are fitted with water-saving devices. The hotel's surrounds have been designated a protected bird habitat by the League for Bird Protection, while buying from artisan farmers emphasises Hôtel Les Orangeries' support for the local community

With its unique brand of sincere hospitality and eco luxury, Hôtel Les Orangeries presents a luxurious base from which to explore at leisure the natural and historical wonders of the Poitou region.

rooms
15 rooms and suites

food
organic French

drink
natural wines, organic liqueurs and herb teas

features
landscaped garden and fruit orchard • outdoor pool • games room • complimentary wireless Internet access • satellite television

green features
careful reburishment of building • use of natural materials during renovation • electro-powered bikes • energy saving measures • rainwater harvesting system • support of the local farming community • all produce is sourced responsibly within a 30 km (19 mile) radius • within designated protected bird sanctuary

nearby
nature trails • Abbey Church of Saint-Savin-sur-Gartempe • old Poitiers • Montmorillon

contact
12, Avenue du Dr Dupont
86320 Lussac-les-Châteaux, France •
telephone: +33.549.840 707 •
facsimile: +33.549.849 882 •
email: orangeries@wanadoo.fr •
website: www.hotel-lesorangeries.com

le domaine de saint-géry

THIS PAGE (FROM TOP): *The pool is a delight in the summer months; great lengths have been taken to restore the country estate.*

OPPOSITE (FROM LEFT): *La Cave is named for its unique vaulted ceiling and cream stone walls; savour the distinct taste of organically cultivated truffles.*

When Pascale and Patrick Duler first laid eyes on the Saint-Géry estate in 1985, the sprawling compound lay in ruins. Over the next few years, the Dulers painstakingly revived the rundown grounds, planting thousands of trees over 64 hectares (158 acres) of land and restoring the traditional stone buildings, pigeon lofts and grain silos to their original pristine states. Today, Le Domaine de Saint-Géry is an intimate country house and a luxurious outpost from which to explore the region of Quercy Blanc in southwestern France.

The Duler domain offers only five rooms and suites, each with its own distinct architecture and décor. La Cave occupies a cut-stone vaulted cellar, with its ceiling forming a unique low arch. Soft lighting gives the room a romantic air, while guests can enjoy garden views from the two terraces, one of which opens onto the lush grounds. Le Cantou's large windows invite in abundant sunlight, while the serene La Fontaine enjoys a location close to the fragrant garden where fig and lemon trees are planted. La Métairie showcases the country house's traditional charm, while the two-storey Les Figuiers is a good fit for larger groups.

There is little wonder that the restaurant takes pride of place at the hotel, considering that Patrick is also its chef. Simplicity brings out the best in quality ingredients, and Patrick's creations emphasise the original flavours of meat, fresh herbs and vegetables used—even exotic additions such as wild flowers. Limited seats ensure haute cuisine in an exclusive setting, assuring guests that each dish is prepared with the chef's full consideration. Locally sourced, organic wines and cheeses will delight gourmands, while time-honoured French creations such as foie gras seared in truffle jus are on hand to titillate tastebuds.

montcuq en quercy **france**

This highly prized fungi is cultivated at the hotel's organic truffle plantation, and one is free to explore the compound at leisure. Guests can also stroll along nature trails that will take them through oak woods, grassy fields and the wild orchid reserve, with bicycles on hand for those wishing to go further afield. Instead of wasting electricity, the heated pool uses firewood from the estate's trees and offers picturesque views of the French countryside. In colder months, guests can work out in the climate controlled fitness room, while those who want to relax can head to the library to enjoy a good book. The smoking salon is an especially tempting prospect in the late evenings, exuding an old world charm in which guests can mingle with a cigar and glass of cognac in hand.

The estate understands the importance of protecting its natural heritage. As such, the upkeep of the Saint-Géry compound is based on a biodynamic philosophy, an organic farming method that focuses on cultivating beneficial relationships and restoring the equilibrium between animals, plants and land within a self-sustainable environment. For instance, the management uses only organic processes to maintain its woodlands and truffle plantation, while the eco lodge is powered by renewable energy and avoids using chemicals in its garden or pool.

With the Dulers' whole-hearted devotion to the environment, the natural beauty of Le Domaine de Saint-Géry will surely remain to attract visitors for generations to come.

rooms
5 rooms

food
organic traditional French

drink
selection of organic wines and brandies

features
1,000-sq-m- (10,764-sq-ft-) natural pool · fitness room · smoking salon · library · organic truffle plantation · estate shop · walking trails · spa · bicycles

green features
biodynamic philosophy · refurbished original structure · organic vegetable garden · reforestation · uses renewable energy sources · no chemicals used in gardens or pool

nearby
Cahors · Le Lot · Lauzerte

contact
Lascabanes, 46800 Montcuq en Quercy, France ·
telephone: +33.5.6531 8251 ·
facsimile: +33.5.6522 9289 ·
email: pascale@saint-gery.com ·
website: www.saint-gery.com

hôtel le morgane

Created for today's hip and savvy traveller, Hôtel Le Morgane is a boutique hotel set in downtown Chamonix, France. Setting the elegance of a luxury hotel against an awe-inspiring tableau of glaciers, lush forests and sheer granite cliffs, the mountain retreat attracts nature and sports lovers seeking to cultivate a certain *art de vivre*.

The stylish abode recently underwent a complete facelift to create a contemporary look that juxtaposes nature with luxury. Stone and untreated wood play a large role in interiors: floors are tiled with slate, while granite from the valley and brushed oak wood furnish public and private spaces. Elegant and cosy, rooms are installed with modern amenities such as flat-screen televisions and wireless Internet access. Each room features a king-size bed and contemporary furnishings, among which include creations from design maestros Antonio Citterio and Philippe Starck. Natural light floods through full-length windows, offering guests unhindered views of the mountain peaks and undulating forests Chamonix is famed for.

During renovations, Hôtel Le Morgane took the opportunity to minimise its energy consumption and bring down its ecological footprint. Solar panels have been installed to supplement electricity, while low-voltage bulbs save on energy usage. Water-based varnishes and solvent-free paints also contribute to healthy and hypoallergenic indoor spaces and keep environmental impact low. As part of its

THIS PAGE (FROM LEFT): *Clean lines give bedrooms a classic finish; cuddle up by the cosy fireplace.*
OPPOSITE (FROM LEFT): *The use of natural woods reflects Hôtel Le Morgane's alpine surrounds; a spa session lets one enjoy the pure air while indulging in the latest beauty treatments.*

chamonix mont-blanc **france**

daily operations, the hotel uses eco-friendly chemicals and has established a responsible disposal programme where waste is separated and recycled where possible.

The critically acclaimed Bistrot is yet another reason for guests to rave about. Mickey Bourdillat is a celebrated chef in his own right, steering the restaurant to earn its first Michelin star in 2007. Reputed for his simple yet inventive French cuisine, Chef Bourdillat's table features fresh organic produce sourced from the local region.

For indulgence on a different front, head to the Spa. Boasting facilities such as a pool, steam room and sauna, one can indulge in customised beauty treatments in a tranquil atmosphere.

To truly appreciate the retreat's charming alpine setting, head up into the mountains. Extreme sports abound in the form of ice climbing and snowboarding, while gentle nature trails allow guests to admire the stunning environs at a leisurely pace. Even the cosmopolitan crowd is provided for, with Chamonix's baroque churches, chic boutiques and rustic bistros enabling one to sightsee in style.

Hôtel Le Morgane redefines high-end mountain accommodation by offering a green alternative couched in refined luxury. And with the eco retreat proffering such guilt-free, sensory experiences, there is little wonder guests find it so difficult to leave.

rooms
56 rooms

food
Le Bistrot: contemporary French

drink
open bar of wines, beers, selected spirits and soft drinks

features
the Spa • pool • snow sports • meeting facilities • day-trips and excursions

green features
solar power generator • use of local produce • eco-certified detergents • recycled chemical containers and bottles

nearby
Mont Blanc • Parc National des Ecrins

contact
145, Avenue de l'Aiguille du Midi, 74400 Chamonix Mont-Blanc, France •
telephone: +33.04.5053 5715 •
facsimile: +33.04.5053 2807 •
email: reservation@hotelmorganechamonix.com •
website: www.morgane-hotel-chamonix.com

hi hotel

This intimate hotel-playground in downtown Nice features a distinctive conceptual ingenuity that makes it an icon on its own. Designed by Matali Crasset, Hi Hotel's 38 rooms are a deconstruction of luxury expectations that proves there's plenty of surprise left to be teased out of the old four walls and a bed.

Every room is modelled on one of nine evocatively named templates, designed by Crasset at a level that goes beyond colour schemes and furnishings. Instead, they are functionally different experiences encouraging guests to find multiple uses for everyday objects. In 'Techno Corner' accommodations, a swivelling flat-screen television doubles up as a partition between bedroom and bathroom, a role assignment that makes a theatre seat out of the sleek bathtub. 'Rendez Vous' is an open-plan space that appears dedicated to bathing, with a large lava stone tub taking pride of place indoors and a private outdoor terrace with shower. A few modular adjustments later, and the canary-yellow chambers become efficient offices, or stylish living rooms. Transformations in 'Happy Day' are even more dramatic. What appears to be a cosy pastel-green living room hides an alcove that, when opened, reveals the other half of the couch/bed and makes a bedroom out of a lounge.

THIS PAGE: *A profusion of colours greet guests at every turn.*
OPPOSITE (FROM LEFT): *Hi Hotel's rooms showcase contemporary design at its most innovative; the rooftop pool terrace offers unhindered views of the ocean.*

nice **france**

This flexibility extends to the hotel's facilities. Happy Bar reveals an exoskeletal cage that provides seating and a frame for towering video projections to accompany the music of live DJs. The rooftop pool doubles as an outdoor observation point with views to the Alps over the rooftops of Nice, complete with deck chairs and waterbeds. Espace Hi Body Spa offers hammams and massage rooms crafted in futuristic style from 21st-century materials.

The cleverness of the Hi Hotel's design approach is not limited to finding a balance of form and function; it also incorporates a sense of ecological responsibility—after all, what could be more modern? Recycled materials are used everywhere from the paper in the office to the containers in the kitchen, with disposable packaging avoided wherever possible. Guests wishing to see the city may make use of bicycles as an alternative to car rentals and public transportation. The hotel also believes in organic farming and production as an answer to some of today's environmental problems, and, as a result, cotton staff uniforms, the building's coat of mineral paint, the entire canteen restaurant's menu, and even the garden's fertilisers, are all naturally derived.

The greatest pitfall contemporary designer hotels face is an over-reliance on unusual qualities as too much distance between norms and innovations risks alienation. Hi Hotel deftly sidesteps this concern by centering its creativity on the already familiar—a matter of new ideas presenting themselves in everyday situations. By the time one reaches the end of a stay, life itself may seem just that little bit different.

rooms
38 rooms

food
Hi Food: organic • Hi Sushi: Japanese

drink
Happy Bar

features
Espace Hi Body Spa • rooftop pool terrace • rental of bicycles • conference facilities

green features
use of recycled materials • vegetable-based shampoo and shower gels • organic products • energy and water saving practices

nearby
beach • downtown Nice

contact
3 Avenue Des Fleurs, 06000 Nice, France •
telephone: +33.49.707 2626 •
facsimile: +33.49.707 2627 •
email: hi@hi-hotel.net •
website: www.hi-hotel.net

domaine de murtoli

THIS PAGE: *Domaine de Murtoli's sprawling green compound.*

OPPOSITE (FROM LEFT): *Refurbished interiors make for cosy quarters; savour fine Mediterranean fare amid intimate surroundings.*

If ever there was a place that signified nature's triumph over the excesses displayed by much of the modern travel industry, it would have to be Corsica. Where else could one find a landscape so beautiful, polished by centuries of exposure to sea and sky, that holidaymakers treat it with careful reverence, and wasteful enterprises restrict themselves out of a sense of duty and conscience? This is not a place where celebrities come dressed in their public personae, this is where they come to be themselves.

Some of the best views are to be found at the Domain de Murtoli, a 2000-hectare (4942-acre) expanse of virtually untouched landscape. Due to its size and the nature of Corsica's geographical diversity, a number of widely varied scenes can be found within this estate. One border runs along the edge of the sea for a dozen kilometres, while gardens, fruit orchards and the flourishing Ortolo River valley make up the interior. Down by the pristine beach lies a collection of restored Corsican homes and farmhouses, each one a magnificent villa with its own character. Notably, no other developments are visible from anywhere along the perimeter of the property; one feels as far from urban life as possible, yet the nearest town is only a 15-minute drive away.

The Murtoli's 16th-century stone buildings have been painstakingly upgraded through traditional means by architects Stéphane Lucchini and Thomas Fourtané, with modern amenities sensibly incorporated where possible. Belying the hardiness of their weathered facades are warm interiors with such touches as elegant chestnut parquet flooring and handmade local furniture. Some like the Persia villa are suited for two, while others can house between four and eight guests. Most units feature a large private swimming pool, as well as a sauna, spa and steam room facilities.

sartène **france**

rooms
6 farm manors • 6 refurbished former outhouses • 1 hamlet with 3 former outhouses

food
cave restaurant: traditional Corsican • beach restaruant: light Mediterranean

drink
creek café bar • lounge at the creek

features
private beach and creek • beauty treatments • massage services • al fresco dining available in the garden • private pools • open kitchen • hunting • fishing • nature walks • boat rentals

green features
restored Corsican buildings • farm-supported restaurant • organic kitchen garden • protected estate with 8 km (5 miles) of virgin coastal land •

nearby
beaches • Figari airport

contact
20100 Sartène, France •
telephone: +33.49.571 6924 •
facsimile: +33.49.577 0032 •
email: villas@murtoli.com •
website: www.murtoli.com

Most of the property's green practices focus on conserving the original buildings and environment, but a few significant advances are also made in its kitchen. An organic kitchen garden and nearby farms ensure constant harvest of fresh ingredients. Villa guests may also purchase these supplies for their own use in kitchen-equipped villas, but chefs Bernard Coloma and Alice Monnier make an excellent case for eating out. Having earned a Michelin star at Les Demeures du Ranquet, Coloma is no stranger to high standards, and the broad canvas of the Corsican landscape and its attendant flavours gives his personal style the benefit of added dimension.

Hunting and fishing enthusiasts will find a much wider playing field here than they are normally accustomed to, with game ranging from pigeons, ducks and wild boars to catch from the Ortolo River. The Murtoli is ready to support expeditions with its own teams of experienced staff, hunting dogs and boats. Of course, one may simply enjoy a long walking tour of the grounds, either alone or with a guide, capped off with a luxurious massage on the beach by the experienced resident therapist at the end of the day. Either way, Domaine de Murtoli represents a unique vacation experience that could only happen in Corsica.

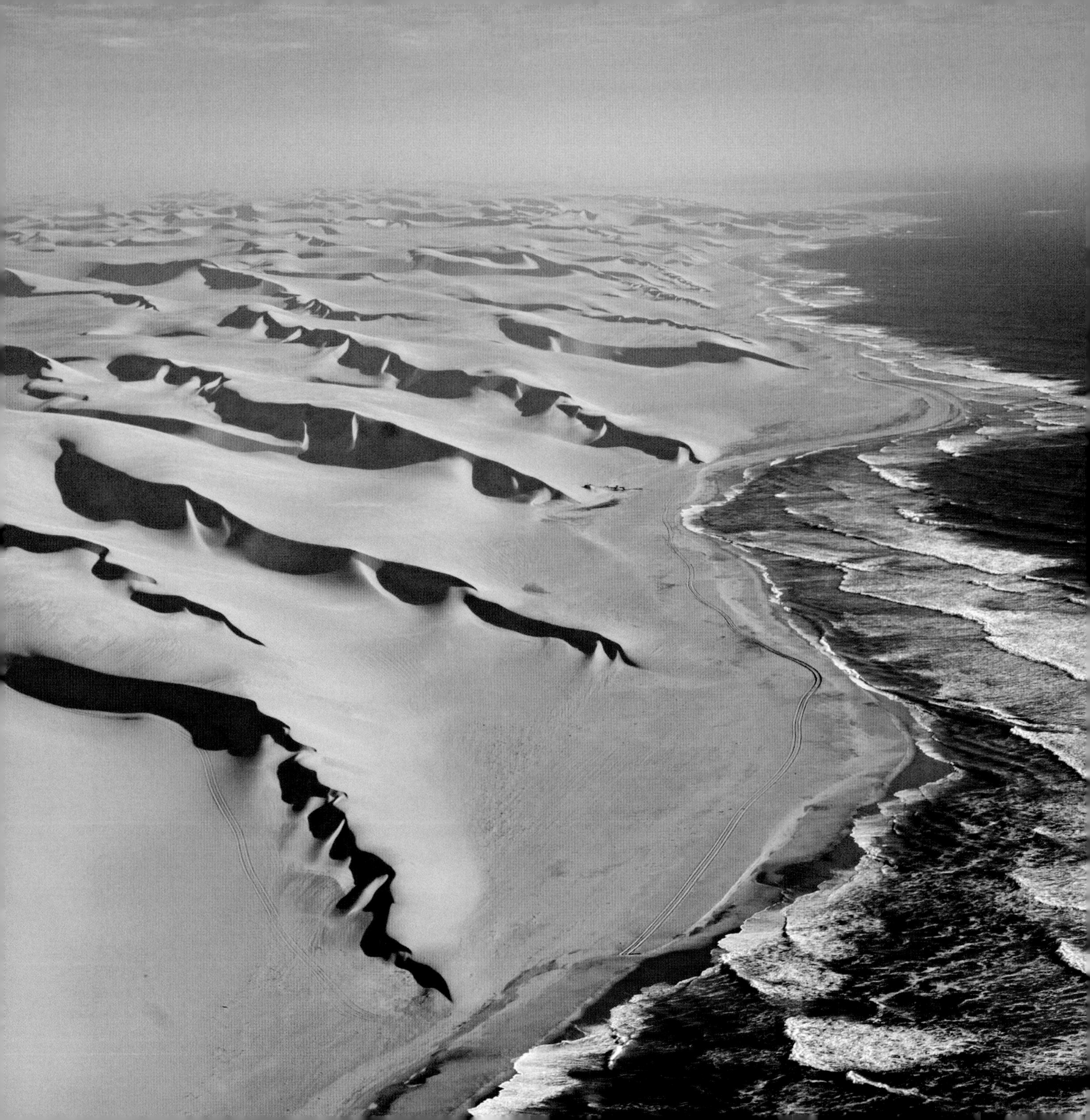

africa+themiddleeast

PORTUGAL
SPAIN
ITALY
GREECE
TURKEY
Origins Dar Itrane
Kasbah Du Toubkal
La Sultana Oualidia
Mediterranean Sea
CYPRUS
LEBANON
SYRIA
IRAQ
IRAN
TUNISIA
Gulf of Sidra
ISRAEL
JORDAN
KUWAIT
Arabian Gulf
MOROCCO
ALGERIA
LIBYA
Lazuli Lodge
Six Senses Hideaway Zighy Bay
WESTERN SAHARA
EGYPT
QATAR
SAUDI ARABIA
U.A.E.
MAURITANIA
MALI
NIGER
CHAD
SUDAN
Red Sea
OMAN
ERITREA
YEMEN
SENEGAL
GAMBIA
Gulf of Aden
GUINEA-BISSAU
GUINEA
BURKINA FASO
BENIN
NIGERIA
DJIBOUTI
SIERRA LEONE
CÔTE D'IVOIRE
GHANA
TOGO
CENTRAL AFRICAN REPUBLIC
ETHIOPIA
LIBERIA
CAMEROON
SOMALIA
UGANDA
Gulf of Guinea
EQUATORIAL GUINEA
KENYA
Borana Lodge
Campi ya Kanzi
GABON
DEMOCRATIC REPUBLIC OF CONGO
RWANDA
CONGO
BURUNDI
TANZANIA
SEYCHELLES
COMOROS
Tsara Komba Lodge
ANGOLA
ZAMBIA
MALAWI
MAURITIUS
MOZAMBIQUE
South Atlantic Ocean
ZIMBABWE
Mozambique Channel
NAMIBIA
MADAGASCAR
BOTSWANA
Legend
Lake
+5000 m
4000–5000 m
3000–4000 m
2000–3000 m
1000–2000 m
500–1000 m
200–500 m
0–200 m
SOUTH AFRICA
Indian Ocean
Cape of Good Hope
0 km
500
1000
1500 km
N

africa + the middle east

a land of contrasts

Africa evokes a thousand untouched landscapes where colourful indigenous tribes live and where the wildest animals roam free. The continent is characterised by vast open spaces, breathtaking scenery and great contrasts—dunes, ocean and mountains that stir the spirit and move the heart. It is a place where it is still possible to see no roads, towns or even trees for hundreds of miles, and suddenly discover a bountiful park filled with magnificent wildlife and fascinating communities.

Africa boasts some of the most fascinating lodges in the world; over the years, it has become the epitome of barefoot luxury, where guests can sleep in style in wonderful outdoor settings while enjoying the same kind of comforts they would at home. Unfortunately, Africa is also a land of great poverty, widespread diseases and severe drought. The ever-increasing human population constantly needs more natural resources, resulting in a significant loss of biodiversity and problems of food availability. The fact that great beauty lies side by side with profound distress means that tourism has a big role to play in Africa: it can be used to alleviate poverty and conserve the environment. Although still somewhat limited in visitor numbers in comparison with other continents, tourism is having a huge impact in Africa as it is the principal foreign exchange earner in most of her countries.

barefoot luxury

The continent actually leads the way in eco-chic travel, through groundbreaking ventures combining conservation and visits to the communities to the benefit of both. Indeed, although some of the tourism establishments in Africa are among the most comfortable on earth, the focus is more often put on the luxury of the experience rather than the experience of luxury. Having breakfast with elephants only a few feet away, going on an afternoon hike with the Maasai, and spending a romantic night under the bright stars—this is what the new breed of enlightened travellers look for. In Africa, being gentle to the environment and concerned for the welfare of the local people goes hand in hand with impeccable service at every turn and stylish interiors. Forget the notion that Africa is synonymous with basic facilities—many safari lodges offer sumptuous canopied beds with fantastic views, long infinity-edge pools and spectacular bathrooms.

communities + conservation

Meeting the peoples and discovering the cultures of Africa can be a moving and profound experience. Most tourism companies now understand that they have to further involve local communities in the success of their operations, and therefore engage them in locally owned or managed tourism projects.

THIS PAGE: *Two giraffes at a sunset rendezvous on the savannah.*
PAGE 80: *Africa is a land of many wonders—not least of them its stunning landscapes.*

This benefits both people and the environment. If African people are given a stake in the safari industry and are allowed to benefit from the income wildlife generates, African game will have a higher value to them alive than dead, thus reducing poaching and other destructive activities. In many parts of Africa, ecotourism has thus reconciled people and wildlife in their competing claims for land. Local governments now channel a portion of the park entrance fees to social welfare and conservation projects, and are training more local people as park rangers and guides than ever before.

Even so, the combined gross domestic product of the 50 sub-Saharan countries is equivalent to that of the state of Virginia in the US. Knowing this, it is easy to understand why there is insufficient internal capital to fund a thorough protection of natural resources. As African governments lack the funds to protect their own heritage, they cooperate with thousands of foreign Non-Governmental Organisations (NGOs) that are dedicated to saving Africa's wildlife and improving people's livelihoods. In Madagascar, the government is committed to tripling the size of its total protected areas in 2005, while NGOs such as Conservation International and the World Wildlife Fund are working hard to strengthen the management of national parks. These same NGOs work in Gabon to help consolidate a network of newly created protected areas that host the most pristine and biologically rich tropical forests in Central Africa. The work of conservation NGOs is of paramount importance in Africa, and many tour operators and lodges cooperate with them. Tourists are also more than welcome to participate in volunteering activities and to make a donation.

Safaris have long been a traveller's favourite, and now that rifles have been replaced by cameras, safari trips are guilt-free as they contribute towards the conservation of the wonderful African wildlife. Luxury safari tents and lodges are also increasingly managed with the environment in mind: water conservation measures and renewable sources of energy are becoming the norm, while in most cases, a portion of the profits from lodges fund the protection of vast wildlife reserves. The luxury lodges of the Ecotourism Association of Kenya have a strong commitment to environmental and community responsibilities, from energy efficiency and reforestation schemes to scouring for local produce and training young villagers for jobs.

THIS PAGE: *The importance of preserving local traditions and cultures becomes clear when you experience them.*
OPPOSITE: *Due to stringent protection measures, scores of wildlife still roam the plains below Mount Kilimanjaro.*

bush and beach

Choosing a holiday destination in Africa is not an easy task, as every country has something unique to offer. If you would like to see the bush, consider Kenya, immortalised as safari country by legendary writers such as Ernest Hemingway and movies such as *Out of Africa*. It is home to the Big Five: the lion, the African elephant, the African buffalo, the leopard and the rhinoceros. The country is also famous for the annual Great Migration of millions of herbivores across the Serengeti-Mara ecosystem and its indigenous people, including the renowned Maasai.

Tanzania is another country of dazzling natural beauty and great safari opportunities. Africa's highest mountain, Mount Kilimanjaro, provides an unforgettable view with its snow-capped peak over verdant plains. Sprawling over 2 million hectares (5 million acres), the world-famous Kruger National Park is South Africa's largest game reserve and one of the finest wildlife sanctuaries on the planet. Botswana's Okavango Delta is another magical oasis, famed for Africa's largest single concentration of elephants and brilliant birdlife.

If you would rather go on a beach holiday, then head east to beautiful Zanzibar Island or try the pristine beachfront of Mozambique with its soft, white sand beaches lined with coconut palms. Other idyllic islands in the azure waters of the Indian Ocean include the Seychelles, Mauritius and the Comoros. Madagascar also boasts spectacular beaches, and it will bring you face to face with its unique flora and fauna: lemurs, baobabs and geckoes. Cut off from the African mainland for millions of years, Madagascar's forests are a naturalist's dream. Further east lie the Maldives, a chain of 1,200 island and coral atolls, which are in danger of disappearing under the waves if the current pace of climate change continues to raise sea levels.

eco-chic in the desert

Stretching from the Red Sea to the outskirts of the Atlantic Ocean, the Sahara covers most of Northern Africa. As large as the US, it is the world's mightiest desert, drawing thousands of visitors in search of adventure. The Sahara is an enlightening and intriguing place, and there is no better way to experience it than through its wonderful eco lodges, kasbahs and tented camps, nestled in the dunes of a tranquil oasis. A camel-back ride with the Bedouins and the pure romance of a candle-lit dinner under a star-studded sky add to the sensory overload that one feels in the Sahara.

The Middle East is another alluring destination for travellers in search of sophisticated luxury in the desert. Far from the artificial image Dubai can sometimes convey, new eco resorts are being developed with the environment in mind. Located on the northern Musandam Peninsula in the Sultanate of Oman, the Six Senses Hideaway Zighy Bay (see pages 89, 104–105) is a perfect example of a luxurious hotel designed to blend in with its natural surroundings. In July 2008, Dubai launched an eco initiative to encourage hotels to reduce their CO_2 emissions by 20 percent by 2011. Another new approach towards promoting sustainable hospitality is the collaboration between local developers and Hollywood celebrities—actor Brad Pitt was recently commissioned to design a new environmentally friendly five-star resort hotel in Dubai.

zero carbon cruise

Egypt is famous the world over for the Pyramids of Giza and the Valley of the Kings, but to truly experience the country's magic, one has to see Egypt from an elegant yacht called a *dahabeah*. A journey down the Nile aboard the carbon-free boat is the essence of eco-chic travel, and it helps preserve an ancient tradition as well: of the 500 boats currently cruising down the Nile, there are fewer than 10 *dahabeahs* left. Another beguiling country for the green traveller is Morocco—savour its rich history, colourful souks and markets, great food and superb eco-friendly accommodation.

an experience to remember

With its pure, raw feel and its vibrant people, Africa offers visitors a feast for the senses—it is a travel experience a thousand miles from the air-conditioned tourist trails in other parts of the world. There are many tribes speaking different tongues, but they all exude the same warm African hospitality and vitality. Close to nature, you and your loved ones can indulge in untamed beauty and timeless sunshine. More importantly, travelling to Africa with eco-minded ventures helps to protect its spectacular wildlife and improve the welfare of locals who share in the benefits of tourism.

THIS PAGE (FROM TOP): Experience history and culture in Egypt.
OPPOSITE: The limestone formations found in the Sahara.

... The Sahara is an enlightening and intriguing place...

africa + the middle east: restaurants

THIS PAGE (FROM TOP): Guilt-free dining need not compromise on luxury; food doesn't have to be boring to be tasty, and good for the environment.

OPPOSITE (FROM TOP): Top-notch service goes with great food at Zighy Bay; enjoy desert hospitality bedouin style at Lazuli Lodge.

nairobi, kenya

Eating with a green conscience is still a fairly new concept in Africa; vegan and vegetarian restaurants are relatively few and far between. Having said that, there are still places to eat guilt-free if you look hard enough. **Chowpaty Pure Vegetarian Restaurant** (4th Parklands Avenue, Parklands, +254.20.374 8884) serves Indian vegan-friendly cuisine from a casual take-out counter.

South Indian favourites such as *masala dosa* can be found here, as well as a variety of fruit juices. **Slush Limited** (Parklands Road, Corner Plaza, Westlands, +254.20.375 1039) has a variety of Chinese, Indian and international vegan-friendly options in a casual environment.

For a memorable eco-dining experience, head to **Campi ya Kanzi** (PO Box, 236-90128 Mtito Andei, +254.45.622 516)—a safari camp located in the foothills of Mount Kilimanjaro, between Kenya and Tanzania. Truly an ecotourism lodge, from the rain-water supply to the solar panel energy source, Campi ya Kanzi offers a fine-dining experience of Italian, international and African cuisine, complete with silver dinnerware and crisp linens. For added drama, there are stunning panoramas of the African landscape.

marrakech, morocco

Earth Café (2 Derb Zawak, Riad Zitoun Kedim, Medina, +212.61.289 402) takes great pride in its usage of fresh and natural ingredients. It offers a variety of international and Moroccan dishes with a selection of vegan-friendly fare.

88 ecochic

cape town, south africa

Lola's (228 Long Street, +27.021.423 9885) is one of the most fashionable restaurants in Cape Town, and it attracts a hip, young, stylish crowd. It has vegan-friendly cuisine and incorporates organic ingredients in its repertoire of salads, pastas, lasagnes, spring rolls, burritos and curries. Food is mainly international with an Asian slant. Many of its patrons hang out here till late as the restaurant's location offers great views of the busy street action.

Organics Alive (42 Palmer Road, Muizenberg, +27.021.788 6012) is an organic green grocer that offers simple vegetarian lunches at its kitchen-style café. Although the café is not generally open for dinner, it can be booked for evening parties and special events. The daily lunch buffet features healthy organic produce such as vegetables, bread and nuts.

Portobello (111 Long Street, +27.021.426 1418) is a very popular restaurant offering good healthy food and great juices in a casual and friendly setting. A daily lunch buffet is available and many of the dishes have a homely touch.

johannesburg, south africa

Earth 2 (1 Olifandes Road, corner of 5th Ave, Emmarentia, +27.011.888 1748) is run by a couple of dedicated ecologists who believe in promoting 'vegan food for a sustainable planet'. That translates to a delicious but healthy offering of pastas, sandwiches, salads and wraps.

Fruits and Roots (Hobart Road, Hobart Corner Shopping Centre, Bryanston, +27.011. 463 2928) is a restaurant and health food store that sells organic foodstuffs, nuts, grains, rice milk, tofus and teas. The restaurant serves healthy light meals alongside some vegan dishes, as well as organic cakes to order.

zighy bay, oman

Zighy Bay in Oman's pristine northern coast offers the ultimate white sand experience on its untouched beaches and breathtaking sand dunes. In addition to striking scenery, visitors you can also dine on organic healthy meals at the luxurious **Six Senses Hideaway Zighy Bay** (Zighy Bay, Musandam Peninsula, +968.2673 5555). The eco retreat offers a wide selection of Asian, international and Middle Eastern cuisine in its three food and beverage outlets.

Enjoy its guilt-free and delicious spa cuisine on the beach, overlooking the waters of the Arabian Peninsula. Or try the Indian curries and Arabic *mezzes* in its fine-dining restaurant.

dubai, united arab emirates

Veg World Restaurant (Gould Souk, Deira, +971.4.225 4455, Bur Dubai, Meena Bazar, +971.4.351 7070) is a casual restaurant that offers some vegan-friendly dishes as well as organic produce that goes into its salads and veggie burgers.

Organic Foods and Café (Sheikh Zayed Road, +971.4.338 4822) stocks a staggering array of organic products that includes fruits, vegetables, dairy products, nuts and bread. It has an organic café on its premises that serves a simple and healthy menu that showcases some flavourful vegetarian dishes.

kasbah du toubkal

THIS PAGE (FROM LEFT): *Spectacular mountain views greet guests from every angle.*

OPPOSITE (FROM LEFT): *Moroccan lamps and ornate carpets turn the lounge into a pasha's den; get a revitalising scrub down at the traditional hammam.*

The Berber community in the village of Imlil, Morocco have a deep respect for the beauty and greatness of Toubkal National Park. Such regard, combined with an impressive warmth and generosity, is evident the moment one steps into the Kasbah Du Toubkal.

A carefree, hardy people, the Berbers are intimately acquainted with their mountainous surrounds and make excellent guides to the region. Kasbah Du Toubkal's location at the foot of Jbel Toubkal—the highest peak in North Africa—provides ample opportunity to discover this for oneself. Adventurous individuals can trek up the mountain, or explore the nearby villages of the Ait Mizane tribe via mountain bike or mule. There is also a traditional community hammam where guests can mingle with locals or while the afternoon away with a hot steam bath or invigorating massage. Mealtimes at the kasbah are communal affairs, serving authentic Moroccan fare to give guests a tasty introduction to local culture.

Kasbah du Toubkal caters to its varied clientele by offering a wide range of accommodation and pricing options. The Garden House is a secluded haven, with three bedrooms that centre on a traditional lounge and kitchenette. Local artworks and hand-carved walnut furnishings add a distinctive Berber flavour to the spacious interiors, while a 12-m (39-ft) plate-glass wall offers dramatic views of a waterfall and the craggy mountains beyond. Berber salons are styled traditionally with rich carpeting and ornate embellishments, and can house families and large groups. Modern distractions such as Internet access and television sets are deliberately absent from the compound, enabling guests to truly appreciate the striking beauty of the rugged landscape.

More a hospitality centre than typical tourist accommodation, Kasbah du Toubkal was established by Discover ltd with the close involvement of the Berber community. The venture was to improve the quality of life in the area while preserving local heritage. The

marrekech **morocco**

rooms
14 double rooms • 1 garden apartment •
1 private house • 15 beds in 3 Berber salons

food
traditional Moroccan

drink
mint teas • byo

features
hammam • library • café • guided treks

green features
High Atlas Tourist Code • responsible waste management • energy conservation measures

nearby
Jbel Toubkal mountain • Marrekech • Ait Mizane villages

contact
BP 31, Imlil, Asni, Marrakech, Morocco •
telephone: +212.24.485 611 •
facsimile: +212.24.485 636 •
email: kasbah@discover.ltd.uk •
website: www.kasbahdutoubkal.com

Moroccan architecture of the compound is derived from its history as the fortified house of a former ruler, and has been lovingly refurbished using only traditional construction methods and labour from surrounding areas. A local team oversees the abode's daily operations, giving it a strong personality that stands out from the mechanical hospitality linked with commercialised establishments.

To conserve the beauty of the Imlil Valley, a High Atlas Tourist code has been established to encourage guests to 'respect local practices, protect the local culture and environment and maintain local pride'. A responsible waste clearance system maintains the cleanliness of the area, while energy conservation measures ensure that there is minimal damage to the fragile mountain environment.

The protected sanctuary is proudly unapologetic about its lack of materialistic extravagances. Instead, guests are rewarded with stunning views of mountains and valleys, the Berbers' genuine hospitality and a chance to experience a unique way of life. As one of the remaining vestiges of Berber lifestyle, Kasbah Du Toubkal is a rare gem worth cherishing.

origins dar itrane

Majestic hills and charming villages provide for the breathtaking scenery and tranquil isolation found at ORIGINS Dar Itrane. Located in the High Atlas mountains and home to the Berbers, the lodge harmonises tradition and modernity to create a culturally rich environment without compromising the comforts that discerning travellers look forward to.

Boasting 17 rooms, spacious roof terraces and panoramic views of the valley, ORIGINS Dar Itrane offers the best of Berber hospitality in an exclusive, authentic setting. Originally an ancient kasbah, the structure was carefully refurbished via traditional techniques and materials such as adobe and wood. Such insistence on local design and construction methods allows the lodge preserve traditional architecture while creating a retreat that exudes exotic charm. For instance, much of the original Moroccan carpentry has been restored, and adorns the windows and furnishings of rooms. Terraces and walkways are also illuminated by candlelight in the evenings, casting an alluring glow over interiors.

The eco lodge's strategic location near Berber settlements acts as an ideal base for hiking excursions. Trekking through the rough terrain will enable visitors to interact closely with locals and be immersed in Berber heritage. Art excursions are also specially crafted to allow guests to try their hand at capturing the rugged mountain range on canvas.

THIS PAGE: *The restored kasbah stands majestically against a mountainous backdrop.*
OPPOSITE (FROM LEFT): *In the evening, candlelit terraces envelop guests in a cocoon of warmth; a relaxing steam bath awaits weary guests at the hammam.*

azilal district **morocco**

In true Berber fashion, the hammam is constructed using ochre coloured tadelakt, a traditional lime coating with natural pigments. To cut down on energy usage, the hammam is heated only in the evenings, welcoming guests with a hot bath after a long day out in the hills. Two cosy living rooms provide a homely environment for visitors to share their experiences over authentic Moroccan cuisine. The lodge's healthy, delicious fare is noted for its simplicity as well as interesting use of local spices. After dinner, guests can browse through the extensive media library or head out to the terrace and admire intriguing rock formations with a cup of hot mint tea in hand.

The lodge extends its commitment to responsible tourism through local sustainable projects. Waste is sorted out daily for responsible disposal. Staff are also educated in the need for environmental conservation. Walking, cycling, donkeys and mules are preferred over vehicular travel to minimise pollution of the environment. Guests also contribute via a token maintenence fee of three euros, which goes into a development fund for the nearby Ait Bougmez valley.

At ORIGINS Dar Itrane indulgence comes not in materialistic forms. Instead, it is felt through the warmth of the Berber community, an untainted landscape, distinctive cultural experiences and unique accommodation.

rooms
17 rooms

food
Moroccan

drink
non-alcoholic beverages • BYO

features
private patios • rooftop terraces • 2 communal living rooms • media library • traditional hammam • day-trips and excursions

green features
waste and water management • recycling programme • protection and promotion of Berber culture • community development projects in Ait Bougmez valley

nearby
Ait Bougmez valley • Ouzoud Cascades

contact
Dar Itrane, Imelghas village, Bougmez Valley, Tabant community, Azilal District, Morocco •
telephone: +33.47.253 7219 •
facsimile: +33.47.253 2481 •
email: sejour@origins-lodge.com •
website: www.dar-itrane.com

la sultana oualidia

THIS PAGE: *The boutique hotel's traditional architecture sets the tone for an exotic getaway.*

OPPOSITE (FROM LEFT): *A private balcony and jacuzzi invites one to lounge in the sultry weather; enjoy glittering views of the sea.*

Widely considered the tour de force of Morocco's finest architectural and engineering talents, La Sultana Oualidia hotel and spa has garnered a strong following since it began receiving visitors in 2007. The boutique hotel's rising castle walls and traditional layout are built to resemble an ancient Moorish fortress, while its modern sophistication and exclusive luxuries have seen the jet-setting crowd flock to this previously obscure seaside locale.

The stately, buff-coloured exterior of La Sultana Oualidia uses the forms of traditional Moroccan architecture to grand effect, exuding a majesty that extends throughout the abode. Local materials such as rassingua—a type of shell-limestone unique to Oualidia—wood, and stone have been utilised to design public spaces, providing a muted backdrop to the courtyard garden where tall palms, cacti and African daisies flourish in a rich profusion of colours. Above, multiple rooftop terraces act as vantage points from which one can appreciate the unparalleled vistas of the nearby lagoon, salt marshes and towering cliffs.

The hotel offers 11 exclusive rooms and suites, each with a private balcony and outdoor jacuzzi. Guests will find the interiors' warm beige tones and pastel accents cheerfully reminiscent of the sun-drenched coast nearby, while tadelakt-coated walls and ancient marble flooring evoke an air of rustic elegance. Rooms draw inspiration from artworks by Régis Delène-Bartholdi, and are individually decorated with ornate carpeting, iron-wrought vessels and intricate furnishings to reflect the artist's poetic depictions of desert life. Amid such lavish settings, guests can appreciate contemporary comforts such as plasma televisions with satellite programming and a complimentary non-alcoholic minibar—yet another example of the hotel's meticulous attention to detail.

oualidia morocco

Ingenious engineering has enabled La Sultana Oualidia to attain full sustainability through its water and waste management. All water is sourced locally and undergoes desalination before being used, while pools are maintained by ionisation—a process that kills bacteria and prevents algae from growing—in place of environmentally damaging chemicals. In an updated version of an ancient system, sewage is broken down by vegetation before being used as fertiliser. There is also an underground treatment area that processes wastewater from the bathrooms and kitchens to be used for irrigation.

A stunning representation of modern and traditional Morocccan luxuries can be found at the spa, a vast cavern nestled at the heart of the hotel. Carved stone columns surround a heated indoor pool, reaching up to the vaulted roof. Such exotic surroundings set the scene for a revitalising spa session: stressed individuals can choose to unwind at the hammams with a steam bath or indulge in the latest beauty treatments to the soothing sounds of running water. The restaurant is equally impressive; here artistically presented seafood and locally grown produce capture the full-bodied flavours of Moroccan cuisine.

La Sultana Oualidia hotel and spa is much more than a sanctuary for weary minds and bodies—it is an exemplary model of green designer living for other luxury establishments to emulate.

rooms
4 rooms • 7 suites

food
Moroccan and fresh seafood

drink
The Lounge

features
spa • outdoor pool • private jacuzzi • high-speed Internet access • complimentary non-alcoholic minibar • satellite TV • library • meeting facilities • private beach

green features
full water sustainability • waste management • pools are maintained by ionisation • wastewater used for irrigation purposes

nearby
Safi • El Jadida • Boulaouane Castle • golf • watersports • local market place

contact
Parc à Huîtres N°3, 24000 Oualidia, Morocco • telephone: +212.23.366 595 • facsimile: +212.23.366 594 • email: reservation@lasultanahotels.com • website: www.lasultanaoualidia.com

borana lodge

Borana Lodge lies on the edge of the Samangua Valley and offers panoramic vistas stretching from the Lewa Plains to the Ngare Ndare Forest—the very sort of landscape that Hemingway describes in *Green Hills of Africa*. Built in 1992 by local artisans, the lodge uses only indigenous building materials and dead wood found on the ranch. The result is a sumptuous retreat that is in keeping with its surroundings: the lodge gives the impression of having sprung from the rocks upon which it was constructed.

Eight African-style chalets make up Borana Lodge's accommodation. Awash in a palette of warm earth tones, spacious interiors feature the artistic side of Kenyan culture with local paintings and sculptures displayed throughout the lodge. Interiors are specifically designed to cater to guests' need for privacy, with an open fireplace, a cosy bedroom, a generous en-suite bathroom and exceptional views creating a secluded haven from the outside world.

The main lodge and fireplace provide a charming environment for guests to mingle over cocktails. The camaraderie continues in the elegantly appointed dining room, where guests dine together on organic produce harvested from the gardens. Al fresco meals are available out on the pool verandah, where the isolated nature of the vast African savannah sets the tone for intimate dining affairs.

Kenya's untamed landscape and flourishing wildlife makes for rich pickings. Explore Borana Ranch on horseback with a stable of agile

THIS PAGE (FROM LEFT): The privately owned reserve allows guests to observe wildlife up close; interiors are cosily furnished.
OPPOSITE (FROM LEFT): The pool melds into the rocky surroundings; thatched-roof cottages bring a rustic vibe to the African ranch.

kenya **africa**

breeds to choose from. Equestrian guides take guests game spotting as they venture through hard terrain and verdant forest. Polo is a popular sport in the region, with specially bred ponies for enthusiasts to play a few chukkas with the locals. Immersing oneself in the African bush is an ideal way of experiencing wildlife at its most uninhibited, and guests can embark on overnight fly-camps where tents, showers, fine wine and three-course dinners await after a day roughing it out in the wild. Individuals desiring to appreciate the area's abundance in comfort can do so with a soothing massage followed by an afternoon at the infinity pool, from which one can spot elephants and buffalo slaking their thirst in the reservoir below.

Such enriching adventures have been made possible due to the ranch's commitment to protect its environment. A wildlife fund has created a flourishing game sanctuary in the region with various conservation projects. The ranch has also been awarded the Virgin Holidays Responsible Tourism Award for efforts in alleviating poverty through generating employment, improving school facilities and funding a mobile clinic.

Borana Lodge is renowned for its striking natural beauty, exclusivity and thriving wildlife, but adding to the experience is the fact that guests give back to the community just by staying at the ranch. Indeed, luxury ecotourism does not get more authentic than this.

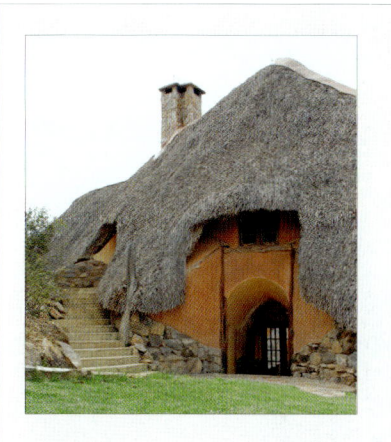

rooms
8 cottages

food
fresh organic produce

drink
juices and wines

features
private fireplace · infinity pool · game blind · massage services · polo · day-trips and overnight excursions

green features
local natural materials used in construction · organic farm · wildlife conservation fund · mobile clinic · community development projects

nearby
Borana Ranch · Mount Kenya · Lewa Plains

contact
PO Box 137, Nanyuki, Laikipia, Kenya, Africa ·
telephone: +254.721.557 362 ·
facsimile: +254.62.310 75 ·
email: bookings@borana.co.ke ·
website: www.borana.co.ke

campi ya kanzi

THIS PAGE (FROM TOP): Leopard-print coverlets add a touch of the savannah to cool linen sheets; savour African delights at the foot of Mount Kilimanjaro.

OPPOSITE (FROM LEFT): Guests are treated to spectacular views of the landscape at every turn; Tembo House's cosy quarters exudes an old-world charm.

'A vacation that refreshes and replenishes' is a philosophy that eco-conscious hotels across the world have adopted in a big way. Campi ya Kanzi is one such establishment, giving back to the land and its local people while offering visitors the finest in African luxury.

Located in the foothills of Kilimanjaro, the five-star safari camp is a joint venture between owners Luca and Antonella Belpietro and the Maasai herdsmen. This community-owned eco-tourism lodge spreads across an immense 113,312 hectares (280,000 acres) of stunning and varied African landscape, offering guests a firsthand experience of what bush life is all about.

There is plenty of room for opulence out on the savannah, and Campi ya Kanzi's eight tented cottages give a luxurious edge to 'camping' out in the wild. Constructed from natural materials such as stone, fabric and wood, these thatched roof cottages exude the colonial elegance of a bygone era with canopied beds encased in Italian linen, plush oriental rugs and leather trunks. Generously sized bathrooms with brass fittings and bidets add to the old-world charm. Each unit opens up to a wide verandah with panoramic views of either Mount Kilimanjaro, the Tsavo Hills or the Chyulu Hills, while the ample distance between cottages promises the appreciation of such vistas in absolute privacy.

Innovation and stylish living come hand in hand at Campi ya Kanzi, and its owners go to great lengths to make sure that the reserve is self-sufficient. The state-of-the-art solar panel system provides abundant

kenya africa

electricity, while water—the camp's scarcest resource—is cropped and stored to provide running water for the entire camp. Relying on green technology keeps the impact on the environment minimal, thus maintaining the fragile balance between Mother Nature and the man-made world.

Recreational activities at Campi ya Kanzi take on a different spin from the conventional facilities offered in five-star establishments. Embark on an adrenaline-packed game drive in an open landrover to nearby Tsavo National Park, where more than 30 different mammal species inhabit; set out on a foot safari where knowledgeable Maasai trackers reveal the rich flora and fauna of the land; search for elephant herds as a plane trip gives guests a bird's-eye view of the land. These activities are accompanied by a sumptuous picnic for guests to tuck in while looking out across the plains of the savannah.

The day's excitement generates the buzz that goes on at Tembo House. The safari camp's restaurant and lounge sets the tone for an affable evening, as guests mingle and recount their experiences with a glass of champagne or Italian wine in hand. Dinner is a sensory experience, with authentic Italian and African creations—prepared on eco-friendly charcoal fires and harvested from the camp's organic vegetable garden—enhanced by chandeliers, crystalware and candlelight.

At dusk, with the African skies overhead taking on a dramatic purple hue, one can't help but agree that Campi ya Kanzi offers an experience that is truly magical.

rooms
8 tented cottages

food
Tembo House: African, Italian and international

drink
Tembo House: lounge

features
privately owned Maasai Reserve • tented lodges • library • wine cellar • satellite phone • forest walks and game drives with Maasai trackers • mobile camping, with game drives or game walks

green features
solar power • water collection from roofs for camp's use • organic vegetable garden • eco-friendly charcoal used in food preparation • waste management

nearby
Amboseli National Park • Chyulu Hills • Mount Kilimanjaro • Tsavo National Park

contact
PO Box 236-90128 Mtito Andei, Kenya, Africa •
telephone: +254.45.622 516 •
facsimile: +254.45.622 516 •
email: lucasaf@africaonline.co.ke •
website: www.maasai.com

tsara komba lodge

THIS PAGE: *The island resort is hidden amid dense foliage.*
OPPOSITE (FROM LEFT): *Rich natural woods and soft lighting give rooms a calming atmosphere; enjoy dramatic island views alongside delicious cocktails.*

Breaking away from the monotony of city living, Tsara Komba Lodge offers a slice of Madagascan island life in a tropical paradise. The secluded island retreat is framed against Nosy Komba's lush forest background and soft white sands, providing a laid-back locale from which to discover the natural world in-depth or to simply luxuriate amid the Lemur Island's picturesque surrounds.

Comprising of only eight lodges, the property offers an exclusive sojourn in an exotic setting. Each lodge measures 95 sq m (1,022 sq ft) to 75 sq m (807 sq ft) and has been tastefully constructed from natural materials such as rosewood and sohihy. Inside, polished dark wood floors and a canopied four-poster bed give interiors a classic elegance while providing a soothing ambience to chill out in. Warm reds and yellows add a cheerful vibrancy to rooms, alongside local artworks—made from lime and natural pigment—that emphasise the resort's tropical island appeal. Thatched roofs are built high above to enable air circulation, while a hardwood patio overlooking the beach allows one to admire the surrounding island scenery in privacy.

Such easy access to Nosy Komba's pristine shoreline provides ample opportunity for various water activities such as scuba diving, cruising round the Mitsio archipelago and

nosy be **madagascar**

fishing off local pirogues. Guided excursions bring visitors face to face with Madagascar's iconic native lemurs, as well as tropical flora and fauna along the way. Other attractions include tours to the ylang-ylang plantations, and Ambanja Market to soak up the cheerful ambience of local village life. Lucky guests might even chance upon dolphins playing in the bay throughout the year or migrating whales between August and November.

Epicureans will not be disappointed with the sumptuous local fare offered at Le TK. With critically acclaimed chef Alain Schieb at the helm, guests can savour innovative fusion fare and local specialities such as Zebu fillets and Madagascan foie gras. Meals are served in the main house, with two open decks looking out to a splendid view of Grande Terre Island creating a magical setting for intimate dinner parties. Le TK bar is an ideal place to unwind, with its wide selection of French, South African and Madagascan wines to be savoured against the dramatic backdrop of the ocean.

The establishment's philosophy of 'Respect for the Environment' can be seen through the deliberate absence of televisions and air-conditioning. Eco-friendly materials such as commercially grown timber and plants are used for landscaping purposes, while metals and plastics are regularly recycled and re-used. Tsara Komba Lodge also aids in sustaining the indigenous community by hiring local staff and educating farmers to phase out slash-and-burn farming and look for greener alternatives.

Tsara Komba Lodge is an ideal blend of eco paradise and island luxury guaranteed to place one next to nature in the greatest comfort. With so much good work done just by staying there, guests will be left with an indelible desire to come back for more.

rooms
8 lodges

food
Le TK: fusion and Madagascan

drink
Le TK bar

features
Liberty Spirit: customised week-long stays • private sun deck • day-trips and excursions

green features
use of commercially grown timber and plants for landscaping • use of natural materials for construction • recycling programme

nearby
Grand Terre Island • Nosy Be

contact
Nosy Be, Madagascar •
telephone: +261.32.074 4040 •
email: resa@highspiritlodges.com •
website: www.tsarakomba.com

lazuli lodge

Located in the Bahareya oasis, four hours travel by bus away from populous Cairo, Lazuli Lodge is a testament to how the simplest pleasures in life can also be the most luxurious.

Visitors do have to do without many amenities that the modern traveller has come to take for granted. There is also no electricity, although hot water is available throughout the day with each room possessing its own heater. In return, however, guests are lodged in enticingly sumptuous rooms and suites, done up in Egyptian cotton and tastefully decorated with local pottery or blown glass. The lodge was built entirely with natural materials sourced from the area, in keeping with the retreat's philosophy of respect for the environment and its local inhabitants.

As darkness falls, countless candles dot the dunes, creating a scene of surreal beauty enhanced by the hushed silence that falls over the land since all boats on the Nile stop their electric generators at night. Relaxing on the terrace with the wind blowing gently through one's hair, the meditative guest will rediscover what the city dweller often forgets—that doing nothing and simply being at one with nature is a delight far too rarely savoured.

THIS PAGE: In the evening, Lazuli Lodge is an oasis of calm.
OPPOSITE (FROM LEFT): Lounge amid multiple throw cushions and abundant natural light; mud walls keep the heat out in the day.

cairo egypt

In the morning, a host of discoveries await. Dromedaries transport guests to view the desert landscape and its palm plantations, while the less intrepid can stroll among the soft sands. In the distance, dahabeyas navigate the great expanse of the Nile by sail, instead of burning up precious fuel resources.

Within the retreat, there is a pool fed by a natural water source. Guests can enjoy a refreshing dip to escape from the heat, taking note that the use of creams or sun oils are prohibited to prevent chemical agents from polluting the waters. Working hard to preserve the purity of the water source it has access to, the lodge uses natural filters made from sand, stones and coal to treat wastewater before discharging it into the Nile.

After the day's exertions, stop by the vegetable garden, where one is welcome to harvest its organically grown produce. These ingredients are then turned into local delicacies such as Molokhia, Egyptian Rice or Koshari Abu Gibba. The rich cuisine is followed by hot Mint teas served in silver pots and local sun-ripened fruits—a delectable way to end any meal.

As one chills out by the bar with a cocktail, there is time to marvel at how seamlessly the retreat has integrated itself into the local culture and scenery, while maintaining a unique character that stands out from other establishments. Lazuli Lodge is an example par excellence of how luxury travel need not be ostentatious; rather it is the return to unspoilt nature that makes a stay here so indulgent.

rooms
17 rooms • 3 suites

food
Egyptian

drink
bedouin-style bar

features
massage services • library • outdoor pool • day-trips and excursions

green features
environment-friendly construction methods • pool supplied by natural spring water • proper wastewater management • use of natural products in daily operations • organic vegetable garden

nearby
Cairo • Libyque Desert

contact
Lazuli, 2nd floor El Moltaka Towers (Tower A) Abbasseya Square, Cairo, Egypt • telephone: +20.2.2403 0891 • facsimile: +20.2.2403 0913 • email: contact@lazulinil.com • website: www.lazulinil.com

six senses hideaway zighy bay

A refuge from the mega commercialisation often associated with Middle Eastern states, 'hideaway' is an understatement when one describes the thrilling isolation of Six Senses Hideaway Zighy Bay. Perched on the tip of Oman's Musandam Peninsula, the exclusive retreat offers an irresistible combination of sun and sea against a dramatic backdrop of rugged mountain terrain of what was originally a seabed.

This is the magnificent view adrenaline junkies take in as they paraglide 488 m (1,600 ft) down the steep, impenetrable Hajar mountains to the entrance of this sandy hued oasis. The resort's architecture is minimalist, with cuboid structures cutting a bold figure amid the vast mountains and turquoise bay.

Local stone, raffia and dark wood accentuate the traditional Omani design of all 79 pool villas, two private retreats and one private reserve, while the main colour palette of brown, beige and camel exudes a rustic elegance.

Such simplicity in design reflects the starkness of the surrounding scenery, a dynamic contrast to the modern, inviting interiors. Inside, an integrated home theatre system, satellite TV and high-speed Internet access are just some of the amenities on hand to ease urbanites into the spirit of things, while a plush king-sized bed, anti-snore pillows and a generous bathtub await to pamper the weary traveller. The resort's philosophy of 'redefining experiences' sees creature comforts spilling outdoors, and

THIS PAGE: *The resort's minimalist architecture harmonises with the stark desert surroundings.*
OPPOSITE (FROM LEFT): *Traditional Omani design and mesmerising mountain views set the tone for a romantic dinner affair; Dining on the Edge offers a bird's eye view of Zighy Bay.*

musandam peninsula **sultanate of oman**

guests are treated to a personal infinity-edge pool, traditional Arabic summer house, al fresco rainshower, private sun deck and dining suite.

In spite of the seemingly barren nature of the Musandam landscape, guests will quickly discover the wealth of activities that will appeal to both the adventurous and laid-back soul. In addition to paragliding, sporting enthusiasts can embark on four-wheel-vehicle drives through towering dunes and undulating canyon trails, or engage in an exciting bout of game fishing. Alternatively, luxuriate in the resort's encompassing serenity with a leisurely Arabic culinary workshop or relaxing session at the world-acclaimed Six Senses Spa.

The resort's sumptuous facilities is further highlighted by the smorgasbord of cuisines featured. Dining on the Sand takes guests on a culinary journey with its myriad of pan Asian, Middle Eastern and Continental flavours. Dining on the Edge showcases sophisticated fine dining with stunning mountain views, while Bites rustles up fresh seafood right by the marina.

The peninsula's intriguing fossil and dead coral formations are especially significant to geologists concerned with the earth's developments. Aware of the rare quality of its location, Six Senses Hideaway Zighy Bay takes various eco-friendly measures to keep the environment in pristine condition. Natural ventilation reduces reliance on energy, while the deliberate absence of landscaping aids in water conservation. To minimise impact on Zighy Bay's flourishing underwater world, only non-motorised watersports are allowed.

Deftly incorporating high living into a striking desert locale untampered by mankind, Six Senses Hideaway Zighy Bay embraces its contrasts with flair—and guests can only benefit from it.

rooms
79 pool villas • 2 private retreats • 1 private reserve

food
Dining on the Sand: Asian, Middle Eastern, Continental • Dining on the Edge: fine dining • Bites: seafood

drink
Drinks on the Edge: bar • Chil-Mood Bar • Vinotheque: wine cellar

features
Six Senses Spa • all villas have pools, sun decks and al fresco rainshowers • wireless Internet access • in-villa dining • library • volleyball court • watersports • paragliding • day-trips and excursions

green features
use of natural materials for construction • water conservation and energy efficiency programme • non-motorised watersports

nearby
Musandam Peninsula • Dubai

contact
Zighy Bay, Musandam Peninsula
Sultanate of Oman •
telephone: +968.2673 5555 •
facsimile: +968.2673 5556 •
email: reservations-zighy@sixsenses.com •
website: www.sixsenses.com

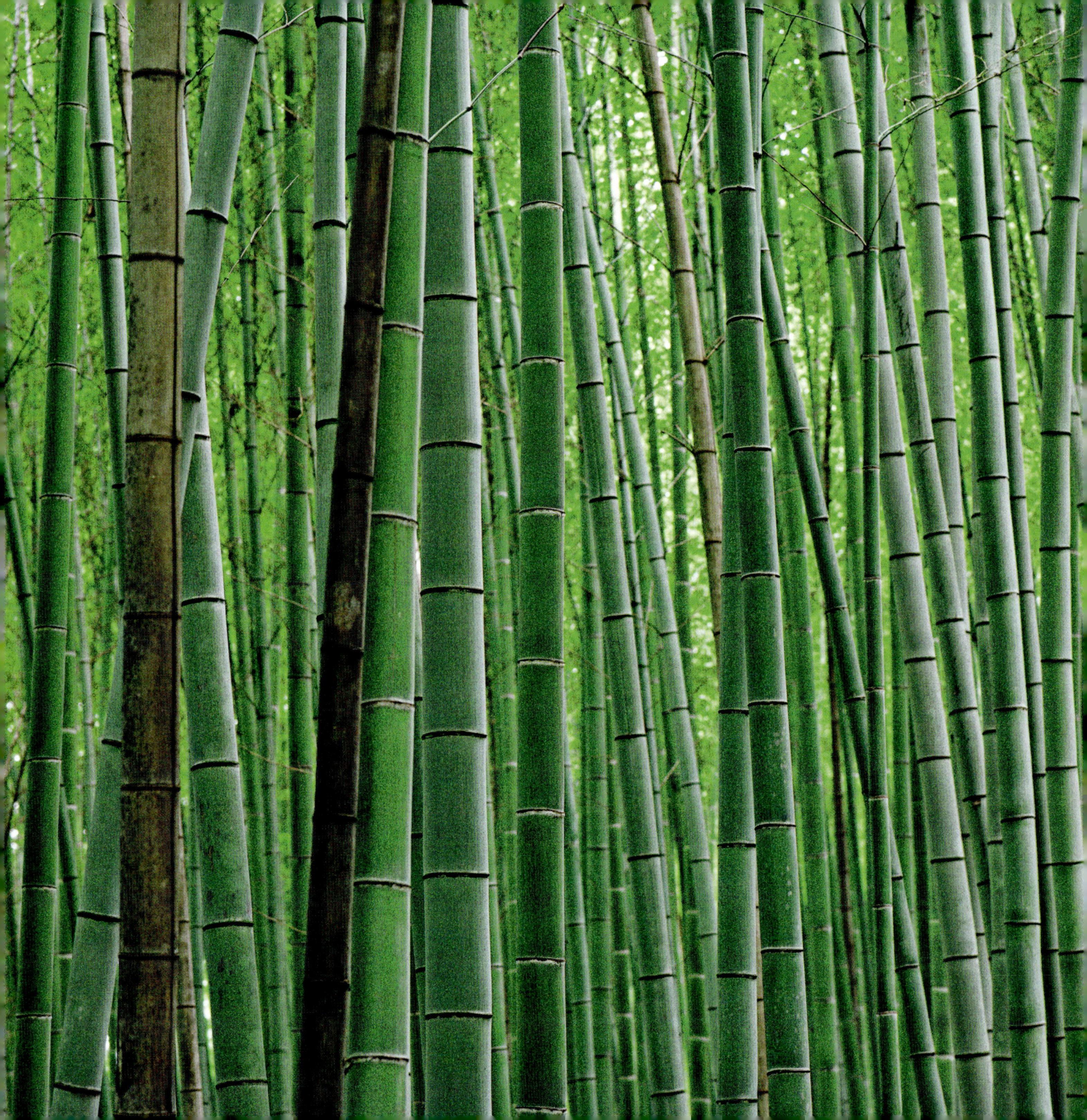

asia + the pacific

Map of Asia and Oceania

Countries and Regions

Asia: Mongolia, North Korea, South Korea, Japan, China, Pakistan, Nepal, Bhutan, Bangladesh, India, Myanmar (Burma), Vietnam, Laos, Taiwan, Thailand, Cambodia, Philippines, Sri Lanka, Maldives, Malaysia, Brunei, Singapore, Indonesia, East Timor

Oceania: Australia, Papua New Guinea, Solomon Islands, Vanuatu, Fiji, New Zealand

Seas and Oceans

Pacific Ocean, Indian Ocean, Sea of Japan, Yellow Sea, East China Sea, South China Sea, Philippines Sea, Bay of Bengal, Andaman Sea, Gulf of Thailand, Sulu Sea, Celebes Sea, Java Sea, Banda Sea, Arafura Sea, Timor Sea, Coral Sea, Tasman Sea, Great Barrier Reef, International Date Line

Resort Locations

- Four Seasons Tented Camp Golden Triangle
- Banyan Tree Ringha
- Six Senses Hideaway Ninh Van Bay
- Evason Ana Mandara + Six Senses Spa–Nha Trang
- El Nido Resorts
- Hotel Majestic Saigon
- The Dune Eco Beach Hotel
- Anantara Dhigu Resort + Spa, Maldives
- Soneva Fushi by Six Senses
- Soneva Gili by Six Senses
- Six Senses Destination Spa Phuket
- Anantara Phuket Resort + Spa
- Evason Phuket + Six Senses Spa
- Six Senses Hideaway Yao Noi
- Six Senses Hideaway Samui–A Sala Property
- Six Senses Hideaway Hua Hin
- Evason Hua Hin + Six Senses Spa
- Jimbaran Puri Bali
- Ubud Hanging Gardens
- Bamurru Plains
- Southern Ocean Lodge
- Paperbark Camp
- Nukubati Island
- Treetops Lodge + Wilderness Experience

Legend

- Lake
- +5000 m
- 4000–5000 m
- 3000–4000 m
- 2000–3000 m
- 1000–2000 m
- 500–1000 m
- 200–500 m
- 0–200 m

Scale: 0 km – 500 – 1000 – 1500 km

asia + the pacific

Asia and the Pacific region is blessed with a wealth of cultures and traditions. Places as unique and diverse as the UNESCO-listed Uvs Nuur Basin in Mongolia, China's Great Wall, the Taj Mahal in India, the temples of Angkor Wat in Cambodia, Indonesia's Borobudur temple complex, Nepal's Sagarmatha National Park (habitat of the rare endangered snow leopard) and Australia's Great Barrier Reef are all truly irreplaceable sources of life and inspiration.

However, the grim reality is that many of these countries' ecosystems are becoming increasingly degraded. According to the United Nations, species are becoming extinct one hundred times faster than the rate shown in the fossil record. If temperatures and sea levels continue to rise, polar bears could disappear from the Arctic, tigers from India and Nepal (the Bangladeshi Sunderbans are already critically endangered), elephants, orangutans, leopards and the Tibetan antelope or chiru will all face a bleak future threatened by disappearing habitats, global warming and human devastation.

The impact of destruction is vast but humans are finally realising that, by allowing the world to inspire us, we become keener to protect it. Sustainable tourism is catching on as today's travellers seek destinations where the well-being of the environment and its inhabitants is an important consideration. In Asia-Pacific alone, huge conservation initiatives are underway. From banning shark hunting in the Maldives to constructing eco villages in China—nature and humankind have been working harmoniously to rebuild the planet one step at a time.

the maldives

Renowned for its pristine waters, white sandy beaches and coral reefs swarming with colourful wildlife, this breathtaking stretch of 1,200 tropical islands south-west of India holds a fragile grip on existence. Because the islands are small and exposed, minor weather disturbances can have major effects on their delicate ecosystems. Maldivians have come to realise that they need to actively protect their environment in order to ensure the islands' survival.

Wildlife in the Maldives is at risk and the facts speak for themselves. Of the seven (worldwide) turtle species that face extinction, five of them are found in the Maldives. Since the government banned turtle fishing in 1995, the turtle population is slowly recovering and

THIS PAGE: *Being eco-conscious also means taking care of cultural icons such as the maginificent Borobodur.*

PAGE 106: *Bamboo, a native grass to Asia, is known to remove harmful greenhouse gases such as carbon dioxide.*

many can be found nesting in the northerly Baa Atoll. The shark population is vital to the stability of the Maldivian ecosystem. As top predators they maintain the health of fish populations by regulating numbers and reducing the spread of disease. However the hunting of sharks' fins—a Chinese delicacy—has drastically decreased its population over the years. The country's leading resorts are lobbying for a nation-wide ban on shark fishing and shark-fin trading, along with a greater enforcement of the laws designed to protect the endangered species in the Maldives.

In an effort to further protect the natural environment, the Maldivian government imposed a tax on tourist beds along with a series of restrictive laws aimed at protecting the islands' landscape. Due to the country's geographical disparity (with isolated islands spread over a massive area), each resort must be completely self-sufficient regarding sewage, electricity and water desalination. Sound waste management solutions, recycling, responsible purchasing and social responsibility projects between resorts and neighbouring islands are just some of the initiatives undertaken by environmentally concerned operators such as Six Senses, Banyan Tree and Four Seasons.

Zero carbon emissions by 2010 is the goal Six Senses Soneva Fushi has set itself. To achieve this, a number of processes have been put in place, including the installation of a deep-sea water air-conditioning system, solar thermal water heating, an energy recovery system (ERI) for a Reverse Osmosis water plant and heat recovery pumps. Operation-related energy and water-efficient measures, waste treatment, energy-efficient four-stroke outboard motors in boats, battery-operated golf buggies, a ban on plastic bottles (guests are provided with reusable glass ones instead) and higher bicycle usage, are further conservation strategies. The group has implemented a scheme to offset carbon emissions from all guest flights and boat travel. In association with The Coverging World, a non-profit charity organisation, the Six Senses wind turbine is expected to generate over US$2 million worth of carbon credits by 2028.

china

A one-hour ferry ride from Shanghai, Chongming Island on the Yangtze River Delta, is crisscrossed with canals and dirt roads and hosts the largest migratory bird sanctuary in China. With plans underway to turn part of its wetlands into the world's first self-sufficient city, the Dongtan Eco-City project will be powered entirely by renewable energy sources and supplied with battery or fuel cell vehicles and solar-powered water taxis.

Tourist attractions will include a leisure park, a science exhibition, an educational centre and a wildlife conservation area. Developed by Shanghai Industrial Investment Corporation, a mix of traditional and innovative measures will be used, such as low-energy air-conditioning and green roofs. Estimates predict that Dongtan will use half the water and create one-sixth the waste of a city of comparable size, with 8 hectares (20 acres) set aside for producing native foods such as corn, rice and fish. Nearby farms will be restored while surrounding wetlands act as a buffer around the city to control ground pollution.

luang prabang, laos

The ancient town of Luang Prabang in the centre of Northern Laos is an exemplary piece of unspoilt Southeast Asia. This picturesque UNESCO-listed town and former seat of kings is an outstanding example of 19th and 20th-century Lao and European colonial architecture. This unique and well-preserved townscape illustrates the seamless blending of these two distinct cultural traditions. There are 34 Buddhist temples located throughout the town, and all are set against a stunning backdrop of lush green mountains and the mighty Mekong river.

There is plenty of cultural heritage to explore here. Royal palaces, Buddhist temples, elephant sanctuaries and indigenous Lao hill tribes can be found throughout the region. There is also the daily *Tak bat* or alms round, a living Buddhist tradition where the city's thousand-odd, saffron-robed monks form a snaking, mile-long queue as they go about collecting daily alms at dawn. Should you want an adrenaline rush, you can also go white-water rafting.

With its low population density, unspoiled diverse ethnic lifestyles and possibly the richest, most extensive network of ecosystems—with over 800 species of birds and more than 100 large mammals including tigers, clouded leopards, gibbons, the Irrawaddy dolphin and silver pheasants—the town is most deserving of its eco status. In place to protect and conserve

THIS PAGE (FROM TOP): *Chinese youths get creative by making reusable shopping bags from old clothes at an eco awareness bazaar; the ancient Laotian town of Luang Prabang.*
OPPOSITE: *Soneva Gili by Six Senses spares no effort in maintaining its green status.*

these natural resources is a network of 20 National Protected Areas that cover almost 14 percent of the country, and is believed to be one of the largest conservation areas in the world.

ulpotha, sri lanka

Built on the site of a deserted traditional village, Ulpotha covers a 5-hectare (12-acre) site at the base of the Galgiriwiya Mountains deep in the jungles of Old Ceylon. Originally conceived as an ecological mission to renew traditional farming practices in the area, Ulpotha is now a favourite destination for those seeking respite from the world—yogis visit from all corners of the globe to run workshops amidst the lush countryside.

The village has evolved organically into what it is today and the locals are very much a part of the experience. The huts are simple, functional and comfortable with local materials used throughout. The swimming pool is a freshwater lake fringed with flowering lilies. Guest numbers are restricted to a maximum of 20 at any one time to preserve the unspoilt beauty. The food is organically grown on site and the village is self-reliant for water. There is no electricity, all waste is recycled and the net carbon footprint is virtually zero. The on-site Ayurvedic clinic is available for guests and also provides a free service to surrounding villages.

Ulpotha is ecotourism at its purest, with the real luxury here being to experience Mother Nature in all her wondrous glory. It is a spiritual and regenerative environment where locals, visitors and nature happily co-exist, and the concept of time and space seems to be suspended in the rhythms of traditional life.

wild earth journeys

A raw passion for wild places led anthropologist Carroll Dunham and photographer Thomas Kelly to spend over 25 years in the Himalayas. Settling into partnership with the local nomads, they founded Wild Earth Journeys (www.wildearthjourneys.com), offering authentic and unashamedly eco-conscious adventures to the deepest, wildest, most remote parts of the Himalayas. From Tibet's renowned Mount Kailas to the heartland of Mongolia, the homeland from where Genghis Khan ruled the world, Wild Earth Journeys roams off-trail to explore deep, green grasslands and mountains, lakes and hidden valleys, and the chance to experience the daily lives of local nomads. It offers the perfect adventure for writers, artists, meditators, yogis, explorers and those who simply want to be free to soak in the sacred wilderness.

THIS PAGE: *Reconnect with nature through yoga and meditation.*
OPPOSITE: *The magnificent plains of Mongolia inspire pure awe.*

From Tibet's renowned Mount Kailas to the heartland of Mongolia...

asia + the pacific: shopping

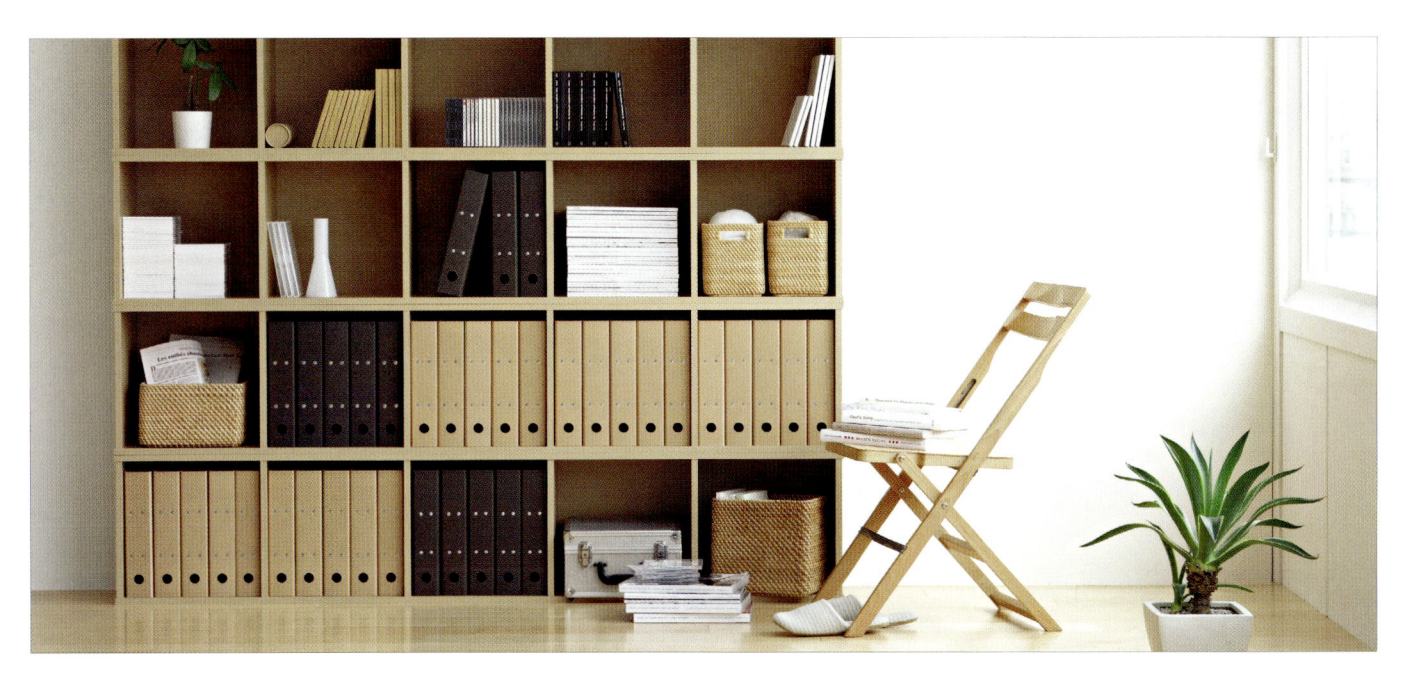

bangkok, thailand
Everybody heads to **Chatuchak Weekend Market** (Thanon Phanon Yothin, +66.2.2724 6356) for a taste of what real shopping in Bangkok is like. Eschew the large malls with the fancy brands for one-of-a-kind creations that are made and designed by Thais themselves. Find out where the fashion section is and you'll be blown away by local ingenuity and creativity. Lots of antique knick-knacks can be found at the market too.

Support local crafts at **Benjarong** (River City Shopping Complex, room 325-326, 23 Trok Rongnamkaeng, Yotha Road, +66.2.237 0077) and get the famous pale green celadon ceramics from **Chiiori** (87 Sukhumvit Road, +66.2.254 4976). World-renowned **Lotus Art de Vivre** (Four Seasons Hotel, 155 Rajdamri Road, +66.2.250 0732/ The Oriental Hotel, 48 Soi 40 Charoenkrung Road, +66.2.236 0400) offers a range of stunning jewellery and exquisite homeware that showcases superb local craftmanship.

kuala lumpur, malaysia
Go through a whole range of recycled items at **Bijou Bazaar** (Akademi Seni Budaya Warisan Kebangsaan ASWARA, 464 Jalan Tun Ismail, +60.03.5630 0064), the Malaysian capital's latest favourite marketplace. Retro furniture sits side by side with used fashion and vintage accessories. Visit bijoubizaar.blogspot.com often to find out details of when the next merchandise fiesta will take place.

Also check out sports and outdoor wear brand **Lafuma** (16 Jalan Telawi, Bangsar Baru, +60.03.2287 1118), which offers a range of sustainable sportswear. Its Pure Leaf Collection features pieces made from eco-friendly products such as 100 percent organic cotton and hemp, or recycled materials like polartec and technowarm micro-fibre.

singapore
Muji—the Japanese brand which translates to 'no brand, good product'—has been encouraging environmental awareness since the 1980s with a range of products that are unvarnished and stylish in their stark simplicity. Muji paper stationery is made from unbleached and recycled paper, and many of the fabrics in its homeware department are unbleached cottons. You can find Muji stores scattered throughout Singapore.

Maki Squarepatch (+65.6292 2248) is a pioneer in Singapore for its planet-saving creations. Designers Enqi and Xin came up with the idea of recreating products—fashion, gifts, accessories and homeware—from 'pre-loved' fabrics. Their philosophy: for every discarded item, there will be someone out there who will love it. There are scarves made from patches of vibrant retro fabric, restyled vintage dresses, bags, tablecloths and blankets. A range of Maki Squarepatch gift items can be found at **Books Actually** (5 Ann Siang Road, +65.6221 1170), **La Libreria** (64A Queen St, Bugis Street Market,

+65.6337 1346), **L'escalier** (391 Orchard Road #04-20 Ngee Ann City, +65.6735 4228) and **The Tango Mango Bookshop** (Changi Airport Terminal 3).

There are few vintage shops in Singapore, so the **Oppt Shop** (www.facebook.com/pages/Oppt-Shop/17300651390) stands out for its offering of fashion from another generation. Find restyled dresses and tops, and accessories galore such as clutches and cigarette cases. Great for gifts too if you have a friend with a taste for the quirky.

Eco-friendly footwear makes headway in the city with **Dopie**—minimalist sandals made of recycled foam rubber—a collaboration between industrial designer Matthew Harrison and eco-friendly shoe company Terra Plana. Available at **Spin the Bottle** (#01-02 The Cathay, Dhoby Ghaut).

Freitag is another international name that has made it to the sunny island. Made from used seatbelts, truck tarpaulin and recycled airbags, the Swiss label has been stomping the fashion scene with edgy one-off bags and wallets. Get a piece at **Actually** (29A Seah Street, +65.6336 7298)

Local designer and design lecturer by day **Vik Lim** recycles lining material and scraps from his friends and tailors and fashions them into handmade 'body jewellery'. Think of his pieces as fancy neck ties that you can throw over a plain tee-shirt. Available at **Front Row** (5 Ann Siang Road, +65.6224 5501)

Curiocity (#A1-02, 38 Bencoolen Street, +65.6334 6022) does its part for the Green Movement with its range of environmentally sound products such as EcoYoga mats, organic Oz brand Maud N Lil cotton

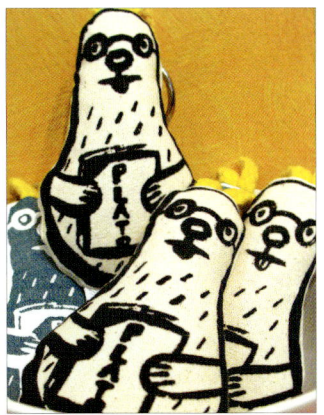

THIS PAGE (FROM TOP): *Quirky toys made from recycled fabric bring eco awareness to indie shoppers; Actually carries eco gems and funky designs from various cult labels.*
OPPOSITE: *Muji as a brand originates from Japan, but has quickly found devoted followers worldwide.*

asia+thepacific:shopping 115

asia + the pacific: shopping

stuffed toys and Hellenique Green Laundry Spin Balls, an alternative to earth-corroding detergents.

The Life Shop (12A Jalan Ampas, #07-02, +65.6732 2366), which offers contemporary furniture with an Asian twist, also carries a range of sustainable furniture, such as chairs and stools that are made from pineapple fibre paper.

australia

Ambra is one of Australia's largest importers of women's hosiery and intimate wear, and the brand now includes an eco-conscious range of underwear and legwear that includes the use of bamboo fibre and organic cotton. Ambra is widely available throughout Australia in **Myer** and **David Jones** stores, selected boutiques and pharmacies.

It is hard not to get excited about **Bird Textiles**, one of Australia's pioneers in sustainable design. Bird handprints its own fabrics on SKAL/CUC certified organic cotton using water-based dyes, and then produces a range of fashion and homewares from the fabrics made. All products are manufactured in Australia using solar power, and Bird became Australia's first carbon neutral business in 2004. The range of over 100 different products includes homeware, accessories and a classic fashion range. You can also buy its fabrics and utilise its custom-made curtain and upholstery service.

The **Bird Textiles Emporium** in Sydney (380 Cleveland Street, Surry Hills, +61.2.8399 0230) is housed in an old heritage listed pharmacy complete with original shopfittings from 1898. Alternatively visit its

THIS PAGE (CLOCKWISE FROM TOP): Impeccable cuts can be found at Aussie eco label Gorman; Bird Textiles' dresses are made from handprinted fabrics and the label also makes their own homeware; Ambra's eco-friendly intimates.
OPPOSITE: the latest spring/summer collection from Bird Textiles.

studio store in Byron Bay (13 Banksia Drive, Byron Bay, +61.2.6680 8633) to see how the brand makes its fabrics.

Ubiquitous Aussie brand **Billabong**, which has made surf wear hip around the world, recently launched a range of Design for Humanity casual wear that is organic and good for the earth. It includes organic cotton tees, board shirts made out of recycled plastic bottles, and recycled boardies. Billabong shops can be found throughout Australia.

Gorman's motto is being 'green and serene', and it achieves that while designing some seriously stylish clothes as well. Its range of organic, sustainable fashion includes classy slips, chic cocktail dresses, comfy knits and tailored shirts in muted shades of dove and ecru.

These translucent colours are achieved with water-based printing and chemical free dyes, while the luxurious textures of its jerseys are achieved with 100 percent organic cotton. Almost all its packaging is recyclable, and a donation is made to Friends of the Earth every time a customer rejects a bag. Gorman can be found in **David Jones** department stores around Australia.

Designer Sam Elsom wants to make desirable fashion without causing environmental havoc. To that end, he designs contemporary creations that are made with organic materials derived by fair trade.

Starting out with just organic tees, the **Elsom** range has now expanded to men's and women's fashion. Dresses are made of silk and jersey with a fluid silhouette, while men's jackets and trousers have a casual cut. Stringently ethical, Elsom sources his materials from cotton farmers who have made the decision to be organic and pesticide-free. His clothes are in demand from Australia to London and are also carried on high fashion website www.netaporter.com. In Sydney, the Elsom brand can be found at **David Jones** (Market Street, +61.2.9266 5544) and **McLean and Page** (Shop 3c 11-27 Wentworth Street, Manly, +61.2. 9976 3277).

Why not send a greeting that grows on the person who receives it? With a 'plantable' card from **Todae** (83 Glebe Point Road, Sydney, +61.2.9660 7266), once the recipient reads the message, he can pop it into a pot of dirt, and watch it grow into a basil plant or a marigold tree.

Eco at Home (507 Willoughby Road, Sydney, +61.2.9958 0412) helps you lead a greener life with all kinds of environmentally friendly home improvement products. Its range includes safe and natural paint, organic hemp linens, chemical-free cleaning agents, power-saving appliances and baby products. All are displayed in a friendly environment where you can seek advice for creating a green home.

Australia-based **Bassike** offers seasonal fashion crafted out of high-quality organic cotton jersey. The brand's silhouettes are simple and fluid and are very much in line with the minimalist taste of the staunchest eco warrior. Bassike can be found in **Incu** (The Galleries Victoria, Shop RG 23-24, 500 George Street, Sydney,+61.2.9698 7416), and **David met Nicole** (382 Cleveland Street, Surry Hills, Sydney, +61.2.8357 2424).

asia + the pacific: spas

Home to undoubtedly the richest spa culture on the planet, the time-honoured healing traditions of the Asia Pacific are firmly grounded in the fundamental principle that energy known as life force flows through oneself to balance and harmonise body, mind and spirit.

From the Indian Ocean to China, Japan, Thailand, Indonesia, Vietnam, the Philippines, Cambodia, Australia and New Zealand, an exotic blend of exotic therapies are offered amid unspoilt natural beauty to soothe and enrich the weariest of minds.

the indian ocean

At many of the exquisite natural retreats dotting India, Sri Lanka and the Indian Ocean's collection of pristine islands, one can enjoy the best of indigenous therapies using deliciously fresh ingredients and expert healing hands.

From the traditional Ayurvedic synchronized *Abhyanga* massage and *Shirodhara* (the pouring of warm medicated oils over the third eye on the face) to traditional Maldivian and Seychellois rituals, authentic healing comes guaranteed.

For a genuine Seychellois experience, the **Rock Spa** of **Frégate Island Private** (Frégate Island Private, PO Box 330, Victoria, Mahé, Seychelles, +248.282 282) utilises fresh organic ingredients that have been harvested on the island or from Frégate's very own hydroponics house. These herbs are then custom-blended into aromatic scrubs, pastes and oils.

The incense-scented spa at **Soneva Fushi by Six Senses** (Kunfunadhoo Island, Baa Atoll, Maldives, +960.660 0304) is every sybarite's delight, with waterfalls trickling into indoor pools and therapy rooms opening onto the ocean as flying fish dart past. A refreshing menu of holistic and traditional treatments comprising all-natural skin foods is available. Many of the ingredients are handpicked in the resort's organic vegetable garden, before being moulded into nurturing recipes for the face and body.

At the spa at **Soneva Gili by Six Senses** (Lankanfushi Island, North Male Atoll, Maldives, +960.664 0304), be soothed by a soul-restoring menu of therapies, signature spa journeys and doctor-assisted Ayurvedic programmes. Afterwards, dine on refreshing spa cuisine at the spa lounge and admire the uninterrupted views of the azure ocean.

The Maldives is a wellness haven—find rejuvenation at the overwater spa at **Anantara Dhigu** (Dhigufinolhu, South Male Atoll, Maldives, +960.664 4100). One of its highlights is the Anantara Detoxifying Signature Treatment which uses mineral-rich Moor mud, steam and lymphatic drainage massage to deeply cleanse the system and reduce fluid retention.

Ulpotha (near Embogama, Kurunegala District, +44.208.123 3603) in Sri Lanka is ecotourism at its purest—a natural, spiritual environment where Ayurvedic therapies are just a small part of the overall regenerative experience.

china

The concept of *qi*, the vital energy that empowers every organ in the body, is fundamental to the understanding of Chinese healing. Traditional therapies like acupuncture, moxibustion, reflexology and *tui na*, or exercise routines such as *qi gong* and *tai chi* help remove blockages and encourage a more harmonious flow of *qi*.

With a constant emphasis on natural ingredients and indigenous spa therapies, the Hot Stone Massage at **Banyan Tree Spa Lijiang** (P.O. Box 55, Lijiang 674100, Yunnan Province, +86.888.533 1111) and **Banyan Tree Spa Ringha** (Shangri-La County, Yunnan Province, +86.887.828 8822) was inspired by *Gui Shi*, Tibet's ancient medical texts.

The stunning landscape alone is reason enough to visit **Crosswaters Ecolodge & Spa** (Mount Nankun Ecotourism District, Longmen, Guangdong, +86.752.739 3666), but eco-conscious visitors will also be happy to find that environmental protection is at the top of the retreat's agenda. The buildings are sustainable, with designs incorporating local bamboo, wood and traditional mud.

The spa menus are created exclusively from home-grown organic ingredients and therapies are created specifically to harmonise the *qi* with nature's seasonal rhythms. These elements combine to restore the energy levels and bring harmony to mind and body.

australia

For more than 40,000 years, the Aboriginal people of Australia have been guardians of the world's oldest living tradition of sacred knowledge, known as the 'Dreamtime.' Their philosophy is to tread lightly on the earth and have the utmost of respect for plants and animals. This is so as the human is regarded as a custodian of the surrounding natural world.

To the Aboriginals, the rainforest is a kitchen, medicine chest and spa and their menu of indigenous therapies includes the rhythmic *Kodo* (or melody) massage, *Mikiri* (deep) facial therapy and the purifying powers of water-based *Yanko* therapy, using the freshest water from local river beds to deeply cleanse, nourish and realign the body's energy fields.

A secluded waterfall on the grounds of the **Daintree EcoLodge & Spa** (20 Daintree Road, Daintree,

THIS PAGE (CLCOKWISE FROM TOP): *Asian spa therapies often harness the benefits of indigenous spices; Daintree EcoLodge & Spa holds open-air treatments so that guests can luxuriate in natural settings; alluring seaviews set the tone for a blissful spa session.*
OPPOSITE: *Become one with nature at the spa at Frégate Island Private.*

asia + the pacific: spas

Queensland, +61.7.4124 9943) provides pure natural spring water for the calming range of Aboriginal therapies on offer at the spa. They are designed to connect people with the natural vibration of this ancient land.

new zealand

Native New Zealand therapies revolve around the healing benefits of hot mineral springs, alongside local natural ingredients such as Rotorua thermal mud, manuka honey, kiwifruit, apricot, ground almonds, aromatic lavender, fragrant coconut oil and botanical extracts.

At **Treetops Lodge & Wilderness Experience** (351 Kearoa Road RD1, Rotorua, +64.7.333 2066) these healthful ingredients are used in the spa's therapy menu. Set in the heart of a 1,012-hectare (2,500-acre) eco and wilderness park in the hills of North Island, this superb ecoretreat was strategically constructed to seamlessly blend into its natural environment of streams, virgin forest and untamed wilderness.

indonesia

The spiritually unique island of Bali is synonymous with Asia's flourishing spa culture. Many Balinese treatments use ingredients from the island's volcanic mountains, tropical forests and majestic rivers. In the Balinese villages, one tradition that has remained constant is the use of *jamu* herbal tonics, the ancient elixir of life.

An entire beauty regime can be created around *jamu*, from facial masks to hair conditioners, body masks and massage oils. Other indigenous Balinese therapies still widely used today for softer, smoother and more supple skin include *mandi susu* or milk baths, *boreh* (body scrubs) and traditional *lulur*, the time-tested healing synergy of aromatic massage, exfoliating body scrub and floral bath.

Embracing traditional Balinese customs, the signature Ayung Beauty Secrets ritual at the **Ubud Hanging Gardens** (Desa Buahan, Payangan, Ubud, Gianyar, Bali 80571, +62.361.982 700) cleanses, refines and hydrates the skin, leaving it radiantly fresh and glowing. At the **Beach Spa** of **Jimbaran Puri Bali** (Jalan Uluwatu Jimbaran, Bali 80361, +62.361.701 605), shaded by towering palms with only the sounds of gentle waves to accompany the soothing strokes of the masseuse, experience a calmness of both body and soul.

the philippines

Traditional healing remains a fundamental part of Philippine culture, throughout the country's 42,000 villages. This heritage, tempered by Spanish and American colonialism, includes a blend of some of the ancient medical traditions of China, India, Greece and Persia.

The Filipino *hilot* treatment is a combination of time-tested massage techniques. It is the oldest and most popular therapy, and is practised even in the most remote villages today. Harnessing the bio-energies the universe, an assortment of flowers, oils and herbal poultices, *hilot* helps restore overall health and harmony.

Paligo is a bathing ritual therapy using warm decoctions of tropical medicinal leaves and flowers to relieve a range of disorders from lethargy to fertility issues. The *oslob* is a form of steam inhalation therapy using boiling water infused with aromatic medicinal plants and herbs traditionally used to clear the head and calm the mind.

With an emphasis on natural ingredients and traditional therapies, **The Farm** (119 Barangay Tipakan, Batangas, +63.2.696 3795) offers a pure and natural healing environment for cleansing and rejuvenation.

The crystal-clear waters at **El Nido Lagen Island Resort** (18/F, 8747 Paseo de Roxas Street, Salcedo Village, 1226 Makati City, +63.2.750 7600) are home to hundreds of species of marine life, from the smallest nudibranchs and endangered sea turtles to the gentle whale shark.

Deeply respectful of the unspoilt landscape, the spa—nestled amid the cliffs towering over Lagen Island— merges seamlessly with its dramatic surroundings and offers a range of therapies either at the spa, on the beach or in the tree top cabana, a perfect hideaway for sunset massages.

japan

To the Japanese, bathing in an *onsen* or hot spring is as serious a ritual as making tea. When bathing Japanese-style, the tub is used exclusively for soaking—one has showered before getting into the bath. A long, luxurious soak at the end of a tiring day cleanses both body and spirit.

Many *onsen* are close to areas of volcanic activity as bathing in mineral-rich waters is believed to cure a range of illnesses, from nervous disorders and bad circulation to skin irritations, aches and fatigue.

Other uniquely Japanese therapies include shiatsu, which uses a variety of hand movements to improve the flow of *ki* (energy) throughout the body. *Reiki*, an extremely calming form of touch therapy, sees the practitioner transmitting the energy from his own body to the client by placing his hands over or on specific areas of the body requiring attention.

The waters of the hot spring baths at **Tobira Onsen Myojinkan** (8967 Iriyamabe, Matsumoto-shi, Nagano-ken, +81.02.6331 2301) gently calm the skin, and are beneficial in treating a range of disorders from rheumatism to stomach and nervous system imbalances. With the best of wild mountain vegetables, the freshest seafood and organically grown ingredients on the menu, the overall experience is the perfect prescription for weary souls.

thailand

Originally practised by monks, traditional Thai massage or *nuat bo'rarn* is an energising, spiritual and healing activity that is now embraced by many wellness seekers. Dressed in loose, comfortable clothing, they perform the movements on a floor mat. Thai massage has also a part of local Thai lifestyle today as a regular way to relax and prevent disease.

Other indigenous healing and beautifying rituals include body scrubs and masks made from local herbs, flowers and food, which deeply exfoliate and feed the skin. Then there are the traditional Thai herbal wraps which often use mineral-rich

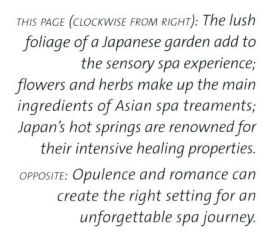

THIS PAGE (CLOCKWISE FROM RIGHT): The lush foliage of a Japanese garden add to the sensory spa experience; flowers and herbs make up the main ingredients of Asian spa treaments; Japan's hot springs are renowned for their intensive healing properties.
OPPOSITE: Opulence and romance can create the right setting for an unforgettable spa journey.

asia + the pacific: spas

THIS PAGE (FROM TOP): *Idyllic surrounds and a deep-muscle massage ensures that all worries melt away; restorative massage is administered by a fully qualified spa professional.*
OPPOSITE: *Holistic wellness is a byword at the Six Senses group.*

mud to cleanse and nourish even the most delicate of skins. The Thai herbal bolus treatment uses spices and herbs which are wrapped tightly in muslin or cotton and infused in steam before being pressed against the skin. This is said to rebalance the body and calm the mind.

Inspired by rural village architecture, the circular, domed treatment rooms of Earth Spa at **Six Senses Hideaway Hideaway Hua Hin** (9/22 Moo 5 Paknampran Beach, Pranburi Prachuap Khirikhan 77220, +66.3261 8200) are built entirely from a mixture of rice husks and straw that remains cool even in high temperatures. Treatments here focus on nourishing the skin with many of the ingredients that are freshly picked at dawn for the day's menu of cleansing and revitalising therapies.

Tucked away on the traditional Thai fishing island of Naka Yai, Phuket, the cutting-edge **Six Senses Destination Spa Phuket** (32 Moo 5, Tambol Paklok, Amphur Thalang Phuket 83110, +66.76.371 400) offers innovative experiences from four spa concepts (Chinese, Indian, Indonesian and Thai).

Ground-breaking fitness programmes, healthy menus and a lush, sustainable living environment combine to offer visitors a complete immersion into an alternative lifestyle that takes into consideration the wellness of the individual as well as the planet.

At the **Evason Phuket & Six Senses Spa** (100 Vised Road, Moo 2, Tambol Rawai Muang District, Phuket 83130, +66.76.381 010), sustaining the local environment is a key philosophy even as it seeks to offer a comprehensive menu of healing therapies. Only the best skin foods and natural products are used.

The signature therapies at the spa at **Six Senses Hideaway Samui— a Sala property** (9/10 Moo 5 Baan Plai Laem, Bophut, Koh Samui, Suratthani 84320, +66.77.245 678) are geared to de-stress the body. Treatments include a range of gentle to invigorating body massages, as well as facial treats that use skin foods from the resort's organic garden.

The resort is set on a headland on the northern tip of Samui Island, and the spa looks out to stunning sea views that calm the weary.

The rejuvenating treatments at the **Anantara Phuket Resort & Spa** (888 Moo 3, Tumbon Mai Khao, Amphur Thalang, Phuket 83110, +66.76.336 100) was designed to reflect the mysticism of the lotus flower, a Thai symbol of enlightenment, rebirth and self-regeneration. The pampering therapies are guaranteed to harmonise and rebalance body, mind and spirit.

The **Six Senses Soneva Kiri Eco-suite** on the island of Koh Kood is a zero-emissions villa built from recycled materials and Forestry Stewardship Council-certified pine and reclaimed teak. It is concrete- and cement-free, and the green roof is home to native flora while also curbing storm water run-off.

Guests can enjoy living the green life in style with a visit to the the spa for some pampering and relaxation. For an even more indulgent experience, arrange for an in-villa massage, complete with soothing music and aromatherapy.

cambodia

A key feature of Khmer healing is the Traditional Khmer Massage, a combination of Thai massage techniques using thumb, palm, heel and stick manipulation to stimulate blood circulation and energy flow throughout the body.

Chub Kchol or cupping employs traditional Chinese medicine techniques to move stagnant *qi* and invigorate the system. Hot herbal compresses are a part of traditional Khmer medicine or *Punlie*, and use a range of indigenous herbs packed in a hot poultice to ease muscle tension and soothe the body naturally.

Many of the treatments at **Hotel de la Paix**'s (Sivutha Blvd, Siem Reap, +855.63.966 000) Spa Indochine and the spa at the **Shinta Mani** (junction of Oum Khum and 14th Street, +855.63.761 998) revolve around traditional Khmer healing methods. Khmer massage, *Chub Kchol, Chab Kchol* (pinching) and indigenous herbal hot compresses are designed to soothe and relax the body. The spa has a floral bath and steam room, and treatments include body scrubs, wraps, floral and herbal baths and the healing stones massage.

vietnam

Indigenous Vietnamese therapies have been known to incorporate native flowers, fruits, spices and herbs such as saffron, tamarind, lemon grass, pomelo and the multi-purpose, highly antiseptic betel leaf in their treatments and remedies.

Still widely used today, these ingredients are integral to Vietnamese traditional massage, facials, and scalp therapies. When treating colds and fevers, massage is combined with a cupping suction treatment along the spine to remove excess heat and toxins, and stimulate the flow of blood and energy through the body.

The Vietnamese Experience Journey at **Evason Ana Mandara—Nha Trang** (Beachside, Tran Phu Boulevard, Nha Trang, Khanh Hoa, +84.58.352 2222) combines traditional body, face and scalp massage therapy. Local flowers and oils are also used during the treatment to cleanse, invigorate and harmonise the system.

Nestled beside a gentle waterfall, the spa at **Six Senses Hideaway Ninh Van Bay** (Ninh Van Bay, Ninh Hoa, Khanh Hoa, +84.58.372 8222) is a paradise for the senses. Guests are soothed by the sound of cascading waters and the aroma of essential oils and incense.

The spa showcases some of Vietnam's speciality treatments together with an extensive menu of signature therapies. Trained therapists create sensory journeys for guests with a range of holistic wellness and pampering treatments to choose from.

Situated in the heart of the city, the spa at the **Hotel Majestic Saigon** (1 Dong Khoi Street, District 1, Ho Chi Minh City, +848.3829 5517) offers a menu of soothing massages, steam baths, facials and foot therapies to restore balance and harmony to the psyche.

anantara dhigu resort + spa, maldives

Situated on the secluded Dhigufinolhu island, Anantara Dhigu Resort & Spa, Maldives is a speedboat ride away and a mere 30 km (19 miles) from the Maldivian capital of Male. To ensure that the boutique resort mirrors the vibrancy of the surrounding verdure, Maldivian architect Mohamed Shafeeq has utilised natural materials and thatched roofs to create an island-style architecture that blends seamlessly into the exotic setting.

The deluxe beachfront villas are a skip away from the turquoise seas. Decorated in soothing beige tones with cobalt blue accents, rooms feature floor-to-ceiling timber-framed glass doors and a four-poster, canopied daybed. Laze the day away with modern-day accoutrements such as a surround sound stereo with flat-screen TV and DVD player, high-speed Internet access—even an espresso machine. Private bathhouse gardens will throw off any remaining inhibitions with an al fresco rainshower and signature Anantara 'made for two' terrazzo tubs inviting one to soak up the sunshine.

Offering all the amenities found in villas, Overwater suites are built on stilts within a private lagoon. Dark teak and red lacquer bring dramatic accents to the room while beds are specially positioned to catch the changing hues of the sea. Bathrooms offer a refreshing perspective of the island, with a glass floor panel looking down to the powder sands and aquamarine waters below. Along with a private wine cellar—some even have an infinity pool—there is little reason for guests to head out of this paradise.

Home to a fascinating, yet delicate eco system, Anantara Dhigu offers a plethora of activities that exposes guests to the island's spectacular ecosystem. Dolphin instruction courses and an in-house marine biologist enable wildlife enthusiasts to learn about the teeming ocean, while watersports facilities allow guests to coast the azure seas. One can also discover Maldives' tropical flora and fauna with the option of bringing along a specially packed picnic. Better yet, take in the unparalleled view of nearby islands while professional therapists knead out any lingering stress at the world-famous Anantara Spa.

THIS PAGE: Overwater suites are designed to bring the Indian Ocean right to one's doorstep.
OPPOSITE (FROM LEFT): Fuddan Fusion Grill offers barbecue specialities together with panoramic vistas; Anantara Spa offers indulgence in a private setting.

south male atoll **maldives**

Such luxuries are made possible due to the island's rich natural environment, and Anantara Dhigu takes great care to keep it in pristine condition. Innovative electricity-saving measures see the resort turning to solar energy and generating hot water for guestrooms through air-conditioning units. Wastewater is recycled and biodegradable chemicals are employed wherever possible. Nurturing nature is an activity that Anantara Dhigu is deeply committed to, and a sea turtle rehabilitation programme has been established to improve the diversity of Maldives' wildlife.

Anantara Dhigu also cultivates its own herbs and vegetables, creating the organic, imaginative flavours found at the resort's various restaurants. Fushi Café offers lavish buffet spreads, while Terrazzo features Italian bistro fare in an intimate ambience. Fuddan Fusion Grill gives guests a taste of local fare with seafood and choice meats smoked over coconut husks and grilled. Located right out at sea, Baan Huraa combines the best of North and South Thai cuisines with stunning ocean views. Just a short boat ride away, sister resort Anantara Veli offers a change of scenery along with sumptuous seafood at 73 Degrees and chilled cocktails at Dhoni.

Getting close to nature is what draws visitors to the sunny islands of Maldives. Anantara Dhigu Resort & Spa Maldives offers precisely that, delivering an unforgettable travel experience by immersing guests right in the heart of this oceanic Eden.

rooms
110 villas and suites

food
Terrazzo: Italian • Fushi Café: international and Maldivian • Baan Huraa: Thai • Fuddan Fusion Grill: barbecue specialities

drink
Aqua Bar

features
Anantara Spa • personal wine cellar • cooking school • surf lessons • watersports facilities • in-house marine biologist • dolphin instruction courses • gymnasium • tennis court • infinity-edge freshwater pool • library • business centre • kids' club • day-trips and excursions

green features
solar energy • generation of hot water through air-conditioning units • wastewater recycling programme • biodegradable chemicals used • sea turtle rehabilitaion programme • organic vegetable garden

nearby
Male

contact
Box 2014, Dhigufinolhu, South Male Atoll
Male, Republic of Maldives •
telephone: +960.664 4100 •
facsimile: +960.664 4101 •
email: maldives@anantara.com •
website: www.anantara.com

soneva fushi by six senses

THIS PAGE: Garden-encased bathrooms and a private stretch of beach give the eco resort a Robinson Crusoe idyll.

OPPOSITE (FROM LEFT): Dark wood interiors and vibrant accents create an alluring ambience; dine in secluded luxury.

It is rare to return fron the exotic islands of the Indian Ocean without having some sort of life-changing epiphany. Thus it was on Kunfunadhoo Island that plans for the Soneva Fushi by Six Senses took form. An ecocentric pioneer in Maldives' five-star scene, Soneva Fushi is one of the first resorts to eschew the polished veneer of conventional hotels and take on a contemporary rustic feel that proved that simple can be chic.

Soneva Fushi champions a 'no news, no shoes' mantra, and with all 65 suites and villas fitted to various degrees of extravagance, guests will see no need to tog their feet on the resort's powder-fine grounds. Much of the abode is hidden among a thick canopy of trees, keeping the natural landscape intact. All units have abundant space in between to ensure utmost privacy, while thatched roofs and garden-encased outdoor bathrooms set the tone for a luxurious castaway experience.

Natural materials such as coconut wood and water hyacinth give interiors a Maldivian character, while cleverly hiding satellite televisions and home theatre systems from view. Herbal pillows accompany the king-sized canopied bed, while a private al fresco sitting area lends itself to engaging views of the nearby Indian Ocean. Indulgent couples will be tempted to stay at the 1,720-sq-m (18,507-sq-ft) jungle reserve, where a spa suite, seawater pool, personal butler service and tree house epitomise the ultimate in barefoot luxury.

At every turn, guests are shown how Soneva Fushi's green policies have contributed to the Eden-like quality of its unsullied locale.

baa atoll **maldives**

Water recycling and sewage management programmes ensure the flourishing of local flora and fauna, while energy saving measures reduce guests' carbon footprint and keep the air pure. Rehabilitated coral reefs provide homes for the tropical fish one encounters while scuba diving, and supping on organic, resort-cultivated produce reminds one anew of Mother Nature's wonders.

Satiating discerning epicureans is a goal Soneva Fushi achieves with panache, and the resort's collection of exquisite restaurants reiterate this. Diverse dining experiences can be found across the island, beginning with Ever Soneva So Down to Earth's Mediterranean and seafood delicacies, Asian buffets and barbecue nights. Sense by the Beach Restaurant invites diners to feast on Peruvian and Japanese fusion dishes, while Mihiree Mitha's Maldivian and international offerings can be enjoyed from live cooking stations. No less outstanding is Fresh in the Garden Restaurant, with its flavourful raw food creations and lush greenery.

A destination in its own right, the world-renowned Six Senses Spa's holistic treatments and therapies will nurse one back to physical and spiritual health. A large reflecting pool make up the spa's central feature, creating a meditative respite for weary individuals.

Much like the environmental rejuvenation nurtured by the resort's eco manifesto, a relaxing sojourn at Soneva Fushi will enable guests to rediscover that elusive equilibrium between the senses.

rooms
65 suites and villas

food
Ever Soneva So Down to Earth: Maldivian, Asian and barbecues • Sense by the Beach Restaurant: Peruvian and Japanese fusion • Mihiree Mitha: Maldivian and international • Fresh in the Garden Restaurant: organic meals • Cinema Paradiso: private dining

drink
Main Bar and So Spiritual • Sense by the Beach: bar • Bar(a)bara Bar • The Wine Cellar

features
Six Senses Spa • satellite TV • high-speed Internet access • gym • outdoor cinema • library • pool • ice cream parlour • treehouse meeting room • water recreation centre • day-trips and excursions

green features
water recycling and sewage management programme • energy efficiency measures • natural materials used in construction • rehabilitated coral reefs • organic vegetable and herb garden

nearby
Male

contact
Kunfunadhoo Island, Baa Atoll
Republic of Maldives
telephone: +960.660 0304 •
facsimile: +960.660 0374 •
email: reservations-fushi@sixsenses.com •
website: www.sixsenses.com

soneva gili by six senses

THIS PAGE: *The villas' Maldivian architecture complements the mesmerising tropical seascape.*

OPPOSITE (FROM LEFT): *Personal butler service and al fresco bathing facilities are part and parcel of the Soneva Gili experience; free-flowing forms and the use of natural materials give the wine cellar an organic feel.*

With over a thousand islands scattered across the Indian Ocean, the Maldives is peerless when it comes to offering the pristine beaches and limpid waters required of a personal beach paradise. Occupying the entire island of Lankanfushi, Soneva Gili has created a luxurious tropical hideaway with a distinctive Robinson Crusoe touch, allowing 'castaways' to indulge in a secluded haven worlds away from the toil of urban life.

Luxury is paramount at Soneva Gili, and being stranded on this exotic location has never sounded more enticing. Radiating from the island are 37 over-water villas, designed to look out to the sea's iridescent hues. In addition, seven standalone Crusoe Residences and a private reserve ensure that nothing interferes with one's appreciation of the oceanic world at large.

Against this azure backdrop, guests are pampered with luxuries of the highest international standards. Thatched roofs, sustainable woods and organic fabrics outfit interiors with a clean, modern look. Plush furnishings and an over-sized canopied bed invite guests to cosy up in the evenings, while al fresco bathrooms and a private water garden bring a whimsical quality to the whole experience. Include the plethora of entertainment options and an exclusive butler service, and guests are left comfortably cocooned in a bubble of contentment.

north male atoll **maldives**

Being in the middle of the ocean makes Soneva Gili perfectly placed for watersports. With an on-site PADI diving centre, novices and professionals alike can discover the thriving ecosystem beneath them. Encounter vast coral gardens thronging with vivid marine life—a rare sight in these times—or ride out the waves with hobie cat sailing and windsurfing facilities at hand. Rejuvenating treatments meted out in stylish comfort can be found at the Six Senses Spa. Perched right over the ocean, treatment rooms feature glass floor panels that look into the shimmering waters below.

Not to be outdone are the resort's dining establishments, with its fine cuisines and vintage wines. Featuring a fusion of East and West creations, The Main Restaurant sees a regular line-up of celebrity chefs hosting sumptuous dinners. Main Bar showcases a different menu daily, while the underground wine cellar with its free-form driftwood dining table transforms any dinner party into a dramatic affair.

Beneath such sophisticated demeanour is a steadfast belief in environmental responsibility. Beginning with the recycling of waste materials in villa construction, the resort's eco-friendly policies extend to using renewable energy sources, growing organic vegetables and phasing out environmentally harmful chemicals. Injecting a green conscience into designer living is no mean feat, and the resort's brand of 'intelligent luxury' has seen Soneva Gili clinching a *Condé Nast Traveller* Readers Spa Award and a placing in the publication's 'World's Top 100' list in 2008.

Saving the earth in style has never been more apt in the light of bleak environmental forecasts. Soneva Gili has risen to the challenge by creating a sustainable Eden, and guests get to be a part of it all.

rooms
37 over-water villas • 7 Crusoe Residences • 1 private reserve

food
Main Restaurant: fusion •
Main Bar: daily changing menu

drink
Main Bar • Gourmet Cellar: wine cellar

features
Six Senses Spa • private pool and water garden • al fresco bathroom • personal butler service • highspeed Internet access • satellite TV • tennis court • on-site PADI dive centre • fitness centre • conference facilities • day-trips and excursions

green features
organic vegetable garden • building materials from renewable sources • energy efficiency programme • wastewater treatment • using eco-friendly chemicals and detergentst

nearby
Male

contact
Lankanfushi Island, North Male Atoll
Republic of Maldives •
telephone: +960.664 0304 •
facsimile: +960.664 0305 •
email: reservations-gili@sixsenses.com •
website: www.sixsenses.com

the dune eco beach hotel

The Coromandel Coast of Tamil Nadu has seen its fair share of visitors from as early as the 16th century. Its lucrative Indian trade saw the establishment of various European settlements in the area, resulting in a nostalgic, colonial charm that pervades the region even today. Located in Pondicherry, The Dune Eco Beach Hotel's pristine beach lets one soak up the old-world glamour in tranquil surrounds, while its contemporary design provides a stimulus for an exciting, unpredictable experience.

Scattered across the 12.1-hectare (35-acre) property are 35 villas and 15 rooms and suites. Artistic expression reigns free at The Dune, and accommodation is individually designed and decorated. From the kaleidoscope of colours created by the traditional glass bangles adorning the Bangle House to the exquisitely carved ceilings of the 150-year-old Kerala House, each abode provides varied insights to Indian culture. All rooms offer sumptuous bedding and alluring garden or sea views, with rooftop gardens and private pools found in selected bungalows. Each unit houses a piece of the past, with reclaimed building material from former South Indian palaces and colonial bungalows used as part of its construction. Solar hot water systems, energy saving bulbs and wastewater treatment plants have also been installed to keep environmental impact low.

A green, healthy lifestyle begins from within, and The Dune promotes this with two restaurants serving health-conscious fusion cuisine prepared from organic produce. F.U.N. (Food U Need) restaurant promotes a hypo-toxic diet, with an emphasis on organic

THIS PAGE: (FROM TOP): *A mixture of old and new gives the eco hotel its eclectic charm; the restaurant's open concept allows natural ventilation.*

OPPOSITE (FROM LEFT): *The retreat's vibrant, contemporary side; kick back by the infinity pool.*

tamil nadu **india**

vegetables and fruits produced from the retreat's two certified farms. The Seafood Bar is also a must-visit, with its extensive array of seafood to be savoured straight from the tandoor or barbecue.

Taking the eco hotel's approach to holistic wellbeing a step further is the Veda Spa. Swamis have traditionally regarded the beachside locale as a place of pilgrimage and meditation, and its picturesque setting is ideal for a rejuvenating spa session. With a comprehensive menu of over 50 therapies, the spa also offers an ayurvedic pharmacy, steam house and beauty treatment centre.

The Dune's historic surrounds make daytrips an activity not to be missed. Pondicherry, a former French colony, will charm visitors with its neo-classical architecture and lively nightlife, while the experimental township of Auroville—where 44 different nationalities have been invited to work and live together—will provide refreshing perspectives on community living. Back at the hotel, guests can participate in tennis, volleyball and horse riding, or simply lounge in the suspended pool overlooking the Bay of Bengal.

Giving back to the community is an ethos the management firmly believes in, and the establishment regularly conducts a rehabilitation plan for tsunami-affected youngsters. The Dune also acts as a base for Artists in Residence, an artists' programme aimed at raising the prominence of the International art scene.

Few hotels have managed to express their care for the environment with such eloquence and heart; with its boutique luxuries, love of art and warm sincerity, The Dune has said it all.

rooms
35 villas • 15 rooms and suites

food
F.U.N. restaurant: hypo-toxic fusion • Seafood Bar: seafood

drink
organic coffee bar • fresh fruit bar • poolside bar • beach bar

features
Veda Spa • Paradise shop • free yoga classes • DVD library and in-room player • guest cell phone • multi-gym • boating • infinity pool • tennis • volleyball • children's payground • animal husbandry • conference hall • day-trips and excursions • artist-in-residence programme

green features
solar-heated water • organic farm and vegetable garden • dairy farm • reclaiming of discarded materials for construction • waste water treatment plant • organic pest control • in-house electrical transport service • complimentary bicycles • organic linen • organic bath amenities • tsunami relief activities and catering school • afforestation project

nearby
Pondicherry • Auroville • Mahabalipuram

contact
Pudhukuppam, Keelputhupet (via Pondicherry University), 605014 Tamil Nadu, India •
telephone: +91.413.265 5751 •
facsimile: +91.413.265 6351 •
email: booking@epok-group.com •
website: www.thedunehotel.com

banyan tree ringha

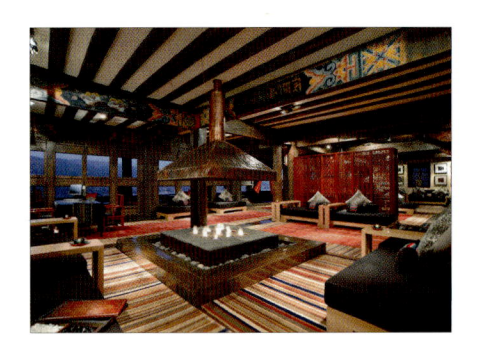

THIS PAGE (FROM TOP): *Enjoy sweeping vistas from the cosy lounge; decked out in Tibetan splendour, interiors feature rich tapestries and handcrafted furniture.*
OPPOSITE (FROM LEFT): *The idyllic highlands beckon guests to live life at a more leisurely pace; Baishuitai, one of the natural marvels found near the retreat.*

Tucked away on a slope in the mountainous Yunnan province, Zhongdian is an oasis of serenity and breathtaking beauty. The region has been designated the official Shangri-La by the Chinese government, and aptly so, for the aura of tranquillity it exudes. At an altitude of 3,200 m (10,499 ft) above sea level, an immediate change in pace can be felt from cosmopolitan life as one contemplates the majestic peaks of the Yangtze range or stop for black shaggy yaks that meander across the highlands. This is a world whose innocence has been preserved in its edenic locale, and can be fully experienced at Banyan Tree Ringha's luxury accommodation and world-class spa.

Viewed from the outside, Banyan Tree Ringha's lodges are harmoniously assimilated into the local environment. The highland escape encompasses refurbished Tibetan farmhouses that were transported log by log to the new site. Inside, rooms are dressed in bold colours, echoing the warm red furnishings and ornate Tibetan carpeting. Modern facilities such as sumptuous bedding and satellite television are paired with traditional wooden hand-crafted bathtubs and finely woven tapestries, while private balconies open up to magnificent tableaus of the mountains or the Ringha River below.

A nod towards traditional Tibetan heritage, the central compound is decorated with impressive pine pillars, exquisite carvings and intricate lacquer work. It is a grand display of Tibetan artistry, one highlighted by the retreat's lavish indulgence on its guests. Indeed, one is pampered in all ways possible, whether with a

yunnan province people's republic of china

soothing spa session with locally inspired treatments such as Tui Na, or a romantic dinner by the riverbank, showcasing seasonal delicacies from Llamo Restaurant, one of Banyan Tree Ringha's two dining establishments.

The integration of Banyan Tree Ringha with its environs goes beyond the merely cosmetic; it extends to being ecologically responsible and giving back to the local community. For instance, the retreat has maintained an ongoing interaction with village residents to tackle waste management problems, and spearheaded tree planting and river cleanup endeavours. Banyan Tree Ringha also sells indigenously made souvenirs, stimulating the local economy while enabling guests to depart with a cherished piece of the Tibetan prefecture.

Treks of varying intensity ranging from the Shudugang Acclimatisation Trek, to the Tsalong Village Trek are available to explore the vast landscape firsthand. Besides being a healthy and environmentally friendly way to discover the area, these excursions include farmhouse visits where guests can sample authentic local cuisine such as home-made yak cheese, and be immersed in the autochthonous culture.

As a rare glimpse into a lifestyle far removed from the stresses and pollution of modern living, staying at Banyan Tree Ringha will elicit renewed appreciation for wide open spaces and fresh air. It brings together the best of nature's creations and a local way of life, evoking nostalgia for the simple pleasures that have become all too elusive today.

rooms
11 lodges • 21 suites

food
Chang-Sa: hotpot and steamboats •
Llamo Restaurant: western and Chinese

drink
Chang-Sa: Chinese wines, sakes and cocktails •
Jakhang Lobby Lounge: teahouse

features
Banyan Tree Spa Ringha • private fireplace and terrace • satellite television • library • conference facilities • meeting rooms • trekking trips

green features
refurbishing of old farmhouses as part of architecture • biological wastewater treatment system • community development projects

nearby
Baishuitai • Gyalthang Dzong • Lijiang • Mount Kawakarpo • Songzanlin Lamasery

contact
Hong Po Village, Jian Tang Town, Shangri-La County, Diqing Tibetan Autonomous Prefecture, Yunnan Province
People's Republic of China 674400 •
telephone: +86.887.828 8822 •
facsimile: +86.887.828 8911 •
email: ringha@banyantree.com •
website: www.banyantree.com

evason ana mandara + six senses spa—nha trang

The colourful, bustling markets and varied streetside delicacies of Nha Trang frequently attract travellers in search of an authentic Vietnamese holiday. Evason Ana Mandara & Six Senses Spa—Nha Trang provides an ideal haven from which to explore Vietnam's multi-faceted character, complete with a stretch of pristine beach to laze the day away should one require some peace and serenity.

The only beachfront resort on Nha Trang, Evason Ana Mandara & Six Senses Spa—Nha Trang is surrounded by verdant foliage shading the 17 villas from the sun and creating privacy for guests. Constructed to resemble a traditional Vietnamese village, the resort features 74 rooms, each with a landscaped garden and pool. A beige colour scheme and dark timber accents give the interior a calm, laid-back ambience to chill out in. Amenities in the form of an oversized canopied bed, a pillow menu, an al fresco rainshower and jacuzzi, satellite television, high-speed Internet access and even a popcorn machine for quiet nights in provide guests with all the modern conveniences expected of a five-star establishment.

Like all Six Senses properties, the Six Senses Spa features a wide range of pampering services in the midst of lush organic gardens. Nha Trang's world-famous clear waters and myriad of marine life is ideal for diving, with a new watersports centre offering full PADI certification. Nha Trang's versatile location also allows guests to enjoy a wide variety of activities. Whether it is an excursion to the

THIS PAGE (FROM LEFT): *Enjoy a slower pace of life amid Nha Trang's serene surroundings; elements of local culture add a warm touch to the rooms.*
OPPOSITE (FROM LEFT): *The resort's lush, tropical setting puts guests in the mood for a holiday; the wine cellar's cosy ambience is perfect for private dinners.*

nha trang vietnam

city, a trek through the forest or a day spent island hopping, knowledgeable staff will ensure that each experience is tailor-made down to the last detail.

Dining at a Six Senses establishment has always been a gastronomic adventure, and Evason Ana Mandara & Six Senses Spa—Nha Trang's restaurants carry on this tradition with panache. Ana Pavilion Restaurant looks out to panoramic views of Nha Trang Bay and offers delectable Vietnamese and international creations for guests to choose from. Themed dinners by the pool such as Beach BBQ and Salt and Seafood evenings can be found at Beach Restaurant, complete with live performances that give an informal introduction to local culture. At night, savour a bottle of wine in the courtyard from Lobby Bar's extensive selection of vintages or a cocktail at the pool bar.

As extravagant as the Evason Ana Mandara experience can be, the resort remains deeply committed to protecting the environment. All villas have been built using sustainable wood and are designed to provide ample natural ventilation, thus reducing the need for air-conditioning. A water recycling programme ensures that the establishment's organic gardens are well cared for, while biodegradable detergents and use of solar energy keep the impact on the environment minimal.

Lying supine on one of the few remaining pristine beaches in the world, guests can't help but notice how the surrounding natural splendour is invariably linked with Evason Ana Mandara & Six Senses Spa—Nha Trang's eco-consciousness—a philosophy the green designer resort executes with style.

rooms
74 rooms

food
Ana Pavilion: Vietnamese and international • Beach Restaurant: themed buffet dinners

drink
Lobby Bar: walk-in wine cellar • Pool Bar

features
Six Senses Spa • al fresco rainshower and jacuzzi • satellite TV • high-speed Internet access • business centre • library • two pools • gym • tennis court • beach volleyball • watersports centre • day-trips and excursions

green features
use of solar energy • self-sufficient water supply • waste water treatment plan • natural ventilation • biodegradable chemicals • herbal and vegetable garden

nearby
Cam Ranh airport • Nha Trang town

contact
Beachside, Tran Phu Boulevard
Nha Trang, Khanh Hoa, Vietnam •
telephone: +84.58.352 2222 •
facsimile: +84.58.352 5828 •
email: reservations-nhatrang@sixsenses.com •
website: www.sixsenses.com

six senses hideaway ninh van bay

THIS PAGE: *Pool villas are built to blend into the rock formations.*

OPPOSITE (FROM LEFT): *An intimate evening meal at Dining on the Rocks is a singular experience; sweeping views of the island accompany one's warm bath; a session at the Six Senses Spa will make guests think twice about returning to the rat race.*

Of all the designer accommodations available in Vietnam, Six Senses Hideaway Ninh Van Bay is one that moves to a different beat. Isolated from dizzying city lights and the roar of rush-hour traffic, the island resort invites guests to take time out from their hectic lifestyles and appreciate the peace and serenity that only Mother Nature can offer.

Accessible only by a 20-minute boat ride, Six Senses Hideaway Ninh Van Bay's secluded location stands out from the populous resort town of nearby Nha Trang. Upon arrival, guests are greeted by a long stretch of white beach unsullied by mass tourism. Dotted along the coast are 58 pool villas, each ensconced in dense green foliage to ensure privacy. Built to reflect its natural surroundings, each unit features thatched roofs, timber beams and dried palm leaves lining the ceiling. Such rustic charm is given an added boost with al fresco bathrooms and open-air living rooms, while private infinity pools, plush bedding and 24-hour butler service bring a touch of extravagance to this secluded haven.

Like all other eco-conscious Six Senses properties, the boutique establishment is designed to blend into its environment, with no plastic, chemicals, bleach or paint used during its construction. Where possible, local bamboo has been used for fences and wall cladding, while the majority of wood used has been recycled. These painstaking efforts

ninh van bay **vietnam**

have earned Six Senses Hideaway Nanh Van Bay accolades at the 2008 Annual Guide Awards, setting an admirable example for others to emulate.

The resort's dedication towards nature preservation may give it a rural outlook, yet guests need not worry when modern conveniences are easily at hand. Satellite television, broadband Internet access and DVD players enable guests to stay in touch, although most will prefer to spend their time outdoors basking in the sun and luxuriating in the island's tranquil splendour.

With the lush island at one's disposal, guests will feel the urge to head out as much as possible. Water sports enthusiasts can take advantage of the bay's limpid waters, while the island's hilly terrain provides guests with an appealing alternative to keep fit. Tucked away in the hillside is the world-renowned Six Senses Spa, offering a plethora of massages as well as local treatments such as Vietnamese facials and baths. From adrenaline-packed jaunts to lazy, indulgent afternoons, Six Senses Hideaway Ninh Van Bay's comprehensive facilities are sure to cater to all tastes.

Should dining be more one's cup of tea, get acquainted with the diverse cuisines offered by the resort. Dining by the Bay capitalises on its panoramic beach views with al fresco seating and a repertoire of local, fusion and international specialities. Dining by the Pool offers Vietnamese and international fare in the glow of candlelight, while Dining by the Rocks presents a smorgasboard of flavours in an intimate setting overlooking the ocean.

For a truly exceptional experience, take a short boating excursion out to the various hidden coves, with a personal chef and waiter in tow. As the sun disappears over the horizon, guests can toast yet another spectacular day spent at Six Senses Hideaway Ninh Van Bay.

rooms
58 pool villas

food
Dining by the Bay: international and fusion •
Dining by the Rocks: fine dining • private dining •
Dining by the Pool: Vietnamese and international

drink
Drinks by the Bay: bar • wine cave

features
Six Senses Spa • private infinity pool • in-villa butler • mini wine cellar • satellite TV • high-speed Internet access • watersports and dive facilities • fitness centre • trekking and nature trails • library • business facilites

green features
designed to blend into surroundings • use of natural and recycled materials • recycled water prorgramme • low energy consumption due to natural ventilated design • use of solar energy • organic vegetable garden • waste recycling

nearby
Nha Trang Bay • Hon Rom • Hon Mot • Hon Mun

contact
Ninh Van Bay, Ninh Hoa, Khanh Hoa, Vietnam •
telephone: +84.58.372 8222 •
facsimile: +84.58.372 8223 •
email: reservations-ninhvan@sixsenses.com •
website: www.sixsenses.com

hotel majestic saigon

THIS PAGE (FROM LEFT): The serenity of the sweeping lobby warmly welcomes travel-weary guests; subdued mood lighting and a five-star ambience relaxes the stressed minds of guests.

OPPOSITE (FROM LEFT): Stained-glass panels radiate coloured light to brighten up the interior and give the room character; dine in elegant surrounds at the Serenade Restaurant.

Having witnessed and withstood the various periods of Vietnam's turbulent history, Hotel Majestic Saigon is undoubtedly one of Ho Chi Minh City's most enduring landmarks. Comprising 175 rooms, six restaurants and bars, this art deco structure sits regally in the heart of the pulsating city, on the picturesque riverside corner of Dong Khoi Street. Much of its 83-year-old façade has been retained, as can be seen from the sweeping arches of the lobby and the private balconies of each room, enabling guests to take in the bustling streetlife of the city below.

Walking through the wrought-iron doors, guests are greeted by an expansive lobby with renaissance period décor, chandeliers, lush carpets, colonial-style chairs and a grand winding staircase to match the impressive interior. Such grandeur and elegance continues into the rooms. Richly appointed, interiors are fitted with old-fashioned telephones and period furniture, although the stained-glass panels hung above the bed and encasing the vanity are easily the main feature. Intricately designed in various shades of colours, these panels bring a touch of sophistication to the rooms, transporting guests back to the opulence of the roaring Jazz Age.

Not everything at Hotel Majestic Saigon is a page from the past though. Plush king-sized beds and crisp sheets ensure a good night's sleep, while a generous bathtub invites guests to luxuriate in a long, aromatic soak. Contemporary technology in the form of flat-screen satellite televisions adorns the rooms. High-speed Internet access have also been incorporated for easy connectivity.

Recreationally, the charming courtyard pool area is far from the madding crowd and is a delightful place to lounge with a cocktail in hand. Folks fancying a quick workout can head to the well-equipped fitness centre, while the spa is just the place to soothe tired muscles before heading back into the hustle and bustle of the city.

Hotel Majestic Saigon offers a wide variety of dining options to tempt the taste buds. There is the Cyclo Café, where a delicious Vietamese buffet spread awaits, while Seranade Restaurant offers fine European cuisine. The all-day dining, al fresco Breeze Sky Bar features chargrilled barbecued specialities alongside an unhindered view of the Saigon River, while guests craving for a refreshing drink can head

ho chi minh city **vietnam**

to the M-Bar situated on the roof, or the timeless Catinat Lounge with its repertoire of classic cocktails and live piano tunes.

In line with preserving the old world charm of Hotel Majestic Saigon, the establishment also actively does its part in protecting the city's environment—now rapidly polluted due to its burgeoning industries. Running an operation as extensive as Hotel Majestic Saigon tends to incur hefty costs, yet the establishment has managed to significantly cut down expenses. Guests are invited to play a part with signs tactfully placed throughout the room as gentle reminders to save water and electricity, while staff members are constantly updated on the various means to cut down on chemical and power usage. The hotel's concerted efforts have garnered a slew of green awards, the most recent being the ASEAN Green Hotel Recognition Award in 2008.

Location-wise, the hotel is hard to beat. The world-famous Ben Thanh Market—where antique furniture, silks and lacquerware are sold—is within walking distance, while the Opera House, Notre Dame Cathedral and Reunification Palace are all a stone's throw away. Exploring the city's busy network of streets and sights will surely be an adventure, and the best place to set foot from must surely be Hotel Majestic Saigon.

rooms
175 rooms and suites

food
Serenade Restaurant: Western •
Cyclo Café: international and Vietnamese •
Breeze Sky Bar: barbecued specialities

drink
Breeze Sky Bar • M-Bar • Majestic Club •
Merry Pool Bar • Catinat Lounge

features
satellite TV • high-speed Internet access •
pool • spa • fitness centre • business centre •
conference facilities • nightclub

green features
water and energy efficiency programme •
solar panel system • waste water treatment •
waste management

nearby
Ben Thanh Market • Notre Dame Cathedral •
Opera House • Saigon River

contact
1 Dong Khoi Street, District 1
Ho Chi Minh City, Vietnam •
telephone: +84.8.3829 5517 •
facsimile: +84.8.3829 5510 •
email: majestic@majesticsaigon.com.vn •
website: www.majesticsaigon.com.vn

evason hua hin + six senses spa

The Six Senses experience has always incorporated high-end living with a deep-rooted love for the environment, and Evason Hua Hin & Six Senses Spa is no exception.

Spread across 9 hectares (22 acres) of lush greenery, the eco resort's 185 rooms are created with indulgence in mind. Rich wood accents and whitewashed walls exude a natural elegance, while artistic lighting gives interiors a romantic quality. Open-plan layouts see the luxuriously appointed bedroom looking out to an expansive verandah, upon which a cosy daybed faces enchanting vistas of the tropical jungle or the sparkling gulf of Siam. For a personal slice of this tropical paradise, choose from any of the 40 pool villas. In addition to private plunge pools, al fresco bathtubs framed by a fragrant garden setting beckon guests to live life au naturel.

Children occupy a special place at Evason Hua Hin, and a kids' club keeps children entertained with cultural excursions and closely supervised 'sleepovers'. With little ones well taken care of, parents will find plenty of time to focus on themselves. Golf aficionados can tee off at any of the six world-class golf courses nearby, while watersports facilities will enable one to discover firsthand the flourishing underwater world. Informative day-trips will appeal to

THIS PAGE (FROM LEFT): *Bright colours create a cheerful dinner setting; fruit trees and vegetables have been planted to beautify the resort and keep it self sufficient.*
OPPOSITE (FROM LEFT): *Plush canopied beds and al fresco bathrooms put guests in a holiday mood.*

pranburi **thailand**

culture buffs, and there is always the option of cycling to Hua Hin Town at one's leisure. To fully experience the eco resort's signature hospitality, spend a day at the Six Senses Spa. Consisting of low lying, thatched-roof huts built over lotus ponds and connected by a network of wooden walkways, the spa's rustic charm and organic treatments attest to the retreat's green outlook.

The success of Evason Hua Hin arises from its pristine surroundings, and the resort has implemented various green measures to ensure that the environment remains unspoilt. Energy efficient light bulbs in place of conventional ones are used to help conserve electricity. Natural ventilation reduces the need for air-conditioning, while pollution is minimised through the use of biodegradable washing detergents and cleaning substances.

An organic vegetable and herb garden provides for the authentic flavours featured at the resort's dining establishments. The Restaurant offers international cuisine and daily changing menus in a picturesque semi al fresco setting. The Other Restaurant educates guests on the intricacies of traditional Thai cuisine, with dishes from all regions of the kingdom recreated masterfully by talented chefs. With an extensive list of vintages, the Wine Cellar is ideal for intimate wine dinners, while the split-level bar serves up a delectable selection of tapas and refreshing cocktails.

Veering away from conventional hotel concepts and taking the path less travelled, Evason Hua Hin has created a sophisticated brand of eco tourism and a boutique beach experience that discerning globetrotters are sure to appreciate.

rooms
145 rooms • 40 pool villas

food
The Bar: Asian tapas • The Other Restaurant: international • The Restaurant: Thai

drink
The Bar • The Other Bar • The Wine Cellar

features
Six Senses Spa • DVD player • stereo system • kids' club • common infinity pool • music library • open-style bathroom • pool villas include plunge pool and outdoor shower • satellite TV • wireless Internet access • conference room • limousine service

green features
natural materials used in construction • organic vegetable and herb garden • energy efficiency programme • responsible waste management

nearby
Hua Hin town • Petchaburi • Sam Roi Yod National Park • the Royal Summer Palace

contact
9 Moo 5 Paknampran Beach, Pranburi Prachuap Khirikhan 77220, Thailand • telephone: +66.32.632 111 • facsimile: +66.32.632 112 • email: reservations-huahin@sixsenses.com • website: www.sixsenses.com

six senses hideaway hua hin

THIS PAGE: The Living Room seats guests amid fragrant lotus ponds.
OPPOSITE (FROM LEFT): Guests will delight in the villas' abundant facilities and sprawling grounds; unwind in secluded comfort at the world-acclaimed Earth Spa.

Hua Hin's quiet seaside town has attracted travellers looking for a change of pace as early as the 1920s, when the Thai royal family built one of its summer palaces there. Creating a secluded haven far from the bustling tourist attractions identified with modern Hua Hin, Six Senses Hideaway Hua Hin stylishly captures the original idyllic charm that has smitten the hearts of many a king.

The retreat encompasses 55 pool villas framed by verdant forest that stretches out to the shoreline. Ranging from 259 sq m (2,788 sq ft) to 380 sq m (4,090 sq ft), rooms feature five-star amenities such as sun decks, outdoor showers, satellite TV and plush beds provide for a luxurious getaway. Private infinity pools melt into the horizon, while a cheery atmosphere is evident in the multi-coloured cushions scattered on daybeds, and generous garden space cordoned off by whitewashed mud walls for privacy.

The resort's signature butler service leaves no whim unattended from arrival to departure. This includes arranging an in-villa dinner for two, or packing a light luncheon for a daytrip. Cultural diversions abound with the Summer Palace just a scenic drive away. A host of nature activities ranging from mountain biking to scuba diving, and the resort's fitness centre and tennis and watersports facilities will certainly work up a healthy appetite in guests.

Offering a profusion of flavours, dining establishments will satiate even the most demanding palate. The Beach Restaurant serves a selection of authentic Mediterranean cuisine and seafood with a stunning view of the Gulf of Siam. Emphasising international favourites, The Living Room redefines al fresco dining with tables placed amid sunken lotus ponds.

As part of Six Senses Hideaway Hua Hin's aim to create a sustainable form of tourism, much of the organic produce served at the table is harvested from the resort's grounds. Responsible waste management keeps the impact on the environment minimal, while the establishment uses only environmentally friendly chemicals and detergents.

Perhaps an excellent representation of Six Senses Hideaway Hua Hin's eco policies is the world-acclaimed Six Senses Earth Spa. Dome-shaped and entirely made of mud, the Earth Spa updates the traditional royal seaside retreat with its irreverent architecture and exclusive therapies. Each dome is designed with low entrances to the outside water to allow breezes and energy to flow in, while ventilation from the top keeps guests cool. Meditation caves allow one to soak in the positive *chi* in privacy, while skin food in the form of organic treatments and carefully concocted essential oils give tired bodies a well-deserved boost.

Luxuriating in the tranquillity of a tropical beach is becoming increasingly difficult to find in an ever-shrinking world. However, guests need not be concerned as Six Senses Hideaway Hua Hin's beach paradise is always on hand for one to get away from it all.

pranburi **thailand**

rooms
55 villas

food
The Living Room: international •
The Beach Restaurant: Mediterranean

drink
The Bar • Wine Cellar

features
Six Senses Earth Spa • butler service • gym • kids' club • open-air bathroom and shower • private infinity pools • satellite TV • tennis courts • conference facilities • watersports centre

green features
waste management programme • use of natural materials during construction of villas and spa • organic vegetable and herb garden • use of biodegradable chemicals

nearby
Sam Roi Yod National Park • Hua Hin town centre • nature trails

contact
9/22 Moo 5 Paknampran Beach, Pranburi Prachuap Khirikhan 77220 Thailand •
telephone : + 66.32.618 200 •
facsimile : + 66.32.632 112 •
email: reservations-huahin@sixsenses.com •
website: www.sixsenses.com

six senses hideaway samui—a sala property

THIS PAGE: Built into the hillside, luxurious pool villas feature amazing views of the island.

OPPOSITE (FROM LEFT): The natural landscape is kept intact to give villas an idyllic appeal; interiors are adorned with a host of modern amenities.

Jostling with fellow tourists for beach space may be the unfortunate outcome of many a tropical holiday. With this in mind, savvy travellers would do much better to head for Koh Samui's rambling hills and check into Six Senses Hideaway Samui for an enticing getaway experience.

Sitting on the tip of the island's sheer cliffs, the luxury resort has 66 villas built into the hillside and unhindered ocean views to wake up to. Local wood is used to blend each unit into the lush forest, while lightweight natural materials such as bamboo and rattan provide natural ventilation and give villas an air of captivating rusticity. Juxtaposed with this simplistic, no-frills setting is a range of world-class accoutrements that cater to every desire. Interiors are equipped with a king-size canopied bed, wireless Internet access upon request, plasma screen television, daybed and outdoor shower and dining area. There is also the option of having a private infinity-edge pool looking out to the horizon, although many will agree that the 270° panoramas of the Gulf of Siam and neighbouring emerald islands alone are enough to take one's breath away.

Similarly impressive are the resort's dining establishments. Showcasing some of the most imaginative cuisines on the island, each restaurant is set to surpass the highest expectations. Dining on the Hill serves a wide array of Thai creations and nutritional dishes that guests can enjoy in the warm glow of the setting sun. Looking down on the island from lofty heights is Dining on the Rocks. This award-winning restaurant deconstructs and revamps conventional Asian flavours with finesse, taking guests on a sensory journey as they savour contemporary creations amid the surrounding serenity.

Having a flair for innovation and redefining experiences also extends to Six Senses Hideaway Samui's efforts in environmental conservation. The eco resort produces its own

koh samui **thailand**

bio-diesel to reduce diesel consumption, while a wastewater treatment programme keeps its three organic vegetable gardens well irrigated. Regular beach clean-ups keep the surroundings spotless, while the Green Book—a Six Senses eco manifesto—is placed in all rooms to promote environmental awareness.

Such dedication to Mother Nature creates a pristine beach location from which to enjoy the abundance of activities available. Explore Koh Samui's lush terrain by foot, elephant, car or motorbike, or head down to the soft sands and placid waters for a day out at sea. Excursions to local markets and Thai culinary workshops will appeal to those moving at a more relaxed pace, while lazy afternoons by the pool provide one with the perfect excuse to come home with a glowing tan.

Regardless of how one spends the day, be sure to visit the Six Senses Spa. Effortlessly melding indulgent luxury with the natural world, the spa's spectacular ocean views and lavishly appointed treatment salas are accompanied by a wide range of holistic and traditional treatments conducted by highly skilled therapists. Much like its commitment to the earth, Six Senses Hideaway Samui's signature hospitality and understated style will ensure that every guest will end each day refreshed and invigorated.

rooms
14 villas · 52 pool villas

food
Dining on the Hill: all day dining ·
Dining on the Rocks: Asian fusion ·

drink
Drink on the Hill: bar · wine cellar

features
Six Senses Spa · butler service · central swimming pool · gym · plunge bathtub · private villa infinity pools · open-air bathroom and shower · satellite TV and DVD player · watersports centre · conference facilities · wireless Internet access available on request

green features
bio-diesel production plant · wastewater treatment plant · organic vegetable and herb garden · public awareness programs

nearby
Chaweng · Gulf of Siam and outlying islands

contact
9/10 Moo 5 Baan Plai Laem, Bophut
Koh Samui Suratthani 84320 Thailand ·
telephone: +66.77.245 678 ·
facsimile: +66.77.245 671 ·
email: reservations-samui@sixsenses.com ·
website: www.sixsenses.com

anantara phuket resort + spa

Mai Khao Beach, a serene stretch of beach just 15 minutes away from Phuket International Airport, represents the antithesis to Phuket's bustling sights and sounds. Situated in Sirinath Marine National Park, Anantara Phuket Resort & Spa's secluded location and understated luxury offers guests the best way to experience Mai Khao's unspoilt beauty.

The resort's 83 pool villas are individually framed by the manicured verdure of a Bill Bensley designed garden. Pathways connect the villas and meander down to the beach, giving guests easy access to the crystalline Andaman Sea. Taking on the architecture of a southern Thai village, each villa features an open concept living area, with vibrant Thai silks and indigenous artworks exuding a cheerful tropical atmosphere.

The vaulted ceiling of the bedroom resembles that of a Thai temple, while the king-sized beds and soft sheets lure one to laze in bed just a little longer. The bathroom comes as a pleasant surprise, with the vanity area leading out to an al fresco 'made for two' terrazzo tub seamlessly blending into the private infinity-edge pool. Coupled with contemporary fittings such as high-speed Internet access, a surround sound system with iPod docks, a large LCD television and even a personal wine fridge, being isolated from Phuket's noisy nightlife and hordes of tourists never sounded so attractive.

Constantly at the forefront of luxury accommodation also sees Anantara Phuket taking proactive steps towards making the resort green. Recycling measures have been

THIS PAGE: Each villa is a secluded haven, with landscaped gardens and a private pool to lounge in.

OPPOSITE (CLOCKWISE FROM TOP): Signature al fresco bathtubs are perfect for a romantic sorjourn; the resort's idyllic surroundings gives one the perfect excuse to make dining out a special event.

phuket thailand

implemented where possible, from the re-use of materials such as paper, glass and plastic to the recirculation of wastewater for landscape irrigation. Environmentally friendly chemicals are also used in the treatment of all pools and landscaping, while lighting throughout the establishment has been installed with a timer as part of its energy-saving policy.

Such efforts play a part in maintaining the national park's lush surroundings, and the benefits of doing so go a long way. Critically endangered giant leatherback turtles return periodically to the park's pristine beaches to lay eggs, while the world-famous coral reefs and brightly hued fish in the nearby Similan Islands are just a dive away, offering guests a glimpse of a carefully protected environment and all its wondrous possibilities.

When guests have had enough adventure outdoors, Anantara Phuket welcomes them back in an indulgent fashion. The terraced pools are ideal for lounging in the sun, with oversized daybeds and bespoke cocktails from the Infinity pool bar. Spa addicts will be ecstatic with the Anantara Spa's extensive range of lavish treatments, meted out in any of its five extravagant treatment rooms. Epicureans can tantalise their tastebuds with the resort's two restaurants offering European and Asian creations, while wine connoisseurs will be delighted with The Tasting Room and its vast selection of vintages.

Offering contemporary, sophisticated luxuries in a sumptuous, unspoilt setting, Anantara Phuket's ability to respect its natural surroundings in style is what makes this resort stand above the crowd.

rooms
83 pool villas

food
La Sala: Italian and Thai • Sea.Fire.Salt: seafood and barbecued specialities • The Tree House: Thai fusion tapas

drink
Infinity: pool bar • The Tasting Room: wine cellar • The Tree House: bar

features
private pool • iPod and iPod docking station • LCD television and DVD player • espresso machine • personal wine cellar • wireless Internet access • watersports • three tennis courts • children's club • fitness studio • library • meeting room facilities

green features
wastewater recirculation for landscape irrigation • recycling of raw materials • environmentally friendly chemicals used in pools and landscaping • timer installed on lighting

nearby
Similan Islands • Phang Nga Bay • Koh Phi Phi • Sirinath Marine National Park

contact
888 Moo 3, Tumbon Mai Khao Amphur Thalang, Phuket 83110 Thailand •
telephone: +66.76.336 100 •
facsimile: +66.76.336 177 •
email: phuket@anantara.com •
website: www.phuket.anantara.com

evason phuket + six senses spa

Devoting an afternoon to picture-perfect beaches is a dream many overworked urbanites harbour. Offering endless days of glorious sunshine, pristine coastlines and absolute privacy, Evason Phuket & Six Senses Spa invites guests to throw off the cares of the day and step into a world of unrivalled eco-luxury.

Sitting atop 26 hectares (64 acres) of virgin parkland, Evason Phuket's 260 rooms are scattered throughout a resplendent garden setting. Island charm and luxury living are seamlessly integrated into the resort, and are further reflected in its open-style interiors. Awash in tones of cream and sand, bedrooms are a portrait of serenity. Full-length windows draw in the sun's rays, while a daybed allows one to bask in the balmy weather. The outside world is just a click away, with modern conveniences such as satellite TV and high-speed Internet access keeping guests in touch with loved ones. Pool villas have the additional perks of a personal pool and private garden, while the Honeymoon villa redefines extravagance by having the privately owned Bon Island entirely to itself after dusk.

Evason Phuket is especially adept at designing nonpareil experiences, and affable staff are always on hand to ensure one's stay is nothing short of unforgettable. A morning's

THIS PAGE: Lush amenities and total privacy envelop guests in a world of contentment.
OPPOSITE (FROM LEFT): A session at The Six Senses Spa includes a lovely view of the Andaman Sea; candle-lit dinners in the evening make for a truly magical affair.

phuket thailand

worth of adrenaline pumping watersports can be followed by a scrumptious champagne picnic. Romantic moonlight cruises can also be organised. The professionally run kids' club will whisk little ones away on an adventure of their own, be it closely supervised tented 'sleepovers' or movie-watching under the stars.

Evason Phuket's green efforts stay true to its core purpose of creating a sustainable environment. The resort's widespread eco-awareness reveals longstanding practices that have kept beachside and oceanic habitats immaculate. A fresh water reservoir allows the resort self-sufficiency, while a waste recycling programme reiterates Evason Phuket's belief in environmental responsibility.

Organic produce and fine dining work in tandem to offer guests a collection of designer restaurants with mouth-watering cuisines. Into the Med features Mediterranean cuisine with a modern twist, while fiery Thai specialities can be found at Into Thai. Into the Beach's casual ambience complements its gourmet pizzas and tapas, while international favourites sit alongside stunning seaviews at Into the View. For a sublime feast of the senses take a scenic boat ride down to Bon Island, where Onto The Island beguiles with its flavourful Thai, European and barbecued creations.

Such gastronomical excess calls for a thorough detox, and guests can recuperate in style at the Six Senses Spa. Going beyond conventional treatments, the spa reaches deeper with its alternative therapies and lifestyle coaches to achieve good health and balance. Body, mind and environment—it's a calm and gentle treatment for all at the Evason Phuket & Six Senses Spa.

rooms
214 rooms • 39 suites • 7 pool villas

food
Into the Beach: Mediterranean • Into Thai: Thai • Into The Med: contemporary Mediterranean • Into The View: international • Onto The Island: Thai, European and barbecued specialities

drink
Into The Beach: bar • infinity pool bar • Into Pondering: light refreshment • Into Wines: wine cellar

features
Six Senses Spa • privately owned Bon Island • satellite TV • high-speed Internet access • watersports • bike and boat rental • conference facilities • fitness centre • 3 pools • kids' club

green features
fresh water reservoir • organic herb and vegetable garden • no chemicals policy • waste management • energy efficiency

nearby
Phuket town • Phi Phi island

contact
100 Vised Road, Moo 2, Tambol Rawai Muang District, Phuket 83130, Thailand • telephone: +66.76.381 010 • facsimile: +66.76.381 018 • email: reservations-phuket@sixsenses.com • website: www.sixsenses.com

six senses destination spa phuket

Healing at Six Senses Destination Spa Phuket begins the moment one sets foot on the idyllic island of Naka Yai. Located in Phang Nga Bay off Phuket, the establishment goes beyond usual spa philosophy to create a bespoke spa experience that guests can not only indulge in, but also bring home.

Reflecting the Chinese, Indian, Thai and Indonesian cultures that have influenced the Six Senses brand of treatments, the layout of The 7th Sense Wellness Centre focuses on feng shui to enhance its positive *chi* energy. Upon arrival, guests are given a complimentary wellness consultation along with a customised programme created to maximise the benefits of their stay here. The itinerary could include anything from a sunrise pilates session to an invigorating workout at the jungle gym with a trainer—or even a signature Six Senses Oriental Fusion massage. Under the supervision of specialists from the various healthcare fields, guests will find themselves leaving this cocoon of wellbeing refreshed and revitalised.

Designed to mirror the retreat's 'clean living' aesthetic are 60 pool villas, spread along the beach and tucked into the hillside. Each unit is outfitted with a pool, terrace, sun loungers and a mesmerising view of the sparkling bay. Rooms are decorated in subtle cream tones, with green cushions adding a splash of colour. Landscaping has been created with an eco twist, with organic citrus fruits and herbs grown in the private garden while a bathroom herb garden provides for

THIS PAGE (FROM LEFT): *The 7th Sense Wellness Centre is built to evoke a sense of positive wellbeing; private free-form pools enable guests can take a dip any time of the day.*
OPPOSITE (FROM LEFT): *Mood lighting, soothing colours and plush beds elicit a calming environment for guests to unwind and relax in; lanterns, natural wood and bamboo accents give the Ton Sai restaurant a rustic charm.*

phuket **thailand**

calming, organic baths. For the ultimate in luxury, opt for the Retreat on the Hill, a 2,500-sq-m (26,910-sq-ft) villa featuring a private spa complete with meditation cave, yoga pavilion, wet and dry treatment rooms, gymnasium and relaxation area. All villas feature iPods, and personalised butler service to see to every desire.

Creating a balance in life is what Six Senses is renowned for, and the resort's management believes strongly in maintaining the island's delicate ecosystem. Natural materials have been used during the construction of villas, evident in their sugar palm thatched roofs. In place of environment-damaging chemicals are saline pool systems, organic pesticides and biodegradable pesticides. The establishment produces its own drinking water, bottled in reusable bottles for guests, while a waste water management programme keeps the gardens well irrigated. As part of its conservation efforts, mangrove forests are also replanted to sustain coastal and swamp habitats.

Total wellness begins from within, and the resort showcases nutritious and delicious alternative cuisine. Ton Sai restaurant offers organic creations alongside pescatarian dishes, freshly harvested from the sea and resort grounds. Dining at the Point offers the latest in cuisine trends, with a carefully prepared, innovative raw food menu that preserves the vitamins and enzymes beneficial to one's health. Spa cuisine classes are also conducted regularly at the Cuisine Cave, enabling guests to recreate balanced meals back home.

With its unique concept, specialised spa programmes and exclusive location, a sojourn at Six Senses Destination Spa Phuket is bound to bring guests back on their feet, energised and ready to take on the rigours of urban life.

rooms
60 pool villas • 1 Retreat on the Hill

food
Ton Sai restaurant: pescatarian •
Dining at the Point: raw food

drink
bio-dynamic wine and champagne

features
The 7th Sense Wellness Centre • all villas have pools, sundecks, iPods and personalised butler service • two gyms • infinity pool • library with Internet access • sea sports • day-trips and excursions

green features
saline pool systems • organic pesticides • biodegradable detergents • natural materials for construction • waste water management • replanting of mangrove forests • organic landscape gardens • organic vegetable gardens

nearby
Phuket

contact
32 Moo 5, Tambol Paklok, Amphur Thalang Phuket 83110, Thailand •
telephone: +66.76.371 400 •
facsimile: +66.76.371 401 •
email: reservations-naka@sixsenses.com •
website: www.sixsenses.com

six senses hideaway yao noi

THIS PAGE: *Hidden among lush foliage, each pool villa is presented as a private retreat.*

OPPOSITE (FROM LEFT): *Sago palm thatching ensures that rooms are ventilated naturally; spectacular island views and lush amenities complete the experience of luxury living.*

When it comes to superlative tropical resorts, it is hard to surpass those found in Asia. From al fresco baths and private plunge pools, one can easily imagine that such indulgences were conceived while reposed in the midst of cloudless blue skies and unspoilt beaches. A well-respected name in the luxury travel market, the Six Senses Group has effortlessly incorporated these aspects into the Six Senses Hideaway Yao Noi.

The beachfront retreat exemplifies how luxury can be multifarious and splendidly redefined in many new ways. Listed on *Condé Nast*'s 'Hot list Hotels' and *Travel + Leisure*'s 'The It List' for 2008, Six Senses Hideaway Yao Noi possesses all the qualities that put the sparkle in its five-star rating—arrival by speedboat, sprawling pool villas, designer amenities, personal butler service and opulent spa suites.

All 56 villas are designed with an open-plan layout boasting magnificent views of the sparkling bay and surrounding tropical foliage. Clean architectural lines of the interiors are accentuated by local wood flooring and sago palm leaf thatched roofs, creating a room that tastefully blends past and present Thai heritage together. An infinity-edge pool, Bose sound system, satellite TV and personal espresso machine complete this portrait of extravagance, creating a self-contained haven where guests can chill out in absolute privacy.

The resort's three dining establishments take full advantage of the sultry weather, excellent vantage points and intriguing limestone formations. Feast on flavourful Thai cuisine at The Living Room & Terrace while admiring unhindered views of Phang Nga Bay. Offering authentic Italian creations in an intimate atmosphere, The Dining Room also proffers private dining options nestled among wild mangrove trees and plantation palms. Not to be outdone by its neighbours, The Main House invites guests to dine on

phang nga **thailand**

fragrant regional specialities amid lotus ponds, while a glass duplex wine cellar will surely keep wine aficionados engrossed for the rest of the evening.

As new standards of luxury are constantly established by the resort's accomplished management, eco-conscious guests will be heartened to know that Six Senses Hideaway Yao Noi is also setting the benchmark for an environmentally-friendly designer lifestyle. The villas' rustic character is emphasised by indigenous methods of natural ventilation adopted to keep its guests cool. Wastewater is recycled for irrigation purposes while 'push' valves on showers help reduce unnecessary water wastage. All chemicals and detergents used are biodegradable, while organic herb and vegetable gardens serve the dual purpose of landscaping and supplying produce to the resort's restaurants.

Such dedication towards maintaining a pristine environment ensures that each day spent on this equatorial paradise is nothing short of a sensational experience. Breathe in the pure air and relax as therapists eradicate any traces of fatigue at the world-acclaimed Six Senses Spa; observe the unblemished marinescape while scuba diving; savour the organic fruits of one's labour at a Thai culinary workshop; luxuriate in the adrenaline rush while mountain biking down winding forest trails. The options are endless, and guests will leave Six Senses Hideaway Yao Noi refreshed, recharged and reborn.

rooms
54 pool villas and pool villa suites • 1 hilltop reserve • 1 retreat

food
The Dining Room: Italian • The Main House: Thai and regional Asian • The Living Room & Terrace: Thai, buffet and grill

drink
The Main House: bar • wine cellar

features
Six Senses Spa • butler service • gym • iPod docking station • meeting room • movie and music library • open-air bathroom • private beach • satellite TV and DVD player • tennis court • villa dining • private infinity pool • watersports centre • Thai cooking class

green features
natural ventilation • biodegradable chemicals used • water recycling programme • organic herb and vegetable garden • water and energy saving measures

nearby
Phang Nga Bay • Phuket

contact
56 Moo 5, Tambol Koh Yao Noi, Amphur Koh Yao, Phang Nga 82160, Thailand •
telephone: +66.76.418 500 •
facsimile: +66.76.418 518 •
email: reservations-yaonoi@sixsenses.com •
website: www.sixsenses.com

el nido resorts

If the ultimate beach getaway brings to mind the tropical Eden featured in the cult classic film *Blue Lagoon*, then the hundred white beaches and surrounding clear waters of the El Nido islands will fit the bill nicely. Accessible only by boat, the municipality is perhaps one of the few remaining beachside destinations unravaged by tourism. Only five of its 45 islands have been developed, and it is on the lush Lagen and Miniloc islands that the exclusive El Nido Resorts have built its homes.

Translated to mean 'nest' in Spanish, guests will feel right at home with El Nido Resorts' luxury tropical accommodation and world-class service. Tucked in a cove framed by thick primary forest is Lagen Island Resort, while Miniloc Island Resort hovers on the water's edge with unrestricted views of the sea. Both establishments are a testament to El Nido Resorts' philosophy of sustainable tourism—all rooms and cottages have been constructed using natural materials and recycled wood salvaged from old Filipino houses. Thatched roofs, bamboo and rattan furniture and antique wood floors give the resorts an intrinsically Filipino character, one that not only harks back to the country's rich heritage, but also plays tribute to its indigenous culture.

Soaking up local history need not mean sacrificing contemporary comforts expected of an extravagant seaside holiday. From hillside cottages to seaview rooms, all units

THIS PAGE (FROM LEFT): *Explore the islands' limpid waters and dynamic rock formations; poolside dinners at sundown are a spectacular affair.*
OPPOSITE (FROM LEFT): *Guests will have a difficult time choosing between Lagen Island Resort's elegant charm or Miniloc Island Resort's rustic appeal.*

pelewan **philippines**

are fully air-conditioned, with plush bedlinen and a private verandah alongside exceptional views of either the never-ending horizon or dramatic limestone cliffs.

The multi-faceted islands provide an abundance of activities for guests to engage in. Visitors can admire the fascinating dripstone formations within ancient limestone caves. Exploring the vibrant marinescape is a breeze with a complete line of watersports equipment available at the marine sports centre. Home to multitudinous tropical flora and fauna, the surrounding verdure provides plenty of wildlife spotting excitement for trekkers.

To protect these marvels of nature, El Nido Resorts has taken up the task of implementing a brand of tourism that is eco-friendly. Both resorts process and recycle its used water and solid waste, while selected rooms are powered by solar energy. To aid in coral reef recovery, EcoReefs have also been introduced into the underwater ecosystem. Such green efforts have been internationally recognised and lauded; El Nido Resorts has received the Green Hotel Recognition Award from ASEAN, as well as a placement on *Condé Nast Traveler*'s Green List.

Of course, if staying in is more to one's taste, El Nido Resorts' on-site facilities are designed to indulge and pamper. Lounge by the pool with a cocktail in hand, or unwind at the Stresscape spa with its extensive range of rejuvenating treatments. Mealtimes have a scenic quality about them, and can be savoured at the clubhouse, by the pool—even in a secluded island cove. Whichever direction one's fancy takes, guests can rest assured in the knowledge that with El Nido Resorts' environmental commitments, all this luxury will not, literally, cost the earth.

rooms
Lagen Island Resort: 51 rooms •
Miniloc Island Resort: 50 rooms

food
resort clubhouse: Filipino and international •
beachclubs: picnics and grilled specialities

drink
poolside bar • beach bar • beachclub bars

features
Stresscape spa • wireless Internet access at the resorts' clubhouse • conference facilities • marine sports centre • billiards • foosball • air hockey • table tennis • on-site clinic • outdoor pool at Lagen • day-trips and excursions

green features
use of natural materials and recycled wood for construction • sewage treatment plant • desalination plant • wastewater recycling programme • EcoReefs • use of solar energy

nearby
Entalula Beach Club • Pangulasian Beach Club

contact
18/F, 8747 Paseo de Roxas Street Salcedo Village, 1226 Makati City, Philippines •
telephone: +63.2.750 7600/ +63.2.894 5644 •
facsimile: +63.2.810 3620 •
email: holiday@elnidoresorts.com •
website: www.elnidoresorts.com

jimbaran puri bali

Bali's famed coastlines, chic restaurants, intriguing architecture and thriving arts scene is a one-stop destination for both the culture buff and beach lover. Jimbaran Puri Bali encapsulates the island's multi-faceted character with its warm hospitality and first-rate facilities, enabling guests to experience all that is intrinsically Balinese.

Jimbaran Puri Bali is located along one of Bali's most exclusive beaches. A flourishing tropical garden setting creates an Edenic atmosphere, with bougainvillea, hibiscus and frangipani scenting the balmy air. The tropicana motif continues throughout the compound, with a personal landscaped garden in all 42 rooms to ensure total privacy. Whitewashed walls and natural materials in the form of marble accents, timber beams and thatch roofs make up each villa, exuding an understated elegance that melds seamlessly into the lush surrounds. Such blissful seclusion is enhanced by a wide array of contemporary comforts offered. Satellite television and high-speed Internet access ensure quick connectivity to the outside world. A large sunken terrazzo bathtub and outdoor rainshower beckon one to throw away any remaining inhibitions, while Balinese silks and intricate woodwork add the finishing touches to each self-contained oasis.

A world of indulgence awaits in any of the 22 newly built pool villas. In addition to the standard facilities offered, villas have the added luxury of a private pool amid a traditional Balinese courtyard, with its beachfront location offering unparalleled ocean views.

THIS PAGE (FROM LEFT): *Enjoy the sun in the privacy of one's garden; a Balinese-style layout ensures that rooms have plenty of light.*

OPPOSITE (FROM LEFT): *At dusk, the resort's well-placed lighting creates a romantic ambience; tranquil beach surroundings allow one to get in the mood for a relaxing spa session.*

bali **indonesia**

There are a plethora of avenues to experience Bali's diverse landscape. Sun and surf await those raring to take on the island's world-famous waves. White beaches give way to verdant hills as one moves inland, and are ideal for rock climbing, trekking or mountain biking. Cultural day-trips will introduce the island's fascinating history, where ancient temple visits offer a chance to witness elaborate processions.

Even the most cosmopolitan traveller will be charmed by the string of reputable art galleries found in the Seminyak area. The resort's spa provides a calming sanctuary for one to regain one's spiritual wellbeing, while the horizon-edge pool provides a stylish location to chill out with a cocktail from the Puri Bar. Bali's rich, varied cuisine can be sampled at Nelayan Restaurant, a beachside establishment that invites diners to bask in the glow of the setting sun. For lighter meals, head to Tunjung Café, which offers western favourites in a casual venue overlooking a lotus pond.

The resort gives back to the island with efforts in environmental protection, cultural preservation and community building. Balinese villas are constructed using traditional methods and locally sourced natural materials. Jimbaran Puri Bali also re-uses waste water for irrigation purposes to help lower water consumption. Resort staff regularly pitch in with locals to keep beaches clean, while guests can also do their part in environmental conservation by switching off air conditioning when not in use.

Bali's ever-changing landscapes and fascinating culture will undoubtedly make for memorable trips—however it is Jimbaran Puri Bali's uninterrupted luxury and pristine surroundings that will transform a pleasant sojourn into something quite exceptional.

rooms
8 beachfront cottages • 2 two-bedroom cottages • 32 one-bedroom garden cottages

food
Nelayan Restaurant: Mediterranean and seafood • Tunjung Café: Indonesian and Balinese • breakfast buffet

drink
Puri Bar

features
high-speed Internet access • private garden • satellite television • spa • horizon-edge pool • watersports

green features
traditional architecture preserved • use of environmentally friendly materials • proper waste management • recycling programme

nearby
Seminyak area • golf courses

contact
Jalan Uluwatu Jimbaran, Bali 80361, Indonesia •
telephone: +62.361.701 605 •
facsimile: +62.361.701 320 •
email: info@jimbaranpuribali.com •
website: www.jimbaranpuribali.com

ubud hanging gardens

THIS PAGE : *Ample space between villas ensures total privacy.*

OPPOSITE (FROM LEFT): *Bright colours and Balinese artwork reflect the resort's tropical surroundings; tiered infinity-edge pools offer excellent vantage points to admire the dramatic gorge.*

Perched high on a terraced slope overlooking the picturesque Ayung River, Ubud Hanging Gardens offers a paranomic view over the valley and its lush tropical surroundings. The resort comprises 38 private villas designed in contemporary Balinese style, set on wooden pillars in order to preserve water absorption over the land's surface.

True to the reputation of the Orient Express group it belongs to, Ubud Hanging Gardens is fully equipped to indulge its guests in all manners of indulgent luxuries. Each villa is furnished with a romantic four-poster bed, and boasts its own heated infinity-edge pool where weary visitors may soak away their worldly cares. Pampering spa sessions are also available at Ayung Spa. Here, therapists expertly mete out signature treatments such Ayung Beauty Secrets, which incorporates a vital energy point massage to ease stress, followed by a floral elixir and hydrating gel to keep skin moist and supple.

Gourmands will need little persuasion to tuck in at Beduur Restaurant, where innovative French-Asian cuisine is prepared under the direction of French executive chef Renaud Le Rasle. Against the majestic backdrop of ancient

bali indonesia

temples, one is treated to delicacies such as steamed butter fish wrapped in a banana leaf medley or tamarind crème brûlée.

Ubud Hanging Gardens also caters to the active crowd with a wide range of diversions. One can participate in yoga classes on a deck overlooking the river or cycle along the Batur volcano. Being Bali's arts and cultural capital, a visit to downtown Ubud's art galleries will also prove to be enriching. Children are not left out either, with affable caregivers teaching kite making and Balinese dances to allow harried parents who need a quiet moment to steal away for an hour or two.

The resort is eco-conscious, recently winning the 2008 ASEAN Energy Award to show how environmental awareness can go in tandem with a successful resort business. Simple steps such as using gas instead of electricity, and planting trees to provide shade over open walkways help Ubud Hanging Gardens to use just a fraction of the energy hotels of its size conventionally consume. A stroll through the gardens among its abundant tropical fruit trees and exotic flowers also allows one to marvel at how beautifully the retreat has incorporated local vegetation into a landscape which was once nothing but a barren cliff.

What makes a stay at the resort truly pleasurable is the fact that one's indulgences do not result in an oversized carbon footprint. In Bali, where countless resorts have destroyed natural resources in order to earn the tourist dollar, Ubud Hanging Gardens stands out as a well-planned design that costs the earth little while giving guests all that they are entitled to expect in comfort and luxury.

rooms
38 pool villas

food
Beduur Restaurant: Asian-French • Diatas Pohon Café: light meals •

drink
Bukit Becik Bar

features
Ayung Spa • infinity pool • high-speed Internet access • yoga classes • children's activities • cycling • day-trips and excursions • business services available on request

green features
efficient use of energy • designed with respect to local topography • biotech sewage treatment plant • use of an inclined lift prevents the need to build roads

nearby
downtown Ubud • Batur volcano • Bersakih temple

contact
Desa Buahan, Payangan, Ubud Gianyar, Bali 80571, Indonesia • telephone: +62.361.982 700 • facsimile: +62.361.982 800 • email: reservations@ubudhanginggardens.com • website: www.ubudhanginggardens.com

nukubati island

Nukubati Island is a private, all-inclusive island resort situated inside the Great Sea Reef, off the north coast of Vanua Levu in the Fiji Islands. Framed by a natural magnificence unsullied by pollution, the eco retreat is a remote haven offering white beaches, lush rainforests and flourishing coral reefs.

Stepping off the seaplane onto the island's soft sands, one is immediately captivated by Nukubati's laid-back atmosphere. Coconut groves cast whimsical shadows on the retreat's verdant grounds, while abundant native flora add a dash of colour to the Edenic setting. Four beachside bungalow suites and three deluxe honeymoon bures make up the resort's accommodation. Interiors are elegant, with hardwood floors, custom-made rattan furniture and white louvred shutters bringing to mind Fiji's colonial past. All rooms are fitted with a living room, bedroom with a walk-in wardrobe, a private patio and beach-facing verandah, while honeymoon bures have an additional thatched-roof bure that is ideal for al fresco Fijian massages or intimate dinner affairs.

A sprawling, colonial-style structure just moments from the beach, The Pavilion offers panoramic views of the nearby islands. As the centre for island life, the compound houses a lounge, bar and library. Gourmands desiring to sample traditional South Pacific cuisine will be delighted with the restaurant's flavourful creations. Freshly caught seafood and organic, Nukubati-grown produce takes centrestage, with premium Australian, New Zealand and French vintages on hand to accompany each bite. Taking exclusivity a step further, the entire

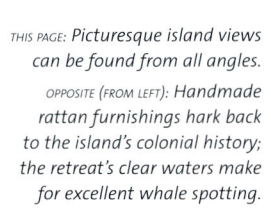

THIS PAGE: *Picturesque island views can be found from all angles.*
OPPOSITE (FROM LEFT): *Handmade rattan furnishings hark back to the island's colonial history; the retreat's clear waters make for excellent whale spotting.*

vanua levu fiji islands

island has been laid at one's feet: meals can be arranged on any part of the island, alongside a full bar service that allows guests to savour a refreshing cocktail wherever they choose.

There is no shortage of adventure at Nukubati, and guests can partake in a bevy of sea sports that the South Pacific is renowned for. Scuba dive among rare tropical fish, ride the waves on a catamaran, or embark on a Fijian spear-fishing excursion. Volleyball and tennis facilities await back on the beach, while a sumptuous picnic for two on a nearby deserted island is undoubtedly the most romantic way to get 'lost at sea'.

The only locally owned luxury retreat in Fiji, Nukubati's ecological sensitivity arises not only out of necessity, but also from the owners' deep love of the island's natural splendour. Nukubati has managed to achieve full sustainability, despite not being connected to the national power grid, main water supply or the main sewage system. The establishment's 350 solar panels power the entire retreat as well as the island's nursing station. Rainwater is carefully collected and stored for use, while wastewater is recycled to ensure that the organic vegetable gardens are well irrigated. The eco resort's dedication to the environment has been recently honoured at the *Condé Nast* World Savers Awards 2008.

Nukubati Island features exclusivity and warm hospitality in true Fijian character. Perfect for an exotic getaway, honeymoon or even a tranquil retreat, the intimacy of this small private island resort is sure to capture any traveller's heart.

rooms
4 beachside bungalow suites •
3 honeymoon bungalows

food
traditional South Pacific • private beach picnics

drink
island-wide bar service

features
privately owned island • library • sea sports • tennis • volley ball • day-trips and excursions • seaplane transfers • boat charters

green features
organic vegetable gardens • use of solar panels and wind generators • recycling and composting programme • rainwater collection • use of LED lights • monitoring of coral reef population

nearby
Great Sea Reef • Suva

contact
Nukubati Island, PO Box 1928, Labasa
Vanua Levu, Fiji Islands •
telephone: +679.603 0919 •
facsimile: +679.603 0918 •
email: info@nukubati.com •
website: www.nukubati.com

bamurru plains

Bamurru Plains, in the untamed floodplains of Australia's Northern Territory, redefines luxury travel. Instead of chauffeur-driven limousines and elaborate spa treatments, think sunset safari drives and reconnecting with nature at its most awe-inspiring. This award-winning wild bush resort bypasses the need for conventional dainties with its faultless service and rich panoramas of biodiversity.

Billed as Australia's finest reserve camp, Bamurru Plains offers a unique way to answer the call of the wild in an inimitably Australian landscape. Each of its nine safari bungalows looks out onto the plains, giving guests uninterrupted views of the surrounding savannah woodland. Inside, timber flooring and pillars dress the room in warm, clean lines, while immaculate linens in sandy hues emphasise the resort's affinity with the earth. Mesh-screen walls admit refreshing breezes from the floodplains and allow unimpeded appreciation of the bush from the comfort of a well-cushioned deck chair.

Technology takes a back seat at Bamurru Plains, and there are no television sets, telephones or Internet access. Instead, the area's flourishing ecosystem takes centre stage, and senses overloaded with daily urban cacophony are quickly refreshed by the sights and sounds of Mother Nature. Guests can embark on an airboat trip on the floodplains for a glimpse of herds of buffalo, or go on an open-top bush drive. After all, Bamurru Plains is located in a region of climatic extremes,

THIS PAGE: *Guests can watch herds of buffalo feeding in the misty floodplains at dawn.*
OPPOSITE (FROM LEFT): *The rooms are decorated in a palette of earth hues, emphasising the resort's close ties to Mother Nature; evenings at the lodge can be spent with fellow guests and a round of cocktails and canapes.*

new south wales **australia**

and one of the highlights here is the resort's showcase of resident wildlife and the annual cycle of environmental rebirth.

Maintaining the sensitive habitats is a priority at Bamurru Plains, and great care is taken to ensure that the land is tampered with as little as possible. Accordingly, the camp was constructed at the edge of the floodplains, while the majority of Bamurru Plains' electricity is solar generated. Reusable water bottles are provided for the guests, while all linen is made from organic cotton and washed with eco-certified detergents.

The Bamurru Plains management help guests heighten their awareness of the environment through the daily operations of the camp and by encouraging them to take part in camp activities. Such practices have brought the establishment accolades such as being on *Condé Nast*'s 'Hot List 2007' and *Travel & Leisure*'s 'world's coolest new places to stay' in 2007.

The toll of roughing it out in the wild is balanced with a liberal dose of Australian hospitality at the lodge. The focal point for dining and socialising, the lodge is equipped with a library, dining area, barbecue pit and infinity-edge pool. In the evening, a selection of Australian wines and canapés on the front deck enhances guests' enjoyment of the laid-back atmosphere before they head inside for a communal dinner of modern Australian cuisine prepared with local produce.

At night, the stars are a mesmerising backdrop undimmed by city lights. It's an adrenaline rush to experience the Australian outback, an adventure made all the more exciting and enriching at Bamurru Plains.

rooms
9 safari bungalows

food
lodge: contemporary Australian

drink
lodge: open bar of wines, beers, selected spirits and soft drinks

features
communal dining room • infinity pool • library • day tours and excursions • meeting facilities

green features
solar power generator • organic cotton linen • eco-certified detergents • recycled chemical containers and bottles • use of local produce • donation to Australian Wildlife Conservancy for every guest

nearby
Arnhem Land • Kakadu National Park • Mary River

contact
Reservations Office: Suite 9, Upper Level Jones Bay Wharf, 26–32 Pirrama Road Pyrmont, Sydney NSW 2009 Australia • telephone: +61.2.9571 6399 • facsimile: +61.2.9571 6655 • email: info@bamurruplains.com • website: www.bamurruplains.com

paperbark camp

The Australian version of the African camp experience, Paperbark Camp is ideal for guests who adore being close to nature as much as they appreciate their creature comforts. Bringing together world-class lodging with fine cuisine and warm hospitality, the retreat has set up camp as a base from which to discover Jervis Bay's clear waters, white sand beaches and lush bush landscapes. Such a boutique camping experience is facilitated by low-impact eco-friendly operations, awarding the camp advanced accreditation with the Ecotourism Association of Australia.

Keeping the forest canopy intact as much as possible, accommodation is created to co-exist seamlessly with the giant, age-old trees. Built on an elevated timber platform, 12 safari-style tents look up into the soaring eucalyptus and paperbark trees that pepper the area. Naturally ventilated and running on solar power, each tent is fitted with an open-air bathroom, plush bed, local furniture and wrap-around hardwood verandah for one to take in the sights and sounds of the bush. Urbanites with any lingering anxieties about camping in the wilderness will change their minds with a stay in any of the four deluxe tents. Designer furnishings and a standalone bath transform tents into chic abodes, while an unhindered view of the sprawling gum tree forest add to the luxe camping experience.

Just a short drive away is the eco tourist's paradise of Jervis Bay, offering diving, snorkelling, surfing and dolphin watching activities. Booderee National Park is a sanctuary to a wide variety of wildlife, and is easily accessible through a network of walking trails. The camp's flourishing paperbark, gum and mangrove forest trails provide opportunities for animal spotting throughout the day. In the early mornings, guests can head out to watch wild kangaroos feed, while possums and nocturnal creatures take over the forest in the evening and can be seen at play. Green modes of transport such as complimentary bikes and canoes are also provided for guests to explore the tidal inlet at their own pace. Better yet, take advantage of the serene forest setting with a massage in the privacy of one's tent.

The Gunyah provides a communal area for dining and relaxing. Designed by architectural firm Nettleton Tribe, the lodge offers a unique vantage point from among the treetops and is naturally cooled by sea breezes. Reflecting the changing seasons is a modern European influenced menu, highlighting the fresh, organic flavours that the Australian coast is renowned for. In summer, guests can dine al fresco under the trees in a delightful bush setting. Winter sees guests moving inward to the open fire, with plush loungers creating a cosy atmosphere for one to curl up in.

Offering tranquillity and relaxation in an artfully designed experience that takes both environment and guest in mind, Paperback Camp is luxury eco camping at its best—not to mention one of the best options for guilt-free hedonism found in the South Pacific.

THIS PAGE (FROM TOP): Spend an entire evening savouring the Gunyah's warm atmosphere and delectable creations; let the soothing sounds of nature accompany one's bath.
OPPOSITE (FROM LEFT): Safari tents are ensconced amid towering trees; Nearby Jervis Bay's clear waters and flourishing marinescape make for exciting scuba diving.

new south wales **australia**

rooms
12 safari tents

food
Gunyah: contemporary Australian

drink
Gunyah: bar

features
spa • conference room • deluxe tents are fitted with designer furnishings and standalone bathtub • complimentary bikes and canoes

green features
eco-friendly construction • solar power • natural ventilation • biodegradable detergents • use of local produce • green modes of transport • reforestation programme

nearby
Booderee National Park • Jervis Bay • vineyards

contact
571 Woollamia Road, Woollamia
New South Wales 2540, Australia •
telephone: +61.2.4441 6066 •
facsimile: +61.2.4441 6066 •
email: info@paperbarkcamp.com.au •
website: www.paperbarkcamp.com.au

southern ocean lodge

THIS PAGE: *Panoramic vistas can be appreciated from every room.*
OPPOSITE (FROM LEFT): *Stylish interiors consolidate the best of modern Australian design and art; dine on fresh organic produce in sophisticated surrounds.*

Set on the ruggedly beautiful Kangaroo Island in South Australia, Southern Ocean Lodge resets the benchmark for green experiential travel. The island has fast established itself as a premiere destination for both nature lovers and the cosmopolitan crowd, with 4,500 sq km (1,737 sq miles) of land acting as a sanctuary for native wildlife.

Amid the flourishing verdure, the curved form of Southern Ocean Lodge juts out from a cliff above Hanson Bay. Every consideration has been given to create a fine balance between nature and luxury, and the lodge's modern, eco-friendly design attests to this. Organic local materials such as recycled timber and white limestone give guests a sense of place, while the compound's clean, strong lines lends itself to showcasing the magnificent coastal panoramas that greet guests upon arrival.

All 21 suites feature king-sized beds, sunken lounges, glass-walled bathrooms and private terraces. A variety of accommodation are available, with the Osprey Pavilion offering indulgences such as a hand-sculpted bathtub and a plunge pool extending out over the coastal scrub. Interiors showcase the best of contemporary Australian design, with notable luminaries from Florence Broadhurst to Khai Liew reflecting the local landscape through their striking timber furnishings and artwork.

new south wales **australia**

The layout of Southern Ocean Lodge is carefully tailored to the local climate, with flow-through ventilation for hot days and, in colder months, glazing to store natural heat. Fireplaces use eco-smart fires fuelled by green energy such as ethanol, while a Biolytix filter system converts wastewater and sewage into clean irrigation water. However, the retreat's green credentials don't end here; out of 102 hectares (252 acres), only 1 hectare (2.47 acres) of land has been cleared for the lodge. The remaining 99 percent has been placed under a Heritage Agreement to prevent future development.

Celebrated as Australia's culinary capital, South Australia's untainted climate inspires artisan growers to produce a bounty of premium, organic food and wines. The fresh seasonal produce is featured in the resident restaurant's daily changing menu, while the cosy open bar and walk-in cellar's selection of premium wines will accompany guests on their gastronomic adventures.

Housed in its own pavilion, the Southern Spa is an oasis of calm framed by verdant foliage and azure waters. Three treatment rooms, a steam room and chill-out lounge promise the ultimate pampering experience with treatments using Australian-made Li'Tya products. Not to be outdone by man-made luxuries are a host of activities where guests can encounter the island's varied wildlife. Known affectionately as Australia's Galepagos, this 'zoo without fences' alllows one to get up close with the natural world via trekking, cave explorations, island hopping and wildlife spotting. Southern Ocean Lodge may be remote, but as anyone who has made the journey will know, it's well worth the effort.

rooms
21 suites

food
contemporary Australian

drink
open bar and walk-in wine cellar

features
Southern Spa · boutique · business lounge · wireless Internet · day-trips and excursions

green features
environment fund · heat pump technology · Biolytix filter system · revegetation · biodegradable detergents · rainwater collection · recycling · eco-smart fires

nearby
Kangaroo Island

contact
Baillie Lodges Sales & Reservations: PO Box 596, Avalon, New South Wales 2107, Australia ·
telephone: +61.2.9918 4355 ·
facsimile: +61.2.9918 4381 ·
email: reserve@baillielodges.com.au ·
website: www.southernoceanlodge.com.au

treetops lodge + wilderness experience

THIS PAGE (FROM LEFT): *Local Rimu wood and stone adorn interiors; guests will be mesmerised by Rotorua's natural wonders.*

OPPOSITE (FROM LEFT): *Hidden amid lush forliage, villas are designed to be private sanctuaries; ornate fabrics and soft lighting give a polished veneer to rooms.*

A luxurious gateway to Rotorua's natural splendour, Treetops Lodge & Wilderness Experience offers an exclusive retreat with world-class amenities where guests can get closer to nature. The 1,012-hectare (2,500-acre) eco lodge is nestled in the heart of towering 800-year-old forests, trout-filled lakes and sweeping valleys—a magical, evocative setting for guests to luxuriate in.

The exclusive lodge's four suites and eight standalone villas are designed to accentuate the bucolic charm of its lush woodland surrounds. Suites are individually decorated with rich fabrics and ornate schist stone and timber furnishings, and have full views of the valley or nearby waterfalls. Scented candles, plush bedlinen and handcrafted New Zealand-made chocolates add an air of decadence to the interiors, while exclusive access to the Lodge Wing Lounge and state-of-the-art kitchen are pockets of luxury in the wild. Standalone villas are replete with a host of modern facilities ranging from a generously sized bathroom complete with spa bath, to a cosy lounge and small kitchenette. Details such as a stone fireplace, woollen throws and indigenous artworks exude a rustic appeal that reflects the estate's picturesque grounds.

High-end living tends to impact the environment heavily, but owner and nature enthusiast John Sax was determined that the eco retreat tread lightly on the land. A comprehensive eco sustainability programme supports the lodge's designer lifestyle concept, beginning with a carefully planned layout that complements the natural landscape. The central guest lodge, in particullar, is built to integrate a spring-fed stream that meanders along and under the structure. Other initiatives include energy conservation, recycling and re-using waste, minimising damage to the environment. These eco-friendly approaches have garnered the retreat various plaudits, namely 'top New Zealand hotel' at *Condé Nast Traveller*'s 20th Readers' Choice Awards, and a finalist placing in leading international travel network *Virtuoso*'s Best of Best Awards in 2007.

Such dedication towards environmental conservation creates an untainted paradise that eco tourists can explore at leisure. The

rotorua **new zealand**

adventurous may opt for geocaching, or track through 70 km (43 miles) of nature trail on horseback, mountain bike or four-wheel drives. The forest food trail, headed by leading local expert Charles Royal, is worth making time for. Guests are taken on a multi-sensory journey, where they can sample Maori cuisine prepared from local organic produce while learning about the medicinal and nutritional properties of native flora and fauna.

Treetops Lodge's idyllic atmosphere sets the scene for a sumptuous dinner affair. Held at the central lodge's grand dining room, chefs tantalise taste buds with health-conscious dishes prepared from organic produce. Whether it is char-grilled salmon or a succulent steak, guests can choose from a diverse array of New Zealand's abundant offerings. Better yet, savour the unique flavours of the New Zealand countryside with any of the local vintages offered. In addition to well-known labels, Treetops Lodge also carries exceptional wines that are produced by boutique, individual vineyards.

Treetops Lodge holds nothing back when it comes to creating a sanctuary to reflect the best of New Zealand hospitality. And with notable publications such as *Travel & Leisure* magazine voting the lodge as 'one of the 25 top hotels in the world in 2009', there is little wonder that this retreat remains a constant favourite among discerning guests.

rooms
4 suites • 8 villas

food
New Zealand fine-dining

drink
extensive list of New Zealand wines

features
central guest lodge • library • communal kitchen • lounge • conference room • day-trips and excursions

green features
use of natural materials • natural surroundings are integrated into lodge's architecture • 70 km hiking trails • 5 trout-fishing streams • 7 waterfalls • energy conversation • recycling and re-using measures

nearby
Rotorua

contact
351 Kearoa Road, RD1, Horohoro Rotorua, New Zealand •
telephone: +64.7.333 2066 •
facsimile: +64.7.333 2065 •
email: info@treetops.co.nz •
website: www.treetops.co.nz

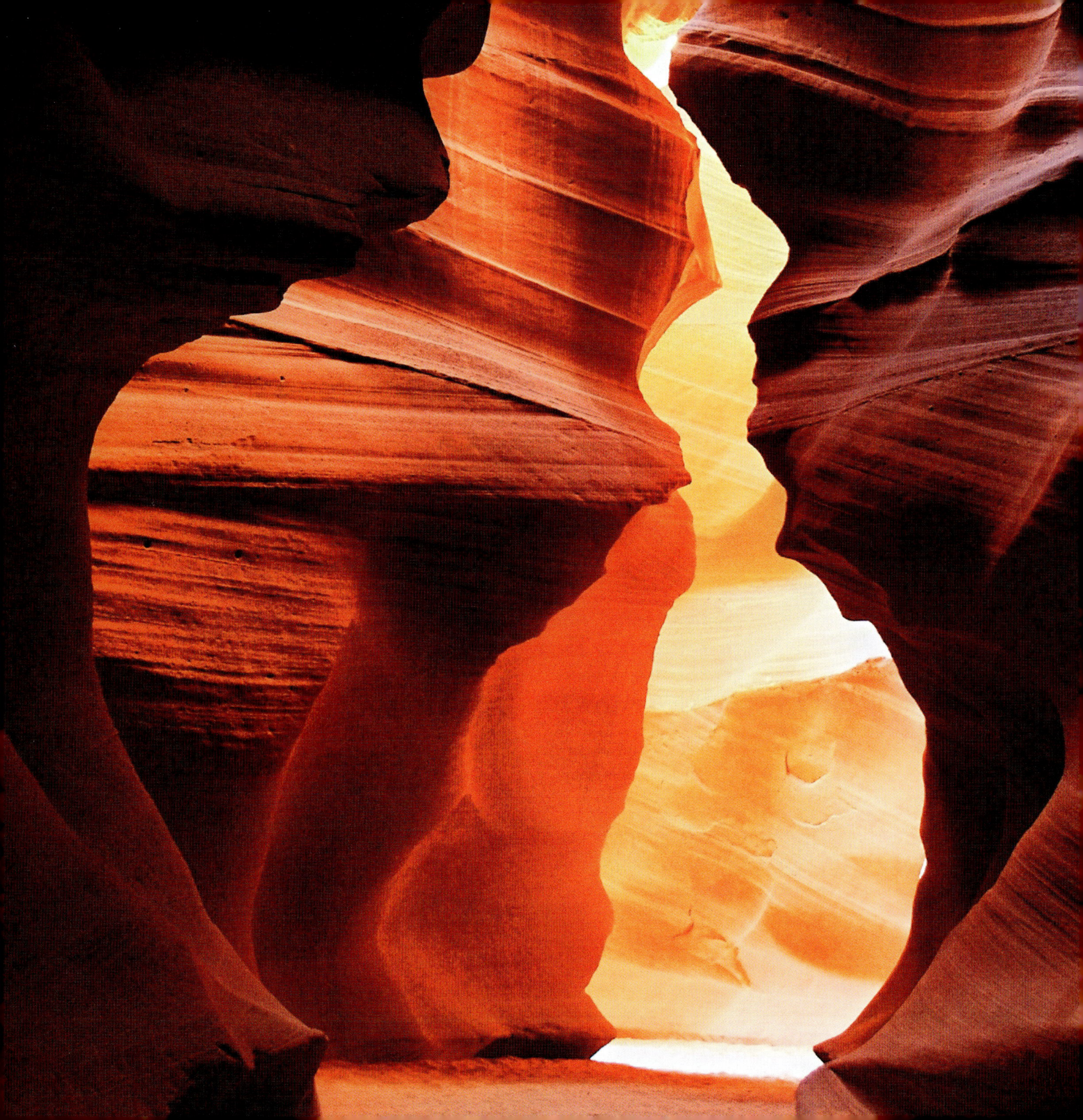

theamericas

Map of the Americas

Oceans: North Pacific Ocean, North Atlantic Ocean, South Pacific Ocean, South Atlantic Ocean, Gulf of Alaska, Gulf of Mexico, Caribbean Sea

Countries:
- Canada
- United States of America
- Mexico
- The Bahamas
- Cuba
- Haiti
- Dominican Republic
- Belize
- Jamaica
- Guatemala
- Honduras
- El Salvador
- Nicaragua
- Costa Rica
- Panama
- Grenada
- Venezuela
- Guyana
- Suriname
- Guyane
- Colombia
- Ecuador
- Brazil
- Peru
- Bolivia
- Paraguay
- Chile
- Uruguay
- Argentina

Locations marked:
- Trout Point Lodge
- Clayoquot Wilderness Resort
- Hotelito Desconocido
- Azúcar
- Hotel Eco Paraiso Xixim
- Laguna Lodge Eco-Resort + Nature Reserve
- Hamadryade Lodge
- Maca Bana
- Pousada Rancho Do Peixe
- Cristalino Jungle Lodge
- Pousada Vila Kalango
- Vila Naiá

Legend:
- Lake
- +5000 m
- 4000–5000 m
- 3000–4000 m
- 2000–3000 m
- 1000–2000 m
- 500–1000 m
- 200–500 m
- 0–200 m

Scale: 0 km – 500 – 1000 – 1500 km

the americas

north america: big parks + green stars

Admiring Yellowstone National Park's Midway Geyser, white-water rafting through the Grand Canyon or having a Rocky Mountain summit all to yourself—it's all possible in the United States of America. Canada, too, has enough highlights to keep you going for several lifetimes, with national parks brimming with wildlife—including bears and lynxes—and a boreal forest that is one of the largest intact forest ecosystems remaining on Earth. Combine the two countries and you have a choice of literally thousands of ecotourism opportunities, from secluded hideaways to national parks, boat trips and cycling holidays, and stargazing and snorkelling.

Ecotourism in North America originally developed around its national parks and protected areas. The US was the first country to establish national parks, beginning with Yellowstone in 1872. Today, an impressive 18 per cent of US territory is under some form of protection. Eco-friendly travel has increased in popularity in the US more than anywhere else on Earth. According to a 2005 survey by the International Ecotourism Society, 13 percent of outbound travellers from the US can be regarded as eco tourists.

This comes as a surprise to many, as North America is often regarded as the most wasteful continent on the planet. With its heavy reliance on fossil fuels, large cars and thousands of fast food outlets, Americans are the most significant emitters of greenhouse gases. The US is the only developed country that has not ratified the Kyoto Protocol Treaty. North America also has the biggest ecological footprint in the world—it uses four times more energy and resources as the earth's ecological capacity to regenerate them. But it is also where some of the most prominent and earliest ecological movements were born—Greenpeace was launched by a group of Canadian activists in the early 1970s. Being green is now the epitome of being hip—politicians and celebrities such as Al Gore, Arnold Schwarzenegger and Leonardo di Caprio are the new public faces of the Green Movement, leading the discussion on climate change and environmental protection—all the while driving hybrid cars. A whole new segment of the population, labelled LOHAS consumers (for Lifestyles of Health and Sustainability), is interested in buying responsible products, including organic food and clothing, green building supplies, socially responsible investing—and, of course, ecotourism and organic spas.

THIS PAGE: The iconic Grand Prismatic Spring at Yellowstone National Park.

PAGE 172: The Grand Canyon is one of North America's most famous natural treasures.

The North American luxury travel industry is going green faster than that of any other continent. Major hotel groups are launching boutique eco hotels. In 2008, Starwood Hotels created a new brand of green hotels called 'Element Hotels'. Built from the ground up, these establishments have been awarded the US Green Building Council's Leadership in Energy and Environmental Design (LEED) Certification—the nationally accepted benchmark for the design, construction and operation of high-performance green buildings. Starwood's philosophy is to satisfy its guests' needs with the environment in mind, using in-room recycling bins, water-efficient faucets and fixtures and eco-friendly paints, carpets and furniture. Guests driving hybrid cars are rewarded with priority parking, and complimentary bikes are provided for both guests and staff.

Fairmont hotels and resorts have been well known for over a decade for their Green Partnership programme, which focuses on improvements in waste management, energy and water conservation, and innovative community outreach programmes involving local groups. Some Hilton hotels have an impressive environmental programme, while the Intercontinental Hotel Group recently unveiled an online 'Innovation Hotel', which showcases some of the best ideas the hotel industry can use when implementing sustainability concepts in the design, development and operation of hotels.

Even ski resorts have taken steps towards greening their operations: The Whistler Ski Resort in Canada and Vail Ski Resort in Colorado are widely regarded as the leading sustainable ski resorts in the world.

Environmental sensitivity is, of course, not restricted to big hotel groups—boutique eco lodges such as Clayoquot Wilderness Resort in British Columbia (see page 190) and Trout Point Lodge in Nova Scotia (see page 192) provide some of the most exclusive and unique vacations in the world while silmutaneously protecting the environment.

central america + caribbean: the birthplace of ecotourism

Central America has only half a percent of the world's land mass—but 10 percent of its biodiversity. With ancient ruins, colonial towns and deserted white-sand beaches, the region is truly a traveller's paradise. Potential visitors to the region face the same dilemma—which

THIS PAGE: *Eco luxury at Clayoquot Wilderness Resort.*

OPPOSITE: *Belize has some of the most astoundingly beautiful diving spots in the world.*

exotic place to choose. Guatemala certainly has the most impressive Mayan ruins, while Belize has brilliant diving spots. Panama is home to some of the most vibrant indigenous people on Earth, and the Osa Peninsula, located in remote Southwestern Costa Rica, hosts the most significant populations of tapirs, puma, jaguars and scarlet macaws. With their sparkling sapphire sea, the Caribbean islands are still the epitome of tropical island chic. Central America and the Caribbean offer myriad slices of paradise.

When it comes to green travel, it is fair to say that Costa Rica has emerged as the region's (and probably the world's) unrivalled leader. A tiny country offering countless adventures, where you can climb a volcano one day, listen to howler monkeys the next and finish the week off snorkelling in its warm blue waters. Its eco-chic appeal not only comes from its sumptuous natural assets and wonderful hospitality, but also from the fact that its peaceful government has created uniform sustainable tourism standards and training programmes—guaranteeing the true sustainability of its eco lodges.

The Certification in Sustainable Tourism Program, or CST, is a product of the Costa Rican Tourism Institute, which was designed to differentiate tourism businesses based on the degree to which they comply with a sustainable model of natural, cultural and social resource management. It is now widely regarded as the best national sustainable tourism accreditation scheme in the world, with award-winning eco lodges such as Lapa Rios and Finca Rosa Blanca regularly cited as examples of best practices.

Guatemala, with its 2 million hectares (5 million acres) of tropical lowland forest and dozens of Mayan archaeological sites, is emerging as another great ecotourism destination. The beautiful Laguna Lodge on the shores of Lake Atitlan (see page 200) is a perfect example of a lodge that blends into its natural environment, being constructed only from volcanic stone, adobe, wood and palm. Panama does not have as many eco lodges, but is considered a birdwatcher's paradise with more than 900 bird species—more than all the bird species recorded in North America. The Yucatán Peninsula in Mexico is famous for Cancun and Tulum, but only the well-travelled know that it also boasts a very high concentration of coastal dunes, lagoons and mangrove swamps that provide a mosaic of habitats for jaguars, sea turtles and monkeys. Hotel Eco Paraiso Xixim, one of the most eco-friendly resorts on the continent, is located right in the middle of this natural paradise (see page 198).

south america: a kaleidoscope of contrasts

South America also offers an infinite assortment of cultures, landscapes and climates. You could keep returning to it and never repeat the same eco-chic experience. It is a place for superlatives: it hosts the world's highest waterfall, its longest river, its driest desert and its largest rainforest.

Covering an area larger than the US, and spanning over nine countries, the Amazon is one of most outstanding ecotourism destinations on Earth. Over a third of the planet's species live in its wilderness, and new animals and plants are discovered on a daily basis. The Amazon also harbours the largest freshwater reservoir in the world, producing one-fifth of the world's oxygen, and is home to many diverse indigenous populations and fascinating cultures. Fantastic eco lodges will help you connect with the forest, its people and its spirit—nightly medleys will make you forget any city's hustle and bustle. Cristalino Jungle Lodge, in the Southern Brazilian rainforest, has become an internationally famous destination for eco tourism lovers, combining rustic comfort with a high respect for nature (see page 210). Hamadryade Lodge, near Napo in Ecuador, is another stunning tribute to the forest, where guests are pampered and nature cared for (see page 204).

Astonishing biodiversity defines the Galapagos Islands, which have been a favourite destination for wildlife enthusiasts since Charles Darwin expounded his Theory of Evolution some 200 years ago. Thanks to the conservation efforts of the Ecuadorian government, it is still possible to spot giant Galapagos tortoises and prehistoric marine iguanas on black lava rocks. Many luxury ecotourism cruises travel through the islands, providing the revenue that ensures the preservation of this unique national park. The most impressive landscapes in South America, however, lie in the western part of the continent, in the massive peaks of the Andes. The longest mountain range in the world, the Andes stretches 7,250 kilometres (4,200 miles) from the equator to the glaciers of Patagonia. But if you're looking for spectacular beaches, then head for Brazil. The country that invented the samba boasts several world-class eco-chic seaside resorts. Pousada Rancho do Peixe (see page 208), Pousada Vila Kalango (see page 206) and Vila Naiá (see page 212) provide stylish cabins, fine food and wonderfully romantic holiday experiences. Dine under the stars, wake to birdsong and swim with the dolphins. The Americas await you.

THIS PAGE: *Birds circle the air in the Galapagos Islands.*
OPPOSITE: *The magnificent glaciers of Patagonia, Argentina.*

...*the glaciers of Patagonia.*

the americas: restaurants

new york, usa

Some of the trendiest restaurants in New York with their own movie star following are vegetarian or vegan. Even carnivores are happy to visit them for taste of the city's hip vibe—and some of the world's best variety of healthy and organic food. **Franchia** (12 Park Avenue, Manhattan, +1.212.213 1001) describes itself as a modern Korean-style teahouse and offers vegetarian sushi, and a wide selection of noodle and rice dishes. Reviewers rave about its pumpkin noodles and *kimchi* (Korean pickle) tofu. It also has other varieties of Asian cuisine such as fried dumplings, *phad thai* (Thai fried noodles) and various curries.

Operated by the same people behind Franchia, **HanGawi** (12 East 32nd Street, between 5th and Madison Avenue, Manhattan, +1.212.213 0077) is one of the more popular vegetarian restaurants in New York. Within a cosy, stylish décor filled with antiques and Asian artefacts, HanGawi offers an all-vegan menu with an emphasis on mountain roots, greens and grains. Dine on claypot tofu, multi-grain rice, *kimchi* tofu and mushroom pancake. Unlike most vegetarian restaurants, the desserts are noteworthy as well, especially its vegan cheesecake.

Vegans on the go can grab a quick bite and drink at **24 Carrots** (244 W 72nd Street, Manhattan, +1.212.595 2550) that serves up organic grub with an emphasis on juices and raw food. Specialities are the raw pizzas and the delicious raw pumpkin pie. **Angelica Kitchen** (300 E 12th Street, Manhattan, +1.212.228 2909) is one of those bustling New York eateries that one heads for to absorb some of the city's buzz—and you'll leave with a natural high after some of its energy-packed health meals. It offers vegan, macrobiotic and organic food with exotic salads, sandwiches and soups. If you're dining or travelling alone, you'll be glad to know that there is a communal table here so that you can eat with and meet other fellow vegans. Especially outstanding is the range of desserts here; deserving of special mention is the Fruit Kanten Parfait and Maple Tofu Whip.

Blossom (187 9th Avenue, between 21st and 22nd Street, Manhattan, +1.212.627 1144) is where vegans in New York head to for special celebrations. Its specialities include black-eyed pea cakes, seitan marsala, and pumpkin gnocchi. Its vegetarian cheesecake also draws the crowd.

Bonobo's Vegetarian Restaurant (18 East 23rd Street, Manhattan, +1.212.505 1200) is one of those places that you go to because you love the taste of vegetables, and not because being vegetarian is a 'lifestyle choice'. It specialises in raw, organic food that is so creative even fast food junkies are drawn to it. Recommended for first-timers to raw cuisine is the carrot pâté, which is naturally tasty—as are many other items on its menu. Bonobo's doesn't try to mimic regular food with mock meat dishes but creates a cuisine that is unique and actually makes raw vegetables taste exciting.

Pure Food and Wine (54 Irving Place, New York 10003) prides itself on being the city's most innovative—some would say best—raw food restaurant. By their definition, that means dishes where nothing is heated beyond 48°C (118°F), locking in the ingredients' natural nutrients and enzymes. It's an entire lifestyle that some adhere strictly to, but ordinary food lovers peeking into the sleek, modern restaurant will find plenty to fall in love with. With dishes such as truffle mushroom squash pasta with macadamia cream, recipes are easily as creative as the presentations. A large wine list with vegan and biodynamic varieties completes the package.

Gobo (401, Avenue of the Americas, 8th Street, +1.212.255 3242 and 1426 3rd Avenue, at E 81st Street, Manhattan, +1.212. 288 5099) is one of the more fashionable spots in New York where the hip and trendy can eat healthily while ogling one another's designer togs. It serves up organic and vegan-friendly Asian-inspired dishes such as braised tofu, and avocado tartare with wasabi lime sauce. Highly recommended is the grilled eggplant sandwich. Gobo is where organic food is given gourmet treatment.

Kate's Joint (58 Avenue B, at 4th and 5th Street, Manhattan, +1.212.777 7059), serves healthy vegetarian food in a junk food disguise, such as the 'un-turkey' club with fries and tofu buffalo wings. Great for takeaways and food on the go.

Red Bamboo (140 West 4th Street, at Washington Square and 6th Avenue, Manhattan, +1.212.260 7049) is one of the busiest vegan-friendly restaurants in New York—tables on Friday and Saturday evenings are almost impossible to get, so reservations are a must. Serving up a mix of international, Caribbean and Asian lacto-free and vegan-friendly dishes, Red Bamboo's specialities include vegetarian renditions of

THIS PAGE: *Pure Food and Wine is the place to go for delectable eco cuisine in chic surrounds when you're in New York City.*
OPPOSITE: *HanGawi is a popular Korean restaurant serving vegetarian food.*

the americas: restaurants

THIS PAGE (FROM TOP): Counter's cosy interior comes with a scrumptious vegan menu and an array of organic liqeuers and homemade infusions.

OPPOSITE: The use of sustainable materials in Abode's interior design does not detract from the restaurant's swank factor.

chicken nuggets (served with excellent honey mustard sauce), and bamboo ribs that are created out of vegetables such as bamboo shoots instead of gluten. It also has a good dessert menu with vegan-friendly chocolate cakes with caramel sauce as well as a range of soy ice-creams. It is small and usually packed but the crowds don't seem to mind, waiting for tables in queues outside.

Counter (105 1st Avenue, at 6th and 75th Street, Manhattan, +1.212.982 5870) is where the beautiful (thin) New Yorkers hang out. It serves vegan-friendly European cuisine with an American twist. A typical example would be a raw shepherd's pie and vege 'meatloaf'. Some recommended dishes are the wild rice risotto cakes with mushroom ragu and creative desserts that include the raw nut cake in lavender broth.

Sacred Chow (227 Sullivan Street, between Bleeker and West 3rd, Manhattan, +1.212.337 0846) is a small vegan restaurant with its own fans who go there for its daily breakfast, sandwiches and pastries. It also serves up vegan-friendly tapas which have received rave reviews.

Los Angeles, usa

Bulan Thai Vegetarian Kitchen (7168 Melrose Avenue, at North La Brea Avenue, Los Angeles, +1.323.857 1882) serves very decent Thai food that happens to be vegetarian as well. It has the requisite of any Thai restaurant such as *phad thai* (Thai fried noodles), summer rolls (raw vegetables rolled up in a thin rice-skin wrapper) and curries. Diners return for the authentic green and red curries, and the pepper 'chicken', which is actually asparagus in masquerade.

Shojin (333 S Alameda Street, Unit 310, at 3rd Street, Little Tokyo Square, Los Angeles, +1.213.617 0305) is an upmarket Japanese restaurant that serves organic and natural food in contemporary fusion style.

All dishes are strictly vegan and bento boxes are available as well. Some of the well-received dishes are the grilled seitan roll which is served as an appetiser, as well as the Nasu miso vegetables and three-mushroom pasta. The more authentic desserts are Japanese such as the green-tea moss cake which is light and pleasantly but not overly sweet.

The Vegan Joint (10438 National Boulevard, in the Palms area, Los Angeles, +1.310.559 1357) is small and personal, with its own crowd of followers who go there for its organic, all-vegan 'fast food'. At breakfast, burritos and pancakes are served, while lunch and dinner menus include an array of healthy wraps, veggie burgers, pineapple curry and fried rice.

Abode Restaurant & Lounge (1541 Ocean Avenue, Santa Monica, +1.310.394.3463) is a sensuous celebration of modern American cuisine, executed with flair by Executive Chef Cyril Kabaoglu. His approach blends the use of fresh seasonal ingredients from local, sustainable sources with a master's artisanal sensibilities. The result is fine dining in a relaxed setting modelled around a luxurious mansion.

A main dining room offers seating at black tables with high-backed tangerine leather chairs, while a lounge and private room lie adjacent. Outdoor dining on the terracotta courtyard is a treat. Try the Sonoma Lamb, served three ways with olive tapenade and kabosha squash.

san francisco, usa

Alive! Vegetarian Cuisine (1972 Lombard St, at Webster, Marina district, +1.415.923 1052) provides 'vibrant food for the body and soul' in its menu of vegan, raw and organic dishes. It specialises in raw vegetarian cuisine, which—while it doesn't sound hugely exciting—does attract a crowd of regular meat eaters who want something that tastes fresh and healthy.

A typical dish would be a pesto lasagna with 'cheese' made out of sunflower seeds. It also has a range of healthy smoothies and raw desserts which include a delicious key lime pie. Eco-conscious diners will appreciate its sustainability philosophy: take-out customers get a 10 per cent discount if they bring their own containers.

Ananda Fuara (1298 Market Street, at 9th Civic Center district, +1.415.621 1994) is small and unassuming but the daily crowd that gathers there proves its popularity. It serves vegetarian Indian and Asian meals as well as veggie burgers and sandwiches. The vegan stroganoff is one of their specials that is worth calling up ahead for. And its vegan chocolate cake is said to be the best in the city. Free meditation classes are also available on site.

Café Gratitude (2400 Harrison St, at 20th Street, Mission-Potrero Hill district, +1.415.824 4652) is a 'feel good' joint with a fun menu that is sure to evoke a few laughs. The items on the menu with names such as 'I am Plenty Great' breakfast and 'I am Abundant' sampler platter are never short of positive affirmation. Food is mainly vegan, organic and raw though there are a few items that are cooked. Special mention must be made of its delicious 'sushi' bowl which has Bhutanese red rice, scallions, kale, avocado, nori and a very light Japanese sauce. The smoothies and shakes are great as well and are sure to invoke more positive vibes, especially the 'I am Cool', mint chocolate shake.

Herbivore (in two locations at 531 Divisadero, at Fell Western Addition district, +1.415.885 7133, and 983 Valencia Street, 21st Mission district, +1.415 .826 5657) is a popular and casual vegan restaurant that is bustling during its weekend brunches. It serves vegan American classics in a pleasant setting with sidewalk seating.

Millennium (580 Geary Street, at Jones, inside Hotel California, Union Square, Theatre district, +1.415.345 3900) is the most elegant organic vegan restaurant in San Francisco and with a menu that is as glamorous as its décor. Open for dinner only, Millennium has an extensive cocktail menu that is created with house-infused organic spirits. The Kiwi Gimlet, for example, is a kiwi-parsley infused vodka imaginatively mixed with fresh lime and parsley. Dishes have a gourmet flair with many fusion flavours, and desserts are deceptively

the americas: restaurants

THIS PAGE (CLOCKWISE FROM TOP): *The area of Old San Juan in Puerto Rico; good eco-friendly food can be found all over the world—if you know where to look; The use of traditional cooking methods keep energy usage low.*
OPPOSITE: *Guests at this São Paulo restaurant dine by candlelight during Earth Hour.*

rich and sinful-tasting with a pure soul of vegan ingredients. Even carnivores are hooked.

seattle, usa

Fancy an organic doughnut? Grab a bunch at **Mighty-O Donuts**, (2110 N 55th Street, at Meridian Avenue N, Wallingford district, +1.206.547 0335). Made from mainly organic ingredients, these donuts allow one to indulge one's cravings without feeling too guilty.

More healthy 'junk' food is available at **Pizza Pi Vegan Pizzeria** (5500 University Way NE, at 44th Avenue, University District, +1.206.343 1415) which serves up pizzas with vegetarian toppings. The 'cheese' toppings are as good as the real thing, and the tomato spreads are way better than those found on regular pizzas.

chicago, usa

Alice and Friends' Vegetarian Café (5812 N. Broadway, +1.773.275 8797) is a vegan-friendly, organic restaurant with a predominantly Chinese menu. Its specialities include smoked veggie-duck, spicy barbecue, and almond 'un-chicken'. Try its fresh ginseng shake for a buzz that will energise you all day.

Cousin's Incredible Vitality (3038 W Irving Park Road, at Kedzie/Brown & Blue Line, Irving Park, +1.773.478 6868) is a raw, vegan and organic restaurant with a daily all-you-can-eat salad bar. The *moussaka* and Zoom Burger are worth trying. It also stocks up on seasonal exotic fruit such as durian.

Karyn's Cooked (738 N Wells Street, at Superior in River North, +1.312.587 1050) and **Karyn's Fresh**

Corner (1901 N Halsted, +1.773.296 6990) offer 'conscious comfort food' which means vegetarian, vegan-friendly meals that taste wholesome and homemade. The lasagna and green enchiladas are both worth a try. It also has homemade 'cheese'cake.

Veggie Bite (in two locations: 3031 West 111th Street, at Whipple, +1.773. 239 4367, and 1300 N Milwaukee, +1.773.772 2483) is a vegetarian fast food restaurant which includes 'sinful' creations on its menu such as chili cheese fries, cheese dogs, barbecue bites and burrito supreme. It also has veggie and tofu burgers. Milkshakes made with soymilk are awesome.

antigua

Kalabashe (10 Vendors Mall, at Redcliff Street and Thames Street, St John's West, +268.562 6070) stands out in meat and barbecue-loving Antigua with its vegan menu. The Thai tofu in spicy peanut and coconut sauce, and 'blazing balls of fire' (veg meatballs) are creative and delicious.

jamaica

If you're a vegan in Jamaica, ask for *ital* food and you'll be better understood. At **Livity** (30 Haining Road, Kingston 5, +876.906 5618), you'll get organic vegan fare and it has a juice bar on its grounds too. The list of tofu entrees is impressive, and the ice-creams are made from soy. Friendly owners and staff add to the pleasant dining experience.

puerto rico

Café Berlin (407 San Francisco Street, Old San Juan, at Plaza Colon, +787.722 5205) has vegetarian options on its menu as well as a wide range of fresh raw juices. The Mangito, which is a kind of shake with fresh mango, is superb. The breads served are freshly made on its grounds. And the location is great for those doing their touristy round of the old part of San Juan.

If you're down in Rincon, said to be the Riviera of Puerto Rico, look out for **Natural High Café** (99 Calle Sol, Carr.115, Km 14.3, Rincon, +787.823 1772), a vegan restaurant which is popular among locals, despite the country's meat-loving culture. The organic vegan café menu includes raw vegetable wraps, sandwiches as well as raw vegetarian sushi. Leave space for the vegetarian cupcakes, which are a must.

mexico city, mexico

Vegetariano Madero (Madero 56 1er. Piso, Colonia Centro Historical, at Isabel la Catolica, +52.5521 6880) has branches throughout the city. Offering all-day Mexican vegetarian dining, one can expect egg omelette, *ensaladas* (salads), enchiladas, breads and juices. There are some imaginative vegetarian creations such as 'hamburger' and fries, and chipotle 'beef tips'. Cheese is widely used here so if you're vegan, you'll have to specify beforehand.

Yug (Varsovia 3B, Colonia Juarez, at Paseo de la Reforma, +52.533 3296) offers international vegetarian cuisine and has a juice bar and bakery on its grounds. It is a draw for the working locals of the area, and serves up veggie burgers, sandwiches, salad and Mexican food.

El Natural Saks (Insurgentes Sur 1641, +52.598 7258) is one of the more upmarket restaurants in Mexico City that serves vegetarian food. The cuisine is mainly international and Mexican, and includes a salad bar, fresh fruit and vegetable juices.

rio de janeiro, brazil

South America may not be a cuisine haven for vegans but there are a few decent options in Rio de Janeiro, such as **Reino Vegetal** (Rua Luiz de Camoes, 98, Sobrado Centro, +55.21.2221 7416) which has a young, hip ambience and a local clientele. Although the restaurant is not entirely vegetarian, it has a mean offering of soya burgers and soya chunk stews. **Restaurante Vegetariano Beterraba** (Rua da Alfandega 25A, Centro, +55.21.2253 7460) is another restaurant that has vegan-friendly options on a menu that is not entirely vegetarian. It has a value-for-money daily vegan buffet, and a large variety of stuffed pastries for lunch. The desserts here are good, especially the banana cake.

são paulo, brazil

Apfel (Rua Bel Cintra, 1343, +55.11.3062 3727) has a daily vegan-friendly salad bar with substantial seitan and soya choices on it. Eat al fresco in the garden for a very pleasant meal. **BioAlternativa** (Alameda Santos, 2214, at Cerquira Cesar, +55.11.3898 2871) offers vegan-friendly organic food in its daily buffet. Its seasonal menu, which changes with the season, features vegetarian pilaf, tofu, *yaki soba* noodles, banana curry and mushroom risotto. Its other branch, **BioAlternativa II** (Rua Maranhao 812, at Higienopolis, +55.11.3825 4759), has a health food store on its grounds for the green eater who wants to stock up at home.

the americas: shopping

usa

Find cutting-edge and sustainable furniture at **Brave Space** (449 Troutman Street Studio 2A Brooklyn, NY, +1.718.417 3180)—a showroom that brings together the creations of a group of Brooklyn-based designers. While the designs are *Wallpaper*- worthy, with many crossing the boundaries of art and function, each piece of furniture optimises the use of materials and minimises wastage. Some of the materials used are rapidly renewable bamboo plywood and FSC (Forest Stewardship Council)-certified plywood to ensure that the wood harvested is stringently eco-sensitive.

Plushpod (8211 West 3rd Street, Los Angeles, CA +1.323.951 0748) carries a range of eco-friendly furniture—the pieces are either made of recycled materials or are ethically produced. Sideboards and decorative screens are inspired by marine and forest motifs. A pretty range of children's furniture are also available.

Boris Bally (www.borisbally.com) sees a second life in discarded road signs—he has created chairs out of them which are comfortable, well-made and have a very distinct modern design. They are also easily taken apart and re-assembled, which makes them great for entertaining large groups at home.

The greenest way to go green is to recycle, recycle, recycle, which is why **The Upper Rust** (445 E 9th Street, Manhattan, NY, +1.212.533 3953) is an eco consumer's dream—a junk store of sorts with lots of charm and character. There are gifts galore with plenty of quirky knick-knacks, as well as lots of vintage furniture, prints and pictures and industrial chic tables which will excite home decorators. Similarly, **Cosmo Modern** (314 Wythe Avenue, Brooklyn, NY, +1.718.302 4662) deals with the old and the quirky, but here, the emphasis is on industrial and mid-century modern furnishings. In fact, owner Cosmo rents out his furniture regularly as props to the likes of Barney's, *Vogue* and the *New York Times Magazine* when they require something with a retro twist.

Ryann (www.iloveryann.com) is Brooklyn-based designer Raina Blyer's personal quest to explore ways of making fashion compatible with her environmental interests. The label's chic urban-ready collections are exclusively made from sustainable fabrics such as bamboo, hemp, ahimsa silk, soy fibre and organic cotton.

Baggu (www.baggubag.com) comfortably fills the void between sinful disposable carriers and expensive haute couture bags no one ever ruins with groceries. Founded by a group of designers, its chief product is a simple reusable nylon carrier based on the humble plastic grocery bag, but rendered beautiful in an array of bright colours and daring prints. The classic Baggu holds 11 kg (25 lbs)—as much volume as three regular plastic bags. Limited-edition screenprinted Baggus and fun colours like Electric Purple and Butter will have you using them for more than just trips to the store.

Clary Sage Organics (Pacific Heights, 2241 Fillmore Street, San Francisco, CA, +1.415.673 7300) smells like a dream because of its fabulous range of organic beauty and bath products. Luxurious products such as herbal lip softener and sweet orange

THIS PAGE (CLOCKWISE FROM LEFT): Ryann uses organic materials that correspond with the seasons; cut down on plastic bag usage with Baggu's cheerful reusable bags; a Clary Sage Organics store; a blouse by Clary Sage Organics.

OPPOSITE: Boris Bally's furniture and home accessories are made from recycled materials such as aluminium traffic signs and champagne corks.

the americas: shopping

and honey bar soap are best sellers. There is even a line of organic cotton clothing—for a complete eco splurge.

Eco Citizen (1488 Vallejo Street, San Francisco, CA, +1.415.614 0100) offers high-quality fashion with an organic touch. Owner Joslin Van Arsdale applies her philosophy of eco-conscious consumerism with fair trade practices and sweatshop-free merchandise. And with her experience in fashion photography and art, there's plenty of style in her offerings of tasselled tees, drawstring dresses, and evening clutches made from recycled material. The shop also carries Linda Loudermilk's cutting-edge green fashion among other eco labels.

Straight out from the American Midwest comes **Urban Fox**'s (www.urbanfoxeco.com) range of eco-friendly lingerie. Their collections are as flirtatious and sexy as they come, with playful features such as ruffles and lace windows adorning the handmade designs. What makes them as good for the Earth as they are a pleasure to wear is their stretchy blend of bamboo and organic cotton. When the time finally comes for a new look, dispose of them with a clear conscience: they are biodegradable.

Melissa Dizon is the designer behind **Eairth**—a sleep-inspired ready-to-wear label that is created with natural fibres such as organic cotton jersey, and is dyed by hand using natural processes and ingredients such as tree bark and cardamom. The pieces are hand-embroidered and hand-stitched in Dizon's native Philippines according to fair trade practices. Wrap shirts and slim-cut jersey trousers are some of the pieces that can be found

THIS PAGE (CLOCKWISE FROM TOP): Excellent cuts, attention to detail and fair trade practices make Eairth an ideal choice for a elegant evening out or a casual afternoon with friends; Urban Fox is known for its organic, playful lingerie pieces.
OPPOSITE: Created from synthetic materials, animal-friendly Truth belts are suitable for all occasions.

in her range of comfort wear. Eairth is available at **Steven Alan** (103 Franklin Street, Manhattan, NY, +1.212.343 0692).

Advancing the image of green fashion is the dedication of **Kaight** (83 Orchard Street, Lower East Side, Manhattan, NY, +1.212.680 5630) which stocks trendy eco fashion from designers in the US and UK. As a result of her own need to be style-savvy as well as eco-conscious, owner Kate McGregor brings in ethical fashion that she and her friends will be proud to don at even the most rigorously chic events. There are wax-finished cotton rainclothes in metallic shades, and organic boots here come with stacked heels and platforms, *de rigueur* features for fashionable footwear.

Eco-friendly apparel brand **Nau** blends outdoor and urban fashion sensibility with a range of city fashion that is stylish, highly fashionable and sustainable. Believing that companies have a broader responsibility than simply generating profit, its mission is 'do well by doing good'.

To that end, Nau's clothes use recycled and organic material where possible, and are created ethically. The range can be found at **Lizard Lounge** (1323 NW Irving Street, Portland, OR 97209, +1.503. 416 7576).

The purest of eco-hearted consumers are never snobby about thrift shops; in fact, they embrace them for their recycling practices. Savvy style meisters also know that it is never chic to don anything too new. Thus, **Buffalo Exchange** (1555 Haight Street, San Francisco, CA +1.415.431 7733) has its own following of students, artists and stylists who go there for perfectly worn leather jackets or cowboy boots.

Its ever-changing inventory includes designer wear, vintage clothing, jeans, leather, basics and one-of-a-kind items. Go mad on retro sunglasses, hats and scarves in this packed trove of fashion finds.

canada

Grassroots (408 Bloor Street West, Toronto, Ontario, +1.416.944 1993 and 372 Danforth Avenue, Toronto, Ontario, +1.416.466 2841) sells eco-friendly things for the home, such as good-for-the-earth cleaning products, organic cotton towels and bedding. The company's mission: to offer eco-friendly products that allow people to make positive choices for themselves, their communities and the planet.

Toronto Hemp Company (637 Yonge Street, south of Bloor, Toronto, Ontario, +1.416.920 1980) delivers a nod to the 1960s' flower power era with a wide range of paraphernalia related to the marijuana culture. It has a decent range of hemp gear in stock, such as jewellery, shoes, pants and jackets.

Canadian label **Truth Belts** is proud to be 'genuinely non-leather'. This translates to accessories such as belts and jewellery that promote happy animals. The label's tee shirts is created from environmentally friendly Bamtex (a blend of mainly bamboo fibre with some cotton and spandex) that is breathable, absorbs moisture and is naturally anti-bacterial. The label's bracelets are actually cuffs made of canvas.

TruthBelts can be found at **Panacea: An Eco Shopping Oasis** (588 Bloor Street West, Toronto, Ontario, +1.647.350 3269).

theamericas:restaurants 189

clayoquot wilderness resort

Stretching from the temperate rainforest along North America's west coast to the Pacific Ocean, the Clayoquot Sound UNESCO Biosphere Reserve protects a diverse array of fragile ecosystems, and it is here that one finds the Clayoquot Wilderness Resort. The resort enjoys an especially striking location in the midst of all this natural splendour, being at the junction where the Bedwell River spills into an impressive fjord.

Since its opening in 2001, this eco resort has been the embodiment of 'glamping'—a portmanteau of 'glamorous' and 'camping'. The journey there begins with an hour-long scenic seaplane trip from Vancouver, and ends with a short ride in a horse-drawn wagon.

Upon arrival, any doubts as to whether the woodland resort deserves its reputation as one of the world's best wilderness experiences will surely vanish. Guests are greeted by an enclave of pristine, white canvas tents. Deluxe tents will attract couples looking for an intimate hideaway, while larger tents offer a spacious lounge area with an extra queen-size sofa bed—the accommodation of choice for families. Both options share the same luxurious furnishings: Adirondack-style beds with feather duvets, woodstoves with temperature control, antique furniture, *objets d'art* and fine rugs. Despite being in the middle of untamed nature, the retreat's wood-fired boilers ensure plenty of hot water, while

THIS PAGE: *With cosy loungers, plush bedlinen and every desire seen to, guests easily forget that they are camping in the wild.*

OPPOSITE (FROM LEFT): *The nature reserve allows for plenty of land and water activities; luxuriate in the outdoor sauna amid the pure mountain air.*

british columbia **canada**

off-site electricity generators guarantee the comforts of hair dryers and wireless Internet. Two lounge tents ensure that guests can make full use of their vacation time. Styled after an opulent reading room, the library lounge is actually a high-tech Internet café, while the games tent resembles a Gentlemen's Club and provides a venue for drinks and conversation.

With an emphasis on the natural flavours of locally sourced ingredients, organic creations are presented with flair amid a grand timber cookhouse with an open show kitchen, while the fire-lit ambience in the outdoor lounge makes al fresco dining a delight at night.

The range of activities available is almost overwhelming—guests can have their pick of horse riding, hiking, biking, rock climbing and archery. Alternatively one can go kayaking, fresh- or salt-water fishing, or whale watching at the nearby Cow Bay. For those wanting to try their hand at everything, the resort's efficient staff will put together a customised itinerary to cater to specific preferences.

Weary minds can recharge at the poetically named Healing Grounds, the resort's safari-style wellness centre. Comprising three massage tents and two treatment rooms, an extensive list of treatments using only organic products are on hand to pamper and indulge.

The resort keeps its carbon footprint light with a comprehensive recycling system in place as well as gravity-fed turbines to help generate clean electricity. A part of the guest fees also go to the resort's Environmental Legacy Programme, dedicated to research, and habitat restoration of the nature reserve.

With the sophisticated traveller more environmentally aware than ever, Clayoquot Wilderness Resort's green efforts set a new standard for glamorous, eco-friendly camping.

rooms
12 deluxe tents · 8 family tents

food
organic fine dining

drink
bar

features
Healing Grounds spa · wood-fired saunas · outdoor hot tubs · private lounge areas · horse riding · archery · trekking · biking · kayaking · fishing · whale watching · day-trips and excursions

green features
Environmental Legacy Programme · recycling · organic food · renewable energy sources

nearby
Clayoquot Sound Biosphere Reserve Area · Nuu-Chah-Nulth First Nations Village

contact
Box 130, Tofino, British Columbia
V0R 2Z0 Canada ·
telephone: +250.726 8235 ·
facsimile: +250.726 8558 ·
email: info@wildretreat.com ·
website: www.wildretreat.com

trout point lodge

THIS PAGE: *The Grand Lodge cuts a striking figure in the woods.*

OPPOSITE (FROM LEFT): *Unpolished log walls and handcrafted fittings elicit a rustic elegance; evenings give way to splendid Nova Scotian sunsets.*

The Tobeatic Wilderness Area in Nova Scotia has always called out to individuals with a spirit of adventure, raring to jump off the bandwagon and into uncharted nature as they explore the dense woodland with its secluded lakes, meandering river ways and thriving wildlife. Trout Point Lodge offers a luxurious outpost for guests to get acquainted with such natural wonders in style, both as an exclusive retreat and as a culinary destination.

In true Great Camp tradition, the lodge has been built without a single nail. Giant Eastern Spruce logs, granite and sandstone have been cut with precision and fitted into each other snugly, creating an impressive establishment of a grandeur that complements the surrounding soaring pine, birch and maple trees. With a limited number of rooms, the eco retreat is built with exclusivity in mind. Honey-hued log walls and hardwood flooring exude a rustic warmth, while plush carpeting, tiffany lamps, handcrafted furnishings, Bulgari amenities, stone fireplaces and sumptuous beds await to swathe guests in privileged luxury. Lodgings are also refreshingly absent of televisions, relying instead on the natural surroundings to stimulate one's senses.

The eco lodge's enchanting location sets the stage for a great Canadian wilderness experience. Nature takes over as guests eschew conventional facilities for kayaking, hiking, swimming—even a whale-watching excursion or fishing expedition. Upon return, guests can relax in the outdoor sauna and wood-fired outdoor cedar hot tub, followed by cocktails around the fireplace while exchanging stories of the day's adventures.

Award-winning gourmet Creole and Acadian cuisines await in the dining rooms after an adrenaline-packed day in the woods. Exquisitely prepared seafood and garden fresh produce highlight the region's abundant resources, while local herbs and spices tease out the distinctive flavours of each dish. Epicureans

nova scotia **canada**

can also bring these creations home with a session at the Nova Scotia Seafood Cooking School. This culinary academy is no lightweight, offering vacation programmes that have caught the eye of noted publications such as *Forbes Traveler*, *National Geographic Traveler* and *Food &Wine*.

Located within the UNESCO Biosphere Reserve, Trout Point Lodge takes great pride in protecting the pristine nature of its surroundings. The deliberate absence of air conditioning and the use of energy efficient light bulbs help keep power consumption low. A wastewater treatment system and use of bulk dispensers instead of conventional toiletry bottles significantly decrease the amount of waste generated, while organic vegetable gardens see the eco lodge moving a step closer to full self-sustainability. The resident naturalist also educates guests on the importance of conserving the fragile boreal forest ecosystem—just one of many reasons that has enabled the lodge to clinch the coveted Parks Canada Sustainable Tourism Award.

Combining a unique boutique experience with ecological sensitivity, Trout Point Lodge reawakens the imagination to the great outdoors by affording guests front-row seats to Nova Scotia's natural and cultural heritage.

rooms
10 rooms • 2 suites • 2 cottages

food
Creole and Acadian-style seafood

drink
fine wines from France, Spain and USA

features
Nova Scotia Cooking School • outdoor sauna • wood-fired outdoor hot tub • Bulgari amenities • day-trips and excursions

green features
natural materials for construction • organic vegetable garden • energy-efficient lighting • recycling and composting programme

nearby
Yarmouth • Halifax

contact
89 Trout Point Road, off the East Branch Road and Highway, 203 PO Box 456, Kemptville Nova Scotia B0W 1Y0, Canada •
telephone: +1.902.482 8360 •
email: troutpoint@foodvacation.com •
website: www.troutpoint.com

hotelito desconocido

THIS PAGE (FROM TOP): *A luxury spa can be found within Hotelito Desconocido's rustic surrounds; all rooms possess river views.*

OPPOSITE: *From the bedroom to the bathroom, interiors are decorated individually and allow ample natural light in.*

By definition, luxury hotels offer larger-than-life pleasures and convenience, shuttering away the minutiae of everyday life with a combination of service and automation. Their desirability is unquestioned, but in this new millennium, the lines beg to be redrawn. Consider the paradox of the Hotelito Desconocido in Mexico. It is a hotel that one must drive for hours on unpaved roads to reach, it offers no movies on demand, no telephones, Internet, or even electricity, its accommodation are built from wood, bamboo and clay in the style of traditional Mexican bungalows, and can be said that the 'little unknown hotel' is one of the most exclusive luxury travel experiences one can have today.

Located within a nature reserve along the Costalegre coastline, the 40-hectare (100-acre) resort breaks just about every rule to achieve one remarkable thing: it offers guests a chance to live alongside nature in the absolute primality of an age long past. Amid exotic vegetation, one shares the land with families of marine turtles, over 150 species of rare birds and local flora reverently protected by the ambitious efforts of owner Marcello Murzilli.

The ingenuity of the Hotelito Desconocido's design allows this ecological responsibility to coincide with five-star comfort and service without compromising the environment. There may not be electric lights, but when faced with the glow of a thousand candles and torches lining the walkways at night, one would rather not have a switch anywhere for miles. Ceiling fans keep rooms cool with the same solar power that heats running water for the bamboo showers in each bungalow. Amenities such as shampoos, moisturisers and mosquito

costalegre **mexico**

repellants are all organically formulated and biodegradable, while waste byproducts are largely recycled and given a second lease of life.

From beachfront residences to the Master Suite, each room strikes a finely tuned balance between authenticity and a feeling of wealth that has nothing to do with money. Arising to a sunrise that stretches across one's private terrace, spending the afternoon in a hammock or daybed, and retiring in a room individually decorated with hand-carved furnishings—all goes beyond room service and helicopter transfers, although those are available too.

The new spa was created as part of a series of ongoing renovations to establish even higher standards of service, and utilises ancient wisdom and traditional techniques such as Anma Shiatsu, acupressure, hot stone therapy and French Polynesian-inspired scrubs with sea salt and essential oils.

Likewise, every outdoor activity benefit from the area's rural charms. Kayaking across the rich estuary, horseback rides through lush gardens, swimming in the infinity pool, bird-watching—all these take on new meaning as timeless, exultant acts. That one can have gourmet meals and transcendental full body therapies in a remote hideaway without the benefit of electricity, and hardly think upon the lack, is astounding. As the Hotelito Desconocido continues to improve itself with each day, one witnesses the definition of luxury travel shifting towards a more eco-conscious, environmentally responsible era.

rooms
27 bungalows • 3 eco villas

food
contemporary Mexican

drink
bar

features
spa • infinity pool • yoga • beach sports club • horseback riding • day-trips and excursions

green features
natural sanctuary for wildlife • operates without electricity • organic, biodegradable amenities • solar-powered fans and heating • waste filtration • exclusive use of own-grown produce • biology education department

nearby
beaches • Costalegre • Puerto Vallarta

contact
Playón de Mismaloya, S/N La cruz de Loreto Costalegre, Mexico •
telephone: +52.322.281 4010 •
email: reservaciones@hotelito.com •
website: www.hotelito.com

azúcar

THIS PAGE (FROM LEFT): *Cheerful cushions give a dash of colour to the sun-bleached pool deck; dome-shaped huts cut a quirky figure in the beach landscape.*

OPPOSITE (FROM LEFT): *Designer furnishings make this lounge a stylish place to chill out in; white-on-white interiors are filled with red-cedar fittings.*

Carlos Couturier's hotels have always been about celebrating Mexico's fascinating multicultural beginnings and swanky, contemporary scene. Each establishment is unique in concept, showcasing a refreshing irreverence that the world has come to associate with modern Mexican design. Couturier has brought his reverence for history and tongue-in-cheek aesthetics down to the seaside and created a stylish beachfront establishment known as much for its quaint architecture as for its excellent service.

Named after the famed sugarcane plantations of Vera Cruz, Azúcar's stripped-down appearance stands out among the lush, tropical setting. White-on-white interiors, curved walls and natural materials exist harmoniously with dynamic splashes of colour, enlivening the minimalist abode.

Echoes of Mexican culture are showcased throughout interiors. Indigenous red cedar is found in the doorframes and bed supports, while fibreglass—the luminous material local fishing boats are built with—adorns the bathrooms, sinks and shower doors. Outside, the organic nature of the 20 bungalows is evident in the thatched palm roofs and pebble and seashell accents, resulting in a resort that is both ecologically viable and unpretentiously chic.

vera cruz **mexico**

Each bungalow is outfitted with modern conveniences, and guests can relax in front of the plasma screen television or lather up in the private outdoor shower. Facilities are created to enhance the resort's natural beauty. An open-air lounge invites guests to luxuriate in the sea breeze with an absorbing read. The free-form pool harmonises with its organic surroundings and is complemented by a sun-bleached deck upon which one can lounge with a cocktail in hand. The outdoor Xochicalli Spa is constructed to admit plenty of sunlight, and features a secluded yoga space alongside an extensive array of natural treatments and therapies.

Azúcar's passion for preserving its heritage is mirrored in historically rich Vera Cruz. Culture buffs will be engrossed with El Tajín's ancient Totonac architecture, as well as the intricate handicrafts found at the charming village of San Rafael. The region's jungle terrain offers adrenaline-packed activities such as riverboat safaris, horseback riding and trekking, with an abundance of local flora and fauna to explore along the way. Pristine coastlines beckon one to head out to the nearby islands and discover the rich marine life and flourishing coral reef. Gourmands will need little persuasion to dine at the resident restaurant, where chefs deftly capture the nuanced flavours of the Mexican landscape with artistic flair.

Hearkening back to the simplicities of traditional Mexican life, a stay at Azúcar is to experience Corturier's heartfelt tribute to Mexico's vibrant people and colourful history.

rooms
20 bungalows

food
Mexican and seafood

drink
restaurant bar

features
Xochicalli Spa • private outdoor shower • hammock • private patio • open-air library • free-form pool • games room • chapel • day-trips and excursions

green features
back-to-basics philosophy • use of natural materials

nearby
Vera Cruz • El Tajín archaeological site • San Rafael • Monte Gordo

contact
Km 83.5 Carretera Federal Nautla-Poza Rica
Monte Gordo, Municipio de Tecolutla
Vera Cruz ZC 93588, Mexico •
telephone: +52.323.210 678 •
facsimile: +52.323.210 804 •
email: gerencia@hotelazucar.com •
website: www.hotelazucar.com

hotel eco paraiso xixim

Planning a holiday in wildlife-rich Celestun, Mexico does not necessarily mean roughing it out Robinson Crusoe style. Staying at Hotel Eco Paraiso Xixim allows access to the unique ecosystem of the surrounding Celestún Special Biosphere reserve without sacrificing the necessary creature comforts that make a luxury holiday so enticing.

Developed with a strict eco agenda, the beach resort sits in the centre of the sprawling 60,700-hectare (150,000-acre) reserve, surrounded by coastal scrub, estuary and mangrove swamps—all of which make a fertile habitat for a large variety of animals and plants. Owner Verena Gerber has taken great pains to ensure minimal impact to the sand dunes on which Hotel Eco Paraiso Xixim is built. In fact, only 3,000 sq m (32,300 sq ft) out of the resort's 25 hectares (62 acres) is built up, leaving the majority of the land virtually untouched so as to preserve the nesting grounds of endangered sea turtles in pristine condition.

In spite of its ecological focus and remote location, Hotel Eco Paraiso Xixim features a slew of modern amenities that amply provide for guests' comfort. Each of its 15 rustic cabañas is fitted with an open-concept living room, a cosy bedroom and bathroom complete with a verandah and hammocks to laze in and watch the sun cast its glow over the Gulf of Mexico. The management's green policies replaces rooms' air conditioning with ceiling fans, well-designed air circulation system and age-old Mayan technology, la palapa—thatched roofs—providing ample ventilation throughout the cabaña.

Serving as a central clubhouse for the eco resort, La Casa Club offers a wide range of recreational activities. Guests can engage

THIS PAGE (FROM LEFT): **Hotel Eco Paraiso Xixim's commitment to the environment ensures that guests can luxuriate in style without the intrusion of modern-day encumbrances; thatched roofs utilise ancient Mayan building methods.**
OPPOSITE (FROM LEFT): **In a bid to cut down on energy usage, rooms are naturally ventilated; the resort's unsurpassable location offers guests front row seats to the glittering Gulf of Mexico.**

yucatán **mexico**

in a game of pool or table tennis, explore Mexican culture in greater detail through the books and videos from the library, take a dip in the azure pool nearby and have a frozen margarita at the well-stocked bar. For a sampling of local flavours in a romantic, candle-lit setting, the Casa Club Restaurant's Mexican, Yucatán and international creations are bound to please all palates.

An in-depth exploration of the world-famous reserve is a must, and guests can embark on various ecological tours specially organised by the resort. Cave explorations, bird-watching expeditions, crocodile safaris and jungle trails allow adventurous individuals to relish the adrenaline rush while experiencing firsthand the inlet's rich biodiversity. The resort's onsite learning centre and museum is also a treasure trove of knowledge, introducing inquisitive minds to its fascinating ecosystem.

Hotel Eco Paraiso Xixim is also ideally placed for guests wanting to explore the inlet on their own. Take advantage of the complimentary bicycles and kayaks and head out to the verdant jungle or nearby salt flat lagoons. Alternatively, culture buffs can visit the colonial city of Merida and stroll through archaeological ruins and striking turn-of-the-century architecture.

Holidaying out in the wild need not be an intimidating experience, and the ability to ease guests into the nature of things with knowledgeable staff and personal service makes Hotel Eco Paraiso Xixim a destination resort in its own right.

rooms
15 cabañas

food
Casa Club Restaurant: Mexican, Yucatán and international

drink
Casa Club Restaurant

features
outdoor pool • library • Natural History Museum • ecological day-trips and excursions

green features
construction of resort with little impact on environment • recycling water programme • potable water made with inverse osmosis and ultraviolet rays • cultivation of dwarf coconut and palm tree plantation

nearby
Celestún Special Biosphere reserve • Merida • Uxmal • Kabah • Gulf of Mexico .

contact
Municipio de Celestún, Yucatán, Mexico •
telephone: +52.988.916 2100/+52.988.916 2060 •
facsimile: +52.988.916 2111 •
email: info@ecoparaiso.com •
website: www.ecoparaiso.com

laguna lodge eco-resort + nature reserve

Perched on the shores of Lake Atitlán, one of Central America's most beautiful lakes, Laguna Lodge Eco-Resort & Nature Reserve is framed by lush forests, steep mountains and volcanoes. Avid environmentalists Mayah and Jeffro Brandon started the lodge in 1999, and it now consists of a 40-hectare (99-acre) private nature reserve that protects the local flora, fauna and culture.

The journey begins with a tranquil boat ride to the resort. Laguna Lodge occupies a series of thatch-roofed pavilions, which, true to the owners' vision, have been built using natural materials such as volcanic stone, adobe, wood and palm. The lodge only offers nine suites to ensure that no undue stress from excessive human traffic is placed on the environment. As such, visitors are ensured a peaceful stay in pristine surroundings.

Suites are furnished with king-size beds dressed in sumptuous linens, intricately woven textiles, local artworks and antiques. Green-coloured Guatemalan marble and local organic toiletries adorn the bathrooms, while a private balcony allows guests to enjoy the clean air and clear views across the volcano-rimmed lake.

The lodge's lakefront restaurant, Zotz, offers distinctive gourmet vegetarian cuisine to whet the appetite. The chef's creations emphasise fresh organic produce, local cheeses, legumes and free-range eggs. The result is an ever-changing menu of rich, exotic dishes, accompanied with an eclectic wine list from the Lava Bar. Even the coffee is made from shade-grown, organic beans, sourced from the reserve and local farmers in the vicinity.

THIS PAGE: **Natural materials and intricate artwork reflect the lodge's Guatemalan heritage.**

OPPOSITE (FROM LEFT): **Wake up to captivating views of the lake; the lounge's rustic ambience makes it one of the best spots for guests to relax and unwind.**

solola guatemala

Contact with the outside world is available, but it's a waste to surf the Internet or check the news when one could be exploring the lake on a kayak or a canoe. Hiking trails take trekkers up to the volcanoes or through the forest, both of which are home to a rich array of wildlife and plant species.

The spa makes creative use of its natural environs, with an intimate lakeside sauna and a jetted spa pool set in smooth river rock. A variety of massages and treatments are available, all of them utilising natural oils and locally sourced ingredients.

As an eco destination, Laguna Lodge places high emphasis on sustainability and reducing environmental damage. The lodge's detailed finishing incorporates handmade ceramic tiles, recycled glass, reclaimed lumber and adobe bricks made on site. Mayah and Jeffro have carefully restored some areas of the forest by replanting trees that were cut down to make way for farmland. The lodge also has a waste recycling programme and is powered by renewable energy. Collected rain and lake water is purified for consumption, while grey water is used to irrigate the organic garden. Being socially responsible is also one of Laguna Lodge's roles, and the establishment supports health programmes in the local communities.

As a first-rate establishment that puts nature first, Laguna Lodge Eco-Resort & Nature Reserve pays personal attention to the well-being of its guests, as well as that of the earth.

rooms
9 suites

food
Zotz: gourmet eco cuisine

drink
Lava Bar

features
spa • lakeside sauna • jacuzzi • spa pool • nature interpretation room • fitness centre • wireless Internet access • Spanish lessons • trekking • canoeing • kayaking • day-trips and excursions

green features
organic gardens • energy-efficient lighting • natural materials for construction • recycling and composting measures • use of biodegradable cleaners • support of local health programmes

nearby
Lake Atitlán • Sierra Madre Mountains • local markets • volcanoes

contact
1 Tzantizotz, Santa Cruz La Laguna
Lake Atitlán, Solola, Guatemala •
telephone: +502.7823 2529 •
email: info@fiveleafresort.com •
website: www.fiveleafresort.com

maca bana

THIS PAGE (FROM LEFT): *Golden tans and poolside indulgence come hand in hand at the resort; off the beaten track, Maca Bana's serene beachside locale offers scenic views of Grenada.*

OPPOSITE (FROM LEFT): *Individually decorated interiors exude warmth and personality; Aquarium Restaurant takes advantage of the tropical sun with al fresco dining options.*

Known for its spices, tropical sunshine and colourful culture, Grenada has always drawn its fair share of tourists seeking an exotic getaway with a laid-back, friendly atmoshpere. With its indulgent luxuries, alluring views and genuine, warm service, Maca Bana encompasses all the above while offering guests a distinctly personal take of the island at the same time.

The brainchild of Uli Kuhn and Rebecca Thompson, Maca Bana introduces a green way of life on the Caribbean island that appreciates and supports its beautiful natural surroundings. The seven luxury villas that dot the hillside of this boutique resort are predominantly powered by solar energy, while innovative use of compost aid in the growing of an organic landscape filled with vegetables and fruit.

Art is the chosen medium to translate the Kuhns' love for nature, and all units feature Rebecca's artworks and capture elements of island life. Rooms are thus given an inviting personality, bolstered by views of the Caribbean Sea, the seaside port town of St George's and the hills beyond. Villas are individually decorated and feature air-conditioned bedrooms, four poster beds, cable television, stereo system, wireless Internet access and the option of a walk-in wardrobe and living room. Guests looking for a quiet respite will be delighted with the assortment of books provided for their reading pleasure, while those intending to soak up the sun can head out to the hardwood decks and lounge in the jacuzzi where spectacular views of the coastline can be enjoyed.

grenada west indies

Fully-equipped kitchens easily persuade guests to feel right at home, and one will be tempted to whip up gourmet meals after a morning expedition to the colourful markets of nearby St George's. Culinary enthusiasts can also add to their repertoire by having personal cooking lessons at their villa.

Maca Bana's lush grounds offer an abundance of nature-loving activities that range from watersports to invigorating massages. Those wanting a personalised keepsake of this memorable trip will be queueing up to attend the art classes given by the resort's trained artist. Conducted in the countryside, these art expeditions invite budding artists to put their impressions of the sun-drenched island down on canvas, while the option of a scrumptious picnic will make learning a new skill even more appealing. Such workshops are also a bid on the owners' part to inspire a deeper appreciation of nature as guests sketch and paint verdant bamboo forests, vivid tropical vegetation or windswept bays.

The diverse landscape is mirrored in the island's cuisine, where African, East Indian and European influences are flavoured with Grenada's numerous spices. At the Aquarium Restaurant, this mélange of flavours are aptly captured in the menu designed by Uli and his talented team of local chefs. Diners can sample imaginative dishes made with the freshest seafood caught off the Caribbean Coast and organic produce from the resort's own gardens.

Experiencing Maca Bana's simple luxuries and the owners' heartfelt sincerity will make one see the world anew; even the most cynical traveller will be hard-pressed not to feel inspired.

rooms
7 villas

food
Aquarium Restaurant: Grenadian and international

drink
Aquarium Restaurant: bar • La Sirena Beach Bar

features
fully-equipped kitchen • infinity-edge pool with waterfall feature • personal sundeck with outdoor jacuzzi • spa services • private cooking lessons • art workshops • day-trips and excursions

green features
predominantly powered by solar energy • organic nursery and fruit orchard • use of compost from restaurant & villas on vegetation

nearby
Grand Anse Beach • St George's • Point Salines Airport

contact
Point Salines, PO Box 496, St George's GPO, Grenada, West Indies •
telephone: +1.473.439 5355 •
facsimile: +1.473.439 6429 •
email: macabana@spiceisle.com •
website: www.macabana.com

hamadryade lodge

THIS PAGE: *Contemporary interiors are a sophisticated contrast with the natural surroundings.*

OPPOSITE (FROM LEFT): *The bedroom's cosy feel arises from its mood lighting and local artworks; Hamadryade Lodge's chlorine-free pool demonstrates its dedication to the environment.*

Named after the Greek term for a spiritual guardian of the woods, the Hamadryade Lodge in the Ecuadorian rainforest lives up to its name by adhering to a strict code of respect for the environment. Going beyond the requirements of eco certification bodies and movements, Sebastien and Melanie Cazaudehore founded their exclusive four-bungalow resort deep in the Amazon purely out of love for the location and its unique history.

In a previous life, the lodge's site was used as a gold mine, and the land suffered from deforestation and soil erosion. It lay forgotten until the arrival of a couple who interestingly came to the hospitality industry from academic backgrounds in classical literature, photography, sustainable engineering and anthropobiology. Upon discovering the site, they found it to be the perfect intersection of all their interests, offering them a unique opportunity to work with local communities to rebuild what was once a flourishing and proud landscape.

In an unusual reversal, no trees were cleared in the lodge's construction as the land was already barren. Instead, the couple took to enriching the soil and replanting it with a cornucopia of indigenous trees and flowers. Every decision had to be carefully weighed against its impact on the environment, a task which the couple's interest in local customs and knowledge made considerably easier. For example, they eschewed the thatched grass roofs found in many tourism-oriented resorts. While giving the appearance and sensation of authentic rural living, these roofs come at an ecological cost. When used in local homes where fires are often built indoors, smoke serves to protect and prolong the life of the thatch. In resorts, however, pesticides and diesel oil are used instead. Such small observations have led to the establishment of Hamadryade Lodge as one of the cleanest and most eco-friendly resorts in the region.

misahualli-tena **ecuador**

Replacing those roofs are a series of clean, contemporary habitats designed by the pre-eminent French architects Oliver Donnet and Caroline Tresse. These geometrically elegant structures are not only an attractive foil to the wilderness of their natural surroundings, they also feature design traits that maximise the availability of natural light and fresh, moving air. Luxurious bathroom amenities are even formulated by a local herbologist from organic ingredients. Each bungalow features its own identity drawn from one of the local ethnic groups—the Quichua, Shuar, Huoarani or Cofane, and is decorated throughout with that culture's distinctive art forms and symbols.

Day activities are another great way to appreciate the lodge's rugged location. Trekking routes, rafting, cave tours and visits to local communities along the Napo River reveal secrets that few others have been privileged to see. The Hamadryade also operates a 500-sq-m (5,382-sq-ft) enclosed butterfly garden, an entire ecosystem unto itself that includes birds, insects and giant spiders.

Spending time at the Hamadryade Lodge gives one the feeling of having returned to a place where the word "nature" is not just some fashionable trait, but rather the only responsible option available for a secluded rainforest retreat.

rooms
4 luxury bungalows

food
French and international

drink
cocktails and South American wines

features
chlorine-free pool • butterfly garden • massages • Internet access • Fair Trade boutique • local art and sculptures

green features
purified rainwater used in lieu of river and underground sources • biodegradable amenities • biological septic tank system • ethnocentric approach to co-existing with local communities and environment • day-trips and excursions

nearby
indigenous communities

contact
Venecia Iz, via Misahualli
Misahualli-Tena, Ecuador •
telephone: +593.8.590 9992 •
facsimile: +593.9.287 3878 •
email: lodge@hamadryade-lodge.com •
website: www.hamadryade-lodge.com

pousada vila kalango

THIS PAGE: *Pousada Vila Kalango's architecture blends seamlessly into the tropical landscape.*
OPPOSITE (FROM LEFT): *The bedroom's sumptuous beds and soft lights exude a calming ambience; lounge in tropical comfort.*

With sand just about everywhere, Jericoacoara, Brazil could be mistaken for a desert. However, the glint of azure waters beyond the shifting 30-m (100-ft) -high sand dunes is anything but a mirage. Next to "Jeri's" renowned dunes, Pousada Vila Kalango is an eco-conscious beach resort in which environmental values are reflected in its untainted tropical setting.

Offering only 24 rooms, the emphasis at Pousada Vila Kalango is on creating a deeply personal experience where individual needs and desires are given the highest priority. Guests can choose from either the bungalows, apartments or palafitos—comfort stilt houses built upon eucalyptus pillars—with garden, sand dune or ocean views. All lodgings are constructed using natural materials such as moracatiara timber, red clay and carnauba palm straw, creating a rustic elegance that keeps in harmony with man and his surroundings.

In the morning, guests can take a leisurely stroll in the organic garden, home to many carefully cultivated species of native vegetation. The 19-m (62-ft) -long outdoor pool beckons in the hot afternoon, with refreshing cocktails from the poolside bar on hand to stave off the heat. The clubhouse offers watersports equipment alongside wind- and kite-surfing lessons for intrepid souls raring to conquer Brazil's world-famous waves. The aptly named Beauty Room will relax tensed muscles with soothing salt baths and massages, while wireless Internet access will enable urbanites to stay in touch with the world. Dining is a delicious experience, with the restaurant serving Mediterranean-influenced Brazilian cuisine and accompanied by exquisite wines. At night, guests can take a short drive to downtown Jeri, where lively bars and samba clubs adding to the authenticity of this cultural experience.

jericoacoara **brazil**

rooms
9 palafitos • 8 bungalows • 7 apartments

food
Mediterranean-influenced Brazilian

drink
poolside bar

features
wireless Internet access • clubhouse • pool • massage services • wind- and kite-surfing lessons • watersports equipment • day-trips and excursions

green features
use of local natural materials in construction • biodegradable chemicals and detergents • organic farming and recycling • on-site water treatment station • community projects

nearby
Jericoacoara National Park • Prea Beach • downtown Jericoacoara

contact
30 Rua das Dunas, 62598-000
Jericoacoara, Brazil
telephone: +55.88.3669 2289 •
facsimile: +55.88.3669 2291 •
email: reservas@vilakalango.com.br •
website: www.vilakalango.com.br

Pousada Vila Kalango's daily operations have been designed with the sole aim of protecting the natural environment. In addition to its seamless integration into the tropical forest landscape, lodgings are fitted with solar-powered hot showers to keep energy usage minimal. Biodegradable detergents and cleaning agents are used to reduce environmental impact, and used water is recycled for irrigation purposes via an on-site treatment station. The eco retreat also practices sustainable organic farming and recycling, while community projects such as beach clean-ups ensure that the iconic Prea Beach remains in pristine condition.

Education is a major factor in creating environmental awareness, and the eco retreat organises day-trips and excursions for guests to discover for themselves the rich natural and cultural heritage of Jericoacoara National Park. Conducted by foot as well as on horseback, experienced local guides offer unique insights into indigenous lifestyles and the importance of nature conservation.

Being on the edge of one of Brazil's most famous beaches, Pousada Vila Kalango's tranquil location, characteristic architecture and dedication to the environment ensure that the green retreat is the epitome of eco culture and barefoot luxury.

pousada rancho do peixe

THIS PAGE: *Rancho de Peixe's beachfront bungalows enjoy gorgeous views of the sea.*

OPPOSITE (FROM LEFT): *Bungalows were constructed with natural materials like wood and thatch; lively textiles give the rooms a welcoming atmosphere; with its strong winds, Prea Beach is a parasailing hotspot.*

The landscape around Jericoacoara is as fragile as it is beautiful, and in 2002, it was declared a protected national park to prevent the region from being ravaged further by environmental degradation. It is here that one finds the Pousada Rancho do Peixe resort, nestled on the pristine Prea Beach.

The resort was designed by Gui Mattos, a Brazilian architect well known for his eco-friendly projects. To wit, Pousada Rancho do Peixe is built from only natural local materials in a simple, traditional design that perfectly complements the tropical verdure outside. Walls are constructed with clay bricks, while wooden floors and thatch roofs create an welcoming, laid-back atmosphere.

The eco resort offers only 16 bungalows—eight are scattered along Prea Beach, while the rest are further inland, surrounded by coconut trees. Measuring 80 sq m (861 sq ft) each, they are fitted with one king-size bed and two single beds, allowing them to sleep four guests comfortably. Outside, a large deck and verandah with hammock create a relaxing

jericoacoara **brazil**

space to enjoy cool sea breezes. Inside, local handcrafted textiles in bright, cheerful prints contrast with rich timber floors and furniture.

Cuisine is another big draw. Open all day, the restaurant serves Brazilian specialities with a Mediterranean twist. No pesticide- or preservative-filled dishes here; guests dine on produce from the resort's own organic farm, while fish is bought daily from local fishermen.

Watersports enthusiasts have even more reason to make the trip—Prea Beach boasts some of the best kite- and wind-surfing opportunities in the world. Beginners need not worry about missing out, as experienced instructors will get them out on the waves in no time. Those who prefer staying on land can explore the beach or meander through the sand dunes via horseback, while cultural buffs will be delighted with Jericoacoara town's bohemian vibes, just a short buggy ride away.

Guests wanting to take full advantage of the plentiful sunshine and crisp air should head to the pool for a few laps. There is also a beach bar, where mixologists serve refreshing cocktails. The paradisal setting tempts one to forget all about the outside world, but those who must stay connected will appreciate the complimentary wireless Internet access.

Situated on conserved land, Rancho do Peixe plays a major role in local conservation efforts. The resort uses only biodegradable detergents and soaps, so as to minimise water pollution. Water is recycled wherever possible, and the resort is involved with community projects such as supporting the local farmers and setting up sanctuaries for rare birdlife.

With the pride that Rancho de Peixe takes in caring for its guests as well as for the environment, it is little wonder that it remains steadily on the list of Brazil's top 150 hotels.

rooms
8 beach bungalows • 8 coconut bungalows

food
restaurant: Brazilian fusion

drink
pool bar • beach bar

features
pool • massage • complimentary wireless Internet access • private parking

green features
built from local natural materials • solar panels • natural ventilation • recycling and composting • biodegradable cleaning products • support of local community • organic farm • nature reserve • bird sanctuary

nearby
Jericoacoara National Park • Prea Beach • downtown Jericoacoara

contact
Praia do Preá S/N
62595-000 Jericoacoara, Brazil •
telephone: +55.88.3660 3118 •
email: reservas@ranchodopeixe.com.br •
website: www.ranchodopeixe.com.br

cristalino jungle lodge

THIS PAGE (FROM TOP): *Relax in style on the spacious floating dock; the lodge is located within the world's largest nature reserve.*
OPPOSITE (FROM LEFT): *Bungalows open up to verdant surrounds; a bird's eye view of the Amazon.*

It is customary these days for five-star hotels to offer the "basic" amenities of satellite television, Internet, pools and spas. It takes something truly special for any establishment to stand out, and the Cristalino Jungle Lodge's green designer concept easily rises to the task.

Conventional facilities take a back seat as 12,000 hectares (29,652 acres) of protected private rainforest—within which the award-winning lodge is situated—welcomes nature lovers to explore its multitudinous wonders. The reserve is connected to the Cristalino State Park, a conservation area that protects 184,900 hectares (456,897 acres) of unique flora and fauna, making it one of the richest in the world in terms of biodiversity. About a third of 1,800 Brazilian species of birds, almost 2,000 species of butterflies and mammals such as monkeys, capybaras, deer, and agoutis inhabit this region. Many of them can only be found here due to the barrier effect caused by large rivers in the south, west and east.

The eco lodge offers three accommodation categories to cater to all tastes. Natural materials such as rattan and bamboo adorn standard rooms, which come with either two or three beds. The comfortable superior rooms offer a verandah equipped with a hammock and a private outdoor shower integrated with the environment. The most inspiring option comes in the form of private bungalows, which can house up to four guests and have a separate living room, outdoor terrace and outstanding private outdoor shower.

Having received the *Condé Nast Traveller* World Savers Award 2008, Cristalino Jungle Lodge takes great pains to ensure that guests feel connected to the natural world. In place of air-conditioning, interiors rely on low-energy ceiling fans and natural ventilation. The restaurant and bar offers beautiful views of the surroundings—a perfect setting for guests to savour local specialities and Caipirinhas.

The lodge uses its location on the Cistalino River to grand effect. A 144-sq-m (1,550-sq-ft) floating dock is an ideal base from which to observe river life up close, while watersports enthusiasts can arrange activities

mato grosso **brazil**

such as canoeing. At night, a bonfire in the middle of the dock creates a cheerful spot to relax and admire the lush nature and star-filled sky. A screened tree house also enables one to view tapirs, deer and peccaries at play. Nature tours along the 30 km (19 mile) trail system offer in-depth understanding of the tropical ecosystem, conducted in small groups to keep disturbance to the forest minimal. For a truly unique experience of the Amazonian rainforest, a visit to the Canopy Tower cannot be missed. Soaring to 50 m (164 ft), with waystations at various heights, climbers can look out to panoramic views of the reserve, with the vast forest canopy a blanket of green at one's feet.

The green retreat's daily operations are based on environmental preservation and sustainability. The management has installed a water treatment system, composts organic waste and recycles as much material as it can. Solar panels are used to heat water, while a hydrokinetic generator has also been fitted to provide clean energy, while the Cristalino Ecological Foundation has been established in a bid to support local education alongside research projects that promote awareness for the fragile, yet fascinating ecosystem

Cristalino Jungle Lodge encapsulates the essence of the Amazon with its unique experiences, creating a rainforest sanctuary for guests who want to explore in style.

rooms
22 rooms

food
Brazilian

drink
Cristalino Lodge Bar

features
canopy tower • floating dock • screened treehouse • library • canoes • trail system • day-trips • overnight camping excursions

green features
Cristalino Ecological Foundation • preservation of primary rainforest • use of solar panels for heating water • hydrokinetic generator • recycling programme • composting measures • water treatment system

nearby
Cristalino State Park

contact
Avenida Perimetral Oeste, 2001, 78580-000 Alta Floresta, Mato Grosso, Brazil •
telephone: +55.66.3521 1396 •
facsimile: +55.66.3521 2221 •
email: info@cristalinolodge.com.br •
website: www.cristalinolodge.com.br

vila naiá

Although the Vila Naiá is a relatively young hotel, the holiday experience it offers is on par with—or even surpasses—other more established places. Located in southern Bahia, the hotel enjoys a splendid seaside location on Corumbau Beach, with its 15 km (9 miles) of pure white sand and protected coastal forest. Watersports enthusiasts will especially enjoy its proximity to the beautiful Mato Grosso reef, which is ideal for snorkelling and diving. Guests who prefer to keep their feet dry can get a taste of Brazil's rich culture at the nearby villages, work on their tans by the pool, or relax with a massage in the beachside lounge.

Designed by architect Renato Marques, Vila Naiá is a perfect juxtaposition of the traditional and cutting-edge modern. It offers only four bungalows and four suites, styled to resemble the fishermen's wooden houses which are seen in the nearby villages. All accommodation was built using recycled timber and traditional hand-made roof tiles, with every room enjoying cooling sea breezes. Despite the villa's rustic atmosphere and remote location—it is four hours from Porto Seguro by car, although plane and helicopter rides are also available—it enjoys every modern amenity that luxury travellers have come to expect. Rooms are equipped with king-sized beds, minibars, telephones, air conditioning and wireless Internet access, while the poolside lounge has a large television for guests to stay in touch with the outside world.

In keeping with the hotel's eco-friendly practices, the restaurant does not import ingredients. Instead, fresh greens are grown in Vila Naiá's own organic garden or sourced from the nearby farmers' market. Poultry is farmed locally, and Corumbau's fishermen provide the restaurant with fresh catch daily. The hotel's world-class Brazilian cuisine can be enjoyed almost anywhere on the premises—guests who want a little more privacy or a more romantic atmosphere can opt to take meals in their rooms or even on the beach. After dinner, have a nightcap at any of the hotel's two bars, or wind down at the yoga platform, located in a tower with beautiful sea views.

When it comes to environmental and social responsibility, it is only justice to say that owner Renata Mellão has set an eco-

THIS PAGE (FROM LEFT): Vila Naiá's affable staff will make guests feel right at home regardless of where they hail from; rooms are designed to allow in abundant natural light.

OPPOSITE (FROM LEFT): Take a refreshing dip in the pool; relax in the evenings with a comforting pot of tea.

bahia **brazil**

rooms
4 bungalows • 4 suites

food
Brazilian • seafood

drink
two bars

features
outdoor pool • poolside lounge • massage services • yoga platform • wireless Internet • watersports • day-trips and excursions

green features
5 hectares (12 acres) of protected private reserve • organic garden • solar power • wind generator • recycled materials used for construction • educational programmes

nearby
Corumbau Beach • villages • Porto Seguro

contact
Corumbau, Bahia, Brazil •
telephone: +55.11.3061 1872 •
facsimile: +55.11.3061 1872 •
email: info@vilanaia.com.br •
website: www.vilanaia.com.br

friendly precedent for other establishments in the region to emulate. The hotel was designed to leave minimal impact on the environment. Recycled materials were used in construction, while buildings are raised above the ground by palifittes in order to leave the sand beneath untouched. Non-organic waste is recycled whenever possible. Vila Naiá is also equipped with solar panels and a wind generator, allowing it to generate 'clean' energy for its own use. The hotel hosts an environmental education centre dedicated to the conservation of local species, and preserves 5 hectares (12 acres) of the surrounding forest that is now officially recognised as a protected area.

For such reasons and much more, Vila Naiá is a luxurious haven of peace and tranquillity, promising a stay in Brazil that is the very definition of green designer living.

index

Numbers in *italics* denote pages where pictures appear. Numbers in **bold** denote profile pages.

24 Carrots (restaurant) 180
7th Sense Wellness Centre 152–153

A

Abode Restaurant & Lounge 182–183, *183*
Acorn House (restaurant) 54, *54*
Actually (shop) 115, *115*
Africa and the Middle East 80–105
    Accommodation 90–105
    Restaurants 88–89
Ait Bougmez valley 93
Ait Mizane villages 90
Alice and Friends' Vegetarian Café (restaurant) 184
Alive! Vegetarian Cuisine 183
Alla Vecchia Latteria Di Via Unione (restaurant) 60
Alter Mundi Beaurepaire (shop) 65, *65*
Alter Mundi Paris (shop) 65
Alter Mundi Rivoli (shop) 65
Alternative energy 40
Alternative fuels 39
Amazon 178, 211
Ambra (label) 116, *116*
Ambrose, Jenny 63
Americas 172–213
    Accommodation 190–213
    Restaurants 180–185
    Shopping 186–189
Ana Pavilion Restaurant 136–137
Ananda Fuara 183
Anantara Dhigu overwater spa 119
Anantara Dhigu Resort and Spa, Maldives *41*, **124–125**
Anantara Phuket Resort and Spa 15, 122–123, **148–149**
Anantara Spa 148–149
Anantara Veli resort 125
Andes mountain range 178
Angelica Kitchen 180
Angkor Wat 109
Antigua 184
Apfel (restaurant) 185
Aquarium Restaurant 202–203
Argan 31
Aromatherapy Associates 31
Asda 32
ASEAN Energy Award 161
Asia and the Pacific 106–171
    Accommodation 124–171
    Shopping 114–117
    Spas 118–123
Au Grain de Folie (restaurant) 58
Australia 109, 119–120
Austria 61
Ayung Spa 160–161
Azor Opa 37
Azúcar 196–197

B

Baa Atoll 110
Baan Huraa 124–125
Babaii, David 30
Bach Original Flower Remedies 63
Baggu (shop) 187, *187*
Bamford 30
Bamurru Plains **164–165**
Banana Republic 24
Bangkok (Thailand) 114
Banyan Tree 110
Banyan Tree Ringha **132–133**
Banyan Tree Spa Lijiang 119
Banyan Tree Spa Ringha 119
Baobab 31
Bar, The (Evason Hua Hin) 142–143
Bar, The (Six Senses Hideaway Hua Hin) 144–145
Bassike (brand) 117
Bay of Bengal 131
Beach Restaurant (Hua Hin) 144–145
Beach Restaurant (Nha Trang) 136–137
Beatroot (restaurant) 55
Bechade, Cedric 68–69
Beduur Restaurant 160–161
Belpietro, Antonella 98
Belpietro, Luca 98
Ben Thanh Market 140–141
Benjarong (shop) 114
Berbers 92–93
Beyond Retro (shop) 64
Bibliothe (restaurant) 59
Bijou Bazaar (marketplace) 114
Billabong (surfwear) 117
Bio Hotels 52
BioAlternativa (restaurant) 185
BioAlternativa II (restaurant) 185
Biodegradable 40
Biofuels 40
Bird Textiles 116, *116–117*
Bird Textiles Emporium store 116
Bites (restaurant) 104–105
Blossom (restaurant) 180
Blue Lagoon (movie) 156–157
Blyer, Raina 186
Bon Island 150–151
Bonobo's Vegetarian Restaurant 180
Books Actually (bookshop) 114
Borana Lodge **96–97**
Borobudur 109
Boris Bally 186, *186*
Botswana 85
Boughton, Patsy 71
Bourdillat, Mickey 75
Boyd, Tim 22
Brandon, Jeffro 200
Brandon, Mayah 200
Branson, Richard 39
Brave Space (shop) 186
Brazil 178, 185
Breathe (Barclaycard credit card) 45
Breeze Sky Bar 140–141
British Soil Association 28

Broadhurst, Florence 168–169
Brompton M3L 37
Brooks, Julian 20
Bukit Becik Bar 160–161
Bulan Thai Vegetarian Kitchen (restaurant) 182
Bulgaria 49
Buriti 31
Burma Bar 134–135
Buying green 40

C

Café Berlin 184
Café Gratitude 183
Café Koppel 59
Calvin Klein 24
Cambodia 109, 123
Campi ya Kanzi *85*, 88, **98–99**
Canada 175, 176
Cancun 177
Cape Chamomile 31
Carbon footprint 18, 40
Carbon neutral 15, 16, 17, 40
Carbon offsetting 16, 18, 37–38, 40, 110–111
Carbon-free travel 50
CarbonNeutral Company 38
Caribbean 176–177
Caribbean Sea 202
Casa Club Restaurant 198–199
Catinat Lounge 140–141
Cazaudehore, Melanie 204
Cazaudehore, Stephanie 204
Central America 176–177, 200
Certification in Sustainable Tourism Program (CST) 177
Chab Kchol (pinching) 123
Chang-Sa (restaurant) **132–133**
Chatuchak Weekend Market 114
Chicago 184
Chidoriya 29
China 108, 111, 119
Chongming island 111
Chowpaty Pure Vegetarian Restaurant 88
Chub kchol (cupping) 123
Chyulu Hills 98
Clary Sage Organics *187*–188
Clayoquot Wilderness Resort **190–191**
Clean and Green Resources Asia 42
Clean Water Asia 31
Clerkenwell Kitchen (restaurant) 54
Climate Care 38, 44
Climatesure (travel insurance) 45
Citterio, Antonio 74
Coles (supermarket chain) 32
Coloma, Bernard 79
Come On Eileen (shop) 64–65
Como No (footwear) 65
Comoros 85
Compressed Natural Gas (CNG) 39
Conde Nast Traveler 129, 135, 154, 157, 163, 165, 170, 210

Condé Nast Traveler Green List 157
Condé Nast Traveler 'Hot List Hotels' 154
Condé Nast Traveler Readers' Choice Awards 170
Condé Nast Traveler Readers' Spa Awards 129
Condé Nast Traveler World Savers Awards 163, 210
Conservation International 84
Converging World 111
Co-operative Bank 44
Coromandel Coast 130
Corumbau Beach 212–213
Corsica 78
Costa Rica 177
Cosmo Modern (shop) 187
Costa Rica 13
Costalegre coastline 194
Counter (restaurant) 182, *182*
Cousin's Incredible Vitality (restaurant) 184
Cow Bay 191
Cristalino Ecological Foundation 210–211
Cristalino Jungle Lodge 178, **210–211**
Cristalino Lodge Bar 210–211
Cristalino State Park 210–211
Crosswaters Ecolodge & Spa 119
Cupuacu 31
Curiosity 115
Cuisine Café 152–153
Cyclo Café 140–141
Cyclocity 37
Cyclopia 31

D

Dahabeah 86
Daintree Ecolodge & Spa 119, *119*
Dalmatian coast, Croatia 52
Darwin, Charles 178
David Babaii 4 Wildaid 30, *30*
David Bann Restaurant 57, *57*
David Jones department stores 117
David met Nicole (shop) 117
Delene-Bartholdi, Regis 94
Dewsons (supermarket chain) 32
Desalination 41
Di Caprio, Leonardo 175
Diatas Pohon Café 160–161
Dining at the Point 152–153
Dining by the Bay 138–139
Dining by the Pool 138–139
Dining by the Rocks 138–139
Dining on the Edge (restaurant) 104–105
Dining on the Hill (restaurant) 146–147
Dining on the Rocks (restaurant) 146–147
Dining on the Sand (restaurant) 104–105
Dining Room, The 154–155
Domaine de Murtoli **78–79**

Dopie (footwear) 115
Drink on the Hill (bar) 146–147
Drinks by the Bay 138–139
Dubai 86
Ducasse, Alain 68
Duke of Cambridge (restaurant) 54
Duler, Pascale 72
Duler, Patrick 72
Dune Eco Beach Hotel **130–131**
Dunham, Carroll 112

E

E-85 fuel 39
Eaith (label) 188, *188*
Earth 2 (restaurant) 89
Earth Café 56, 88
Ebay 23
Ecologically sustainable development 41
eCycle 36
Eco (shop) 32, *36*, 62, *62–63*
Eco at Home (shop) 117
Eco Citizen 188
Ecochic (event) 25
Ecochic properties 13–14, 20–21, 51
Ecochic travel 13–14, 51
Ecofashion 24–27
Ecoist (bags) 27, *26*
Eco lodge 18
Ecology Building Society 43
Ecotechnology 23
Ecotourism 49, 175
Ecotourism Association of Kenya 84
Ecuador 178
Edun (apparel) 27, *27*
El (furniture) 22
El Natural Saks (restaurant) 185
El Nido Lagen Island Resort 121
El Nido Resorts **156–157**
El Septimo (restaurant) 61
Electric cars 38–39
'Element Hotels' (Starwood) 176
Elsom (brand) 117
Elsom, Sam 117
Emerging Green Builders 21
Enamore (lingerie label) 63, *63*
Energy efficient 41
Energy-efficient lighting 23
Engine Shed (restaurant) 56
England 52
Environmental footprint 41
Environmental Legacy Program 190–191
Environmental Transport Association 45
Equa (shop) 63
Espace Hi Body Spa 76–77
Europe 46–79
    Accommodation 68–79
    Restaurants 54–61
    Shopping 62–65
European Ecolabel (accreditation scheme) 15
Evason Ana Mandara and Six Senses Spa, Nha Trang 123, **136–137**

index

Evason Hua Hin and Six Senses Spa 142–143
Evason Phuket and Six Senses Spa 122, 150–151
Eveil Café Epicerie Bio (restaurant) 60
Ever Soneva So Down to Earth (restaurant) 126–127

F
Fair Share (shop) 62
Fair trade 18, 41
Fairtrade Labelling Organisations International 41
Farm, The 121
Fetish for Food (restaurant) 56
Field Kitchen (restaurant) 56
Finca Rosa Blanca Coffee Plantation and Inn 177
Flamant Home Interiors 68
Food & Wine 193
Fossil fuels 41
Finland 52
First Out Café-Bar (restaurant) 55
Firth, Colin 34
Food and Agriculture Organisation (UN) 34
Food U Need (F.U.N.) restaurant 130–131
Forbes Traveler 193
Ford Focus 39
Four Seasons 110
Four Seasons Tented Camp Golden Triangle **140–141**
Fourtane, Thomas 78
France 52, 74
Franchia (restaurant) 180
Freecycle 23
Frégate Island Private 118, *118*
Freitag (apparel) 115
Fresh in the Garden Restaurant 126–127
Front Fow (shop) 115
Fruits and Roots (restaurant) 89
Furstenberg, Diane von *24*, 25
Fushi Café 124–125
Fusion Grill (restaurant) 124–125
FutureFashion initiative 25

G
g=9.8 (shop) 65
Galapagos Islands 178
Galgiriwiya Mountains 112
Gault Millau guide 68
Germany 49–50, 52
Go Green Go (ecoclothing) 25
Girasole (restaurant) 59
Giuggioli, Nicola 62
Global Baseline for Sustainable Tourism 15
Global warming 16, 41
Gobo (restaurant) 181
Gore, Al 42, 175
Gorman 116, *116*

Grand Appetit (restaurant) 58
Grand Canyon 172, 175
Grasset, Matali 76
Grassroots (shop) 189
Great Barrier Reef 109
Great Wall of China 109
Greece 52
Green and Black's 34
Green Book (Six Senses) 147
Green building revolution 51 also see Eco properties
Green certification 41
Green Globe 21 18
Green Globe (accreditation scheme) 15, 41
Green Hills of Africa (book) 96
Green Hotel Recognition Award (ASEAN) 157
Green Partnership programme 176
Green technology 22
Greenpeace 175
Green2greener (organisation) 25
GreenLeaf Foundation 41
Greenpeace Visa (credit card) 45
Greens (restaurant) 56
Gregory, Rogan 27
Gunyah (restaurant & bar) 166–167
G-whiz (Piaggio) 39

H
Hamadryade Lodge 178, **204–205**
HanGawi (restaurant) 180, *180*
Hanson Bay 168
Happy Bar 76–77
Hayes Diversified Technology 36
Healing Grounds spa 190–191
Hemingway, Ernest 85, 96
Henderson's Bistro 57
Henderson's Shop and Salad Table 57
Herbal hot compresses 123
Herbivore (restaurant) 183
Hewson, Ali 27
Hi Food 76–77
Hi Hotel (Nice, France) 51, 58, *58*, **76–77**
High Atlas Tourist Code 91
Hiltl (restaurant) 60, **60**
Hilot massage therapy 120
Hin and Veg (restaurant) 59
Hindmarch, Anya 26
Honda 36
  FCX 39
Hotel de la Paix 123
Hotel Eco Paraiso Xixim 178, **198–199**
Hôtel Le Morgane (Chamonix, France) 51, **74–75**
Hôtel Les Orangeries **70–71**
Hotel Majestic Saigon 123, **138–139**
Hotelito Desconocido **194–195**
Howies (shop) 64
Hudson, Kate 30
Hybrid cars 38–39, 41
Hybrid Travelers 45

I
Iceland 49, 52
Il Margutta Vegetariano (restaurant) 59, *59*
Inconvenient Truth, An (documentary) 42
Incu (shop) 117
India 44, 109
Indian Ocean 118–119, 126
Indonesia 109, 120
Industrial Technology Research Institute (ITRI) 36
Infinity (bar) 148–149
"Innovation Hotel" programme 176
Intergovernmental Panel on Climate Change 32
International ecotourism society 18
World Fair Trade Organisation (WFTO) 24
International Tourism Society 40
Into the Beach (restaurant & bar) 150–151
Into the Med (restaurant) 150–151
Into Pondering (bar) 150–151
Into the View (restaurant) 150–151
Into Wines (bar) 150–151
Isinglass (restaurant) 56
Isla del Tesoro (restaurant) 61

J
Jakhang Lobby Lounge (teahouse) 132–133
Jamaica 184
Jamie's Fowl Dinners (TV show) 34
Japan 121
Jbel Toubkal 90
Jericoacoara National Park 207
Jericoacoara town 209
Jervis Bay 166–167
Jil Sander 24
Jimbaran Puri Bali 120, **158–159**
Joia (restaurant) 59
Juazeiro 31
Juicy Jones (restaurant) 60

K
Kaight (shop) 189
Kalabashe (restaurant) 184
Karan, Donna 25
Karavan (shop) 63
Karyn's Cooked (restaurant) 184
Karyn's Fresh Corner (restaurant) 184
Kasbah Du Toubkal **90–91**
Kate's Joint (restaurant) 181
Kelly, Thomas 114
Kemplar Voltaic Solar Backpack 27
Kenya 13, 85
Kieran Timberlake *20*, 21
Kruger National Park 85
Kuala Lumpur (Malaysia) 114
Kuhn, Uli 202
Kyoto Protocol treaty 175

L
L'Auberge Basque 56, 57, **68–69**
L'escalier (shop) 115
La Casa Club 198–199
La Cour Jardin (Le Plaza Athenee) 68
La Libreria (shop) 114–115
La Potager du Marais (restaurant) 58
La Rhune Mountains 68
La Sala (restaurant) 148–149
La Sirena Beach Bar 202–203
La Sultana Oualidia Hotel & Spa **94–95**
La Victoire Supreme du Coeur (restaurant) 58
Lafuma (shop) 114
Lagen Island Resort 156–157
Laguna Lodge Eco-Resort & Nature Reserve 177, **200–201**
Lake Atitlán 177, 200
Lapa Rios Rainforest Ecolodge 177
Larroque, Christian 68
Laura, Ralph 25
Lava Bar 200–201
Lazuli Lodge 13, 89, **102–103**
Le Domaine de Saint-Géry 52, **72–73**
Le Kid (restaurant) 60
Le TK (restaurant) 100–101
Le TK bar 100–101
Leading Hotels of the World 16
Leadership in Energy and Environmental Design (LEED) 176
League for Bird Protection 71
Leahy, Terry 34
Les Demeures du Ranquet 79
Li'Tya products 168–169
Liew, Khai 168–169
Life Shop 116
Lifestyles of Health and Sustainability (LOHAS) 175
Lim, Phillip 25, *25* also see Go Green Go
Lim, Vik 115
Liquefied Petroleum Gas (LPG) 39
Living Room, The 144–145
Living Room and Terrace, The 154–155
Livity (restaurant) 184
Lizard Lounge (shop) 189
Llamo Restaurant 132–133
Lobby Bar 136–137
Loblolly House 21
Lola's (restaurant) 89
Lotus Art de Vivre (shop) 114
Loudermilk, Linda 188
Low Mileage Discount programme 45
Luang Prabang (Laos) 111–112
Lucchini, Stephane 78
Luma (shop) 64, *64*

M
M-Bar 140–141
Maca Bana 202–203
Madagascar 44, 84, 85
Main Bar 128–129

Main House, The 154–155
Main Restaurant 128–129
Majella National Park 52
Maki Squarepatch 114
Maldives 109–111
Man in Seat Sixty-One, The (railway) 23
Manketti 31
Maoz Falafel (restaurant) 60
Marks & Spencer 32, 35
Marques, Renato 212
Marni 24
Marula oil 31
Maruwa Range 30
Mato Grosso reef 212
Mattos, Gui 208
Mauritius 85
MBNA (credit card) 44
McCartney, Stella 25
McGregor, Kate 189
McLean and Page (shop) 117
McDonough, William see William McDonough & Partners
Mediterranean Coast (Spain) 52
Mellao, Renata 212
Mercedes-Benz F600 Hygenius 39
Mexico City 185
Michaelis, Alex 22
Middle East 86
Midway Geyser 175
Mighty-O Donuts (restaurant) 184
Millennium (restaurant) 183
Miller, Gordon 20
Miniloc Island Resort 156–157
Minkoff, Rebecca 26
Mongolia 109, 112
Monnier, Alice 79
More Than Green Wheels 45
Moringa 31
Morocco 86
Mount Kailas 112
Mount Kilimanjario 85, 98
Mozambique beaches 85
Muji (shop) 114, *114*
Mukti 29, *29*
Murzilli, Marcello 194–195
MyRate programme 45
My Green Travels 40

N
Nani Marquina 22, *22*
Napo River 204–205
National Geographic Traveler 193
Natural High Café 185
Natural History Museum 198–199
Naturbar (restaurant) 59
Nau (apparel) 189
Nelayan Restaurant 158–159
Nelsons Homeopathic Pharmacy 63 also see Bach Original Flower Remedies
Nepal 109
Netaporter.com (fashion website) 117
Nettleton Tribe 166–167

index 215

index

New York 180–183
New York Fashion Week 24–25
New Zealand 120
Newman, Nell 33–34
Newman, Paul 33
Newman's Own Organics 33
Non Governmental Organisations (NGO) 15, 84
Nong Yao Restaurant 134–135
North America 175–176
Northern Lights 52
Norway 52
Notre Dame Cathedral 140–141
Nova Scotia 192
Nova Scotia Seafood Cooking School 193
NTUC Fairprice (supermarket chain) 32
Nu jeans 65
Nude 31, *31*
Nukubati Island **162–163**

O
Okavango Delta 85
Oliver, Jamie 34, *34*
Onsen 121
Onto the Island (restaurant) 150–151
Opera House 140–141
Oppt Shop 115
Organic (restaurant) 61
Organic food 41
Organic Foods and Café 89
Organics Alive (grocer and café) 89
Orient Express group 160
Origins 29–30
ORIGINS Dar Itrane **92–93**
Ortolo River 78, *79*
Oscar de la Renta 25
Oslob steam inhalation therapy 121
Osprey Pavilion 168–169
Other Bar, The 142–143
Other Restaurant, The 142–143
Oulanka National Park 49
Our Eco Shop 62
Out of Africa (movie) 85

P
Pachauri, Rangendra 34
Palette London (shop) 64
Paligo bathing therapy 120
Panacea: An Eco Shopping Oasis (shop) 189
Panama 177
Pangea Organics 30
Pantagonia (apparel) 27
Pantagonia glaciers 178
Paperbark Camp **166–167**
Parks Canada Sustainable Tourism Award 193
Philippines 120–121
Philips, Bijou 27
Piccolo Paradiso (restaurant) 59
Pidden, Andrew 42
Pitt, Brad 86
Pizza Pi Vegan Pizzeria (restaurant) 184

Planet 27
Plushpod (shop) 186
Poitou countryside 71
Pondicherry 130
Porto Seguro 212
Porter Electric (Piaggio) 39
Portobello (restaurant) 89
Poulet, Monsieur 65
Pousada Rancho do Peixe 178, **208–209**
Pousada Villa Kalango 178, **206–207**
Prea Beach 208–209
Prince of Wales 33
Punlie (traditional Khmer medicine) 123
Puerto Rico 184–185
Pure Food and Wine (restaurant) 180–181, *181*
Puri Bar 158–159
Pyramids of Giza 86

R
Rain harvester 23
Rainforest Alliance (NGO) 15
RED American Express 44
Red Bamboo (restaurant) 181
Red Door Gallery 63
Red Veg (restaurant) 55
Reino Vegetal (restaurant) 185
Republic of Ireland 50
Responsibletravel.com 18
Responsible tourism awards 18
Restaurant Bona Dea 60
Restaurant, The 142–143
Restaurante Vegetariano Beterraba (restaurant) 185
Reunification Palace 140–141
Rider, Traci Rose see Emerging Green Builders
Ringha River 132
River Nile 86
Riverford Farm (England) 57 also see Field Kitchen
Rock Spa of Frégate Island Private 118–119
Rocky Mountains 175
Rooibos 31
Royal, Charles 170–171
Ruak River 134
Ryann (shop) 187

S
Saab 9-5 39
Sacred Chow 182
Saf (restaurant) 54, 55
Sahara desert 86, *86*
Salmon Nation Visa Card 45
Samses (restaurant) 60
San Francisco 183–184
San Rafael 197
Sao Paulo 185
Sagarmatha National Park 109
Sax, John 170–171

Scandic Hotels 51
Scandinavian countires 50
Schwarzenegger, Arnold 175
Screwhead (furniture) 22
Sea.Fire.Salt (restaurant) 148–149
Seafood Bar 130–131
Seattle 184
Seminyak 159
Sense by the Beach restaurant 126–127
Seranade Restaurant 140–141
Seychelles 85
Shanghai 111
Shanghai Industrial Investment Corporation 111
Shojin (restaurant) 182
Shopbox.com (shopping site) 27
Shorebank Pacific 45
Shinta Mani spa 123
Singapore 114–116
Sirinath Marine National Park 148
Six Senses Destination Spa Phuket 122, **152–153**
Six Senses Earth Spa 4, 144–145
Six Senses Hideaway Hua Hin **144–145**
Six Senses Hideaway Ninh Van Bay 123, **136–137**
Six Senses Hideaway Yao Noi **154–155**
Six Senses Hideaway Zighy Bay 86, 89, 89, **104–105**
Six Senses Hideaway Samui 122, 146–147 Six Senses Resorts & Spas 15, 18
Six Senses Soneva Kiri Ecosuite 123
Six Senses Spas 104–105, 126–127, 150–151, 154–155
Slow Food movement 51
Slush Limited (restaurant) 88
So Organic (shop) 63
Sobosibio (shop) 65
Solar panels 23
Soneva Fushi by Six Senses 15, 110, 118, **126–127**
Soneva Gili by Six Senses 118, **128–129**
South America 178
Southern Ocean Lodge 2, **168–169**
Southern Spa 168–169
Spa, The 134–135
Spa Indochine 123
Spin the Bottle (shop) 115
St George's town 202–203
Starck, Philippe 74
Steven Alan 189
Stuart Haygarth (furniture) 22
Stresscape spa 156–157
Supermarket chains 32
Sustainable development 18
Sustainable living movements 51–52
Sustainable Travel International (STI) 16
Sustainable tourism 18
Sustainable tourism criteria 18

Sustainable Tourism Initiative 41
Sustainable Travel International 18
Sweden 52
Swinton Park **66–67**
SYM 36

T
Taj Mahal 109
Tamil Nadu 130
Tango Mango Bookshop 115
Tanjung Café 158–159
Tasting Room, The 148–149
Tembo House 98–99
Terrapass 40
Terrazzo (restaurant) 124–125
Tesco 32, 34–35
Textile Recycling for Aid and International Development (TRAID; thrift shop) 64
Thailand 121–123
Theory of Evolution 178
Thompson, Rebecca 202
Tien Hiang (restaurant) 58
Tibits (restaurant) 60, *61*
Tobeatic Wilderness Area 192
Tobira Onsen Myojinkan 121
Todae (cards) 117
Together campaign 35
Ton Sai restaurant 152–153
Toronto Hemp Company (shop) 189
Toubkal National Park 90
Tourism for tomorrow awards 18
Town and Country Planning Association 20
Traditional healing 120–121, 123
Traditional Khmer Massage 123
Train network (Europe) 50
Travel + Leisure 154, 165, 170
Travel + Leisure 'The It List' 154
Travelers Insurance 45
Travelodge 51
Tree House, The (restaurant) 148–149
Treetops Lodge and Wilderness Experience 120, **170–171**
Trout Point Lodge 176, **192–193**
Truth Belts (label) 189
Tsara Komba Lodge **100–101**
Tsavo Hills 98
Tsavo National Park 99
Tulum 177

U
Ubud Hanging Gardens 120, **160–161**
Uganda 44
Ulpotha (Sri Lanka) 112, 119
UNESCO 15, 109, 111
UNESCO Biosphere Reserve 193
United Kingdom 50
United Nations 109
United States Department of Agriculture (USDA) 28
Upper Rust, The 186
Urban Fox (label) 188, *188*

USA 175, 186
Uvs Nuur Basin 109

V
Valley of the Kings 86
Vali Ski Resort 176
Van Arsdale, Joslin 188
Veda Spa 130–131
Veg World Restaurant 89
Vegan Joint, The 182
Vegetalia (restaurant) 60
Vegetariano Madero (restaurant) 185
Veggie Bite (restaurant) 184
Velib' 36
Venice 13
Vera Cruz 196–197
Versace 25
Veyrat, Marc 68
Vietnam 122
Villa Naiá 178, *184*, **212–213**
Virgin Holidays Responsible Tourism Award 97
Virtuoso 170
Virtuoso Best of Best Awards 170
VitaOrganic (restaurant) 55
Vivavi (furniture) 22

W
Wallpaper magazine 22, 186
Wal-Mart 32
Water House (restaurant) 54
Whistler Ski Resort 176
Wild Earth Journeys 112
Wilkinson, Guz 22
William McDonough & Partners, Architecture and Community Design 21
Wine Cellar (Evason Hua Hin) 142–143
Wine Cellar (Six Senses Hideaway Hua Hin) 144–145
Working Assets Visa Card 44
World Heritage sites 13
World Wildlife Fund 84
WWF (credit card) 44

X
Xochicalli Spa 196–197

Y
Yangtze River Delta 111
Year of Food and Farming 33
Yellowstone National Park 175
Yerbabuena (restaurant) 61
Yucatán Peninsula 177
Yug (restaurant) 185
Yunnan province 132
Yves Saint Laurent 24

Z
Zanzibar Island 85
Zara 26
Zero carbon cruises 86
Zhongdian 132
Zotz (restaurant) 200–201

picture credits

A & L Sinibaldi/Getty Images front cover (fields), 39 (top)
Acorn House Restaurant 54
Actually 115 (bottom)
AHR/Photolibrary 35
Alter Mundi 65
altrendo nature/Getty Images 43 (top)
Ambra 116 (bottom right)
Anantara Dhigu Resort & Spa, Maldives front cover (villas), 41 (bottom), 124-125
Anantara Phuket Resort + Spa 15, 148-149
Andre Gallant/Getty Images 80
Arctic-Images/Getty Images front cover (aurora borealis), 46
Azúcar 196-197
Baggu 187(top right)
Bamurru Plains 164-165
Banyan Tree Ringha front cover (bath tub), 132-133
Bird Textile back cover (soap flakes), 116 (top and middle right), 117
BODY Philippe/Photolibrary 111 (bottom)
Borana Lodge 40, 85 (bottom), 96-97
Boris Bally back cover (chairs), 186
Bruno De Hogues/Getty Images 84
Campi ya Kanzi 85 (top), 98-99
Cate Gillon/Getty Images 33(bottom right), 52 (top)
Charles Schiller 181 (bottom left)
Charlotte Wood/Arcaid/Corbis 21 (bottom), 23
China Photos/Getty Images 111 (top)
Chiva-Som, Hua Hin 122 (bottom)
Chris Kober/Getty Images 51
Clary Sage Organics 187 (top left and bottom)
Clayoquot Wilderness Resort 190-191
Clemente Gauer/Getty Images 179
Clerkenwell Kitchen 55 (top)
Corbis/Photolibrary 32
Counter 182 (top and bottom)
Cristalino Jungle Lodge 210-211
Daintree EcoLodge & Spa 119 (top right)
Dala Spa 120
Daniel Deitschel 37/Getty Images (bottom)
Darrell Gulin/Getty Images 83
David B Fleetham/Photolibrary 177
David Babaii 4
Wildaid 30 (top)
David Bann Restaurant 57
Dirk von Mallinckrodt/Getty Images 38

Domaine De Murtoli 78-79
Eairth 188 (top left and right)
Eco-age 34 (top), 62, 63 (top)
Ecoist 26 (top)
Edun 27
EIGHTFISH/Getty Images 106
El Nido Resorts 156-157
enamore 63 (bottom)
Evason Ana Mandara + Six Senses Spa-Nha Trang 134-135
Evason Hua Hin + Six Senses Spa 142-143
Evason Phuket + Six Senses Spa 150-151
Federico Veronesi 12
Four Seasons Hotel Tokyo 121 (bottom right)
Four Seasons Resort Maldives at Kuda Huraa front flap (treatment room), 119 (top left)
Four Seasons Resort Maldvies at Landaa Giraavaru 119 (bottom)
Four Seasons Tented Camp Golden Triangle 14
Four Seasons Tented Camp Golden Triangle 140-141
Francesca Yorke/Getty Images 34 (below)
Francois Guillot/AFP/Getty Images 37 (top)
Frazer Harrison/Getty Images for IMG 24
Frégate Island Private 118
Gavin Hellier/Getty Images 42
Gorman 116 (left)
Hamadryade Lodge 204-205
HanGawi 180
Heath Robbins/Getty Images 36
Heinrich van den Berg/Getty Images back cover (al fresco dining), 88 (top)
Hi Hotel front flap (bedroom), 58, 76-77
Hitl 60 (top)
Hola Images/Getty Images 184 (top left)
Hotel Eco Paraiso Xixim 198-199
Hôtel Le Morgane 74-75
Hôtel Les Orangeries 70-71
Hotel Majestic Saigon 138-139
Hotelito Desconocido 194-195
Il Margutta Vegetariano 59 (top)
James Martin 44/Getty Images (below)
Jerry Kobalenko/Getty Images 113
Jewel Samad/AFP/Getty Images 43 (bottom)
Jim Ballard/Getty Images 178
Jimbaran Puri Bali front cover (pillows), 158-159
Jochem D Wijnands/Getty Images 17
Jochen Schlenker/Getty Images front cover (Grand canyon), 172

John Gollings/Arcaid/Corbis 21 (top)
John Macdougall/AFP/Getty Images back cover (mannequins), 25 (bottom right)
Jörg Sundermann 5, 41 (top), 59 (middle), 88 (bottom left and right)
Justin Sullivan/Getty Images 33 (top)
Kadir Audah Abdul/Photolibrary 109
Kasbah du Toubkal 90-91
Kenneth Johansson/Corbis 183
Kent Mathews/Getty Images 45
La Sultana Oualidia 94-95
Laguna Lodge Eco-Resort + Nature Reserve 200-201
L'Auberge Basque
Lazuli Lodge 13, 102-103, 89 (bottom)
Le Domaine de Saint-Géry 72-73
LivingHomes 44 (top)
Louis-Laurent Grandadam/Getty Images 29 (bottom)
Luma 64 (bottom)
Maca Bana 202-203
Maki Squarepatch 115 (top left and right)
Mario Tama/Getty Images 26 (bottom)
Masaaki Tanaka / Sebun Photo/Getty Images 121 (bottom right)
Mascarucci/Corbis 184 (top right)
Mauricio Lima/AFP/Getty Images 33 (bottom left)
Maya Ubud Resort & Spa 121 (bottom left)
Michele Falzone/Getty Images 175
Muji 114
Mukti 29 (top left)
Nani Marquina 22 (top)
Narinder Nanu/AFP/Getty Images 112
Nelson Antoine/Fotoarena/LatinContent/Getty Images 185
Nils-Johan Norenlind/Photo Library 50 (bottom)
Nude 30 (bottom)
Nukubati Island 162-163
Origins 29 (top right)
Origins Dar Itrane 92-93
Paperbark Camp 166-167
Paul Thompson/Getty Images 53
Peter Aaron/Esto 20
Peter Adams/Getty Images 49
Philip Lim 25 (top)
Philippe Bourseiller/Getty Images 87
Pimalai Resort & Spa 122 (top)
Pousada Rancho Do Peixe 208-209

Pousada Vila Kalango 206-207
Pure Food and Wine 181 (bottom right)
Raimund Linke/Getty Images 50 (top)
Reestore front flap (sofa), 22 (below)
Rob Loud/Getty Images 25 (bottom left)
Roger Wright/Getty Images 16
Ronn Motors 39 (bottom)
Ryan McVay/Getty Images 176
Ryann 187 (top middle)
Ryu Kodoma 181 (top)
Saf Restaurant 55 (bottom left and right)
Sean Gallup/Getty Images 59 (bottom)
Six Senses Destination Spa Phuket 152-153
six senses group (bottom left and right)
six senses group front cover (porcupine), back cover (bath tub, jungle retreat, water villa), 28
Six Senses Hideaway Hua Hin 4, 144-145
Six Senses Hideaway Ninh Van Bay 18, 123, 136-137
Six Senses Hideaway Samui-A Sala Property 146-147
Six Senses Hideaway Yao Noi 19, 154-155
Six Senses Hideaway Zighy Bay back flap (outdoor dining), 89 (top), 104-105
Soneva Fushi by Six Senses 126-127
Soneva Gili by Six Senses 110, 128-129
Southern Ocean Lodge back cover (fireplace), back flap (lounge), 2, 168-169
Steve Allen/Getty Images 56 (top)
Swinton Park 66-67
Ted Mead/Getty Images front cover (tree), 31
The Dune Eco Beach Hotel 130-131
Tibits 61 (top)
TRAID 64 (top)
Treetops Lodge + Wilderness Experience 170-171
Trevor Wood/Getty Images 86
Trout Point Lodge 192-193
Truth Belts 189
Tsara Komba Lodge 100-101
Ubud Hanging Gardens 160-161
Urban Fox 188 (bottom)
Uriel Sinai/Getty Images 8-9
Vila Naiá front cover (fireplace), 184 (bottom), 212-213
Winfried Wisniewski/Getty Images 52(bottom)

The publisher would like to thank April Lee, Brandon Lee, Elaine Chew, Gerald Chew and Jocelyn Lau for their help and support during the production of this book.

directory

HOTELS

EUROPE

ENGLAND

Swinton Park
Masham, Ripon, North Yorks HG4 4JH,
United Kingdom
telephone: +44.1765.680 900
facsimile: +44.1765.680 901
email: reservations@swintonpark.com
website: www.swintonpark.com

FRANCE

L'Auberge Basque
D 307, Vieille Route de St Jean de Luz
64310 St Pée sur Nivelle, France
telephone: +33.5.5951 7000
facsimile: +33.5.5951 7017
email: contact@aubergebasque.com
website: www.aubergebasque.com

Hôtel Les Orangeries
12, Avenue du Dr Dupont
86320 Lussac-les-Châteaux, France
telephone: +33.549.840 707
facsimile: +33.549.849 882
email: orangeries@wanadoo.fr
website: www.hotel-lesorangeries.com

Le Domaine de Saint-Géry
Lascabanes, 46800 Montcuq en Quercy,
France
telephone: +33.5.6531 8251
facsimile: +33.5.6522 9289
email: pascale@saint-gery.com
website: www.saint-gery.com

Hôtel Le Morgane
145, Avenue de l'Aiguille du Midi, 74400
Chamonix Mont-Blanc, France
telephone: +33.4.5053 5715
facsimile: +33.4.5053 2807
email:
reservation@hotelmorganechamonix.com
website: www.morgane-hotel-chamonix.com

Hi Hotel
3 Avenue Des Fleurs, 06000 Nice, France
telephone: +33.49.707 2626
facsimile: +33.49.707 2627
email: hi@hi-hotel.net
website: www.hi-hotel.net

Domaine de Murtoli
20100 Sartène, France
telephone: +33.49.571 6924
facsimile: +33.49.577 0032
email: villas@murtoli.com
website: www.murtoli.com

AFRICA + MIDDLE EAST

MOROCCO

Kasbah du Toubkal
BP 31, Imlil, Asni, Marrakech, Morocco
telephone: +212.24.485 611
facsimile: +212.24.485 636
email: kasbah@discover.ltd.com
website: www.kasbahdutoubkal.com

Origins Dar Itrane
Dar Itrane, Imelghas village, Bougmez
Valley, Tabant community, Azilal District,
Morocco
telephone: +33.47.253 7219
facsimile: +33.47.253 2481
email: sejour@origins-lodge.com
website: www.dar-itrane.com

La Sultana Oualidia
Parc à Huîtres N°3, 24000 Oualidia,
Morocco
telephone: +212.23.366 595
facsimile: +212.23.366 594
email: reservation@lasultanahotels.com
website: www.lasultanaoualidia.com

REPUBLIC OF KENYA

Borana Lodge
PO Box 137, Nanyuki, Laikipia, Kenya
telephone: +254.721.557 362
facsimile: +254.62.310 75
email: bookings@borana.co.ke
website: www.borana.co.ke

Campi ya Kanzi
PO Box 236-90128 Mtito Andei, Kenya
telephone: +254.45.622 516
facsimile: +254.45.622 516
email: lucasaf@africaonline.co.ke
website: www.maasai.com

MADAGASCAR

Tsara Komba Lodge
Nosy Be, Madagascar
telephone: +261.32.074 4040
email: resa@highspiritlodges.com
website: www.tsarakomba.com

EGYPT

Lazuli Lodge
Lazuli, 2nd floor El Moltaka Towers (Tower A)
Abbasseya Square, Cairo, Egypt
telephone: +20.2.2403 0891
facsimile: +20.2.2403 0913
email: contact@lazulinil.com
website: www.lazulinil.com

SULTANATE OF OMAN

Six Senses Hideaway Zighy Bay
Zighy Bay, Musandam Peninsula
Sultanate of Oman
telephone: +968.2673 5555
facsimile: +968.2673 5556
email: reservations-zighy@sixsenses.com
website: www.sixsenses.com

ASIA PACIFIC

MALDIVES

Anantara Dhigu Resort + Spa, Maldives
Box 2014, Dhigufinolhu, South Male Atoll
Male, Republic of Maldives
telephone: +960.664 4100
facsimile: +960.664 4101
email: maldives@anantara.com
website: www.anantara.com

Soneva Fushi by Six Senses
Kunfunadhoo Island, Baa Atoll
Republic of Maldives
telephone: +960.660 0304
facsimile: +960.660 0374
email: reservations-fushi@sixsenses.com
website: www.sixsenses.com

Soneva Gili by Six Senses
Lankanfushi Island, North Male Atoll
Republic of Maldives
telephone: +960.664 0304
facsimile: +960.664 0305
email: reservations-gili@sixsenses.com
website: www.sixsenses.com

INDIA

The Dune Eco Beach Hotel
Pudhukuppam, Keelputhupet (via
Pondicherry University), 605014 Tamil
Nadu, India
telephone: +91.413.265 5751
facsimile: +91.413.265 6351
email: booking@epok-group.com
website: www.thedunehotel.com

PEOPLE'S REPUBLIC OF CHINA

Banyan Tree Ringha
Hong Po Village, Jian Tang Town, Shangri-La County, Diqing Tibetan Autonomous
Prefecture, Yunnan Province
People's Republic of China 674400
telephone: +86.887.828 8832
facsimile: +86.887.828 8911
email: ringha@banyantree.com
website: www.banyantree.com

VIETNAM

**Evason Ana Mandara & Six Senses
Spa—Nha Trang**
Beachside, Tran Phu Boulevard
Nha Trang, Khanh Hoa, Vietnam
telephone: +84.58.352 2222
facsimile: +84.58.352 5828
email: reservations-nhatrang@sixsenses.com
website: www.sixsenses.com

Six Senses Hideaway Ninh Van Bay
Ninh Van Bay, Ninh Hoa, Khanh Hoa,
Vietnam
telephone: +84.58.372 8222
facsimile: +84.58.372 8223
email: reservations-ninhvan@sixsenses.com
website: www.sixsenses.com

Hotel Majestic Saigon
1 Dong Khoi Street, District 1
Ho Chi Minh City, Vietnam
telephone: +84.8.3829 5517
facsimile: +84.8.3829 5510
email: majestic@majesticsaigon.com.vn
website: www.majesticsaigon.com.vn

THAILAND

**Four Seasons Tented Camp Golden
Triangle**
PO Box 18, Chiang Saen Post Office
Chiang Rai 57150, Thailand
telephone: +66.53.910 200
facsimile: +66.53.652 189
website: www.fourseasons.com/goldentriangle

Evason Hua Hin & Six Senses Spa
9 Moo 5 Paknampran Beach, Pranburi
Prachuap Khirikhan 77220, Thailand
telephone: +66.32.632 111
facsimile: +66.32.632 112
email: reservations-huahin@sixsenses.com
website: www.sixsenses.com

Six Senses Hideaway Hua Hin
9/22 Moo 5 Paknampran Beach,
Pranburi Prachuap Khirikhan 77220
Thailand
telephone: + 66.32.618 200
facsimile: : + 66.32.632 112
email:
reservations-huahin@sixsenses.com
website: www.sixsenses.com

**Six Senses Hideaway Samui-A Sala
Property**
9/10 Moo 5 Baan Plai Laem, Bophut
Koh Samui Suratthani 84320 Thailand
telephone: +66.77.245 678
facsimile: +66.77.245 671
email: reservations-samui@sixsenses.com
website: www.sixsenses.com

Anantara Phuket Resort & Spa
888 Moo 3, Tumbon Mai Khao
Amphur Thalang, Phuket 83110 Thailand
telephone: +66.76.336 100
facsimile: +66.76.336 177
email: phuket@anantara.com
website: www.phuket.anantara.com

Evason Phuket & Six Senses Spa
100 Vised Road, Moo 2, Tambol Rawai
Muang District, Phuket 83130, Thailand
telephone: +66.76.381 010
facsimile: +66.76.381 018
email: reservations-phuket@sixsenses.com
website: www.sixsenses.com

Six Senses Destination Spa Phuket
32 Moo 5, Tambol Paklok, Amphur Thalang
Phuket 83110, Thailand
telephone: +66.76.371 400
facsimile: +66.76.371 401
email: reservations-naka@sixsenses.com
website: www.sixsenses.com

Six Senses Hideaway Yao Noi
56 Moo 5, Tambol Koh Yao Noi, Amphur
Koh Yao, Phang Nga 82160, Thailand
telephone: +66.76.418 500
facsimile: +66.76.418 518
email: reservations-yaonoi@sixsenses.com
website: www.sixsenses.com

PHILIPPINES

El Nido Resorts
18/F, 8747 Paseo de Roxas Street
Salcedo Village, 1226 Makati City,
Philippines
telephone: +63.2.750 7600/ +63.2.894 5644
facsimile: +63.2.810 3620
email: holiday@elnidoresorts.com
website: www.elnidoresorts.com

INDONESIA

Jimbaran Puri Bali
Jalan Uluwatu Jimbaran, Bali 80361,
Indonesia
telephone: +62.361.701 605
facsimile: +62.361.701 320
email: info@jimbaranpuribali.com
website: www.jimbaranpuribali.com

Ubud Hanging Gardens
Desa Buahan, Payangan, Ubud
Gianyar, Bali 80571, Indonesia
telephone: +62.361.982 700
facsimile: +62.361.982 800
email: reservations@ubudhanginggardens.com
website: www.ubudhanginggardens.com

FIJI ISLANDS

Nukubati Island
Nukubati Island, PO Box 1928, Labasa
Vanua Levu, Fiji Islands
telephone: +679.603 0919
facsimile: +679.603 0918
email: info@nukubati.com
website: www.nukubati.com

AUSTRALIA

Bamurru Plains
Reservations Office: Suite 9, Upper Level
Jones Bay Wharf, 26–32 Pirrama Road
Pyrmont, Sydney NSW 2009 Australia
telephone: +61.2.9571 6399
facsimile: +61.2.9571 6655
email: info@bamurruplains.com
website: www.bamurruplains.com

Paperbark Camp
571 Woollamia Road, Woollamia
New South Wales 2540, Australia
telephone: +61.2.4441 6066
facsimile: +61.2.4441 6066
email: info@paperbarkcamp.com.au
website: www.paperbarkcamp.com.au

Southern Ocean Lodge
Baillie Lodges Sales & Reservations:
PO Box 596, Avalon, New South Wales
2107, Australia
telephone: +61.2.9918 4355
facsimile: +61.2.9918 4381
email: reserve@baillielodges.com.au
website: www.southernoceanlodge.com.au

NEW ZEALAND

**Treetops Lodge & Wilderness
Experience**
351 Kearoa Road, RD1, Horohoro
Rotorua, New Zealand
telephone: +64.7.333 2066
facsimile: +64.7.333 2065
email: info@treetops.co.nz
website: www.treetops.co.nz

THE AMERICAS

BRAZIL

Pousada Rancho do Peixe
Praia do Preá S/N
62595-000 Jericoacoara, Brazil
telephone: +55.88.3660 3118
email: reservas@ranchodopeixe.com.br
website: www.ranchodopeixe.com.br

directory

Pousada Vila Kalango
30 Rua das Dunas, 62598-000
Jericoacoara, Brazil
telephone: +55.88.3669 2289
facsimile: +55.88.3669 2291
email: reservas@vilakalango.com.br
website: www.vilakalango.com.br

Cristalino Jungle Lodge
Avenida Perimetral Oeste, 2001, 78580-000
Alta Floresta, Mato Grosso, Brazil
telephone: +55.66.3521 1396
facsimile: +55.66.3521 2221
email: info@cristalinolodge.com.br
website: www.cristalinolodge.com.br

Vila Naiá
Corumbau, Bahia, Brazil
telephone: +55.11.3061 1872
facsimile: +55.11.3061 1872
email: info@vilanaia.com.br
website: www.vilanaia.com.br

CANADA

Clayoquot Wilderness Resort
Box 130, Tofino, British Columbia
V0R 2Z0 Canada
telephone: +250.726 8235
facsimile: +250.726 8558
email: info@wildretreat.com
website: www.wildretreat.com

Trout Point Lodge
89 Trout Point Road, off the East Branch Road
and Highway, 203 PO Box 456, Kemptville
Nova Scotia B0W 1Y0, Canada
telephone: +1.902.482 8360
email: troutpoint@foodvacation.com
website: www.troutpoint.com

ECUADOR

Hamadryade Lodge
Venecia Iz, via Misahualli
Misahualli-Tena, Ecuador
telephone: +593.8.590 9992
facsimile: +593.9.287 3878
email: lodge@hamadryade-lodge.com
website: www.hamadryade-lodge.com

GUATEMALA

Laguna Lodge Eco-Resort & Nature Reserve
1 Tzantizotz, Santa Cruz La Laguna
Lake Atitlán, Solola, Guatemala
telephone: +502.7823 2529
email: info@fiveleafresort.com
website: www.fiveleafresort.com

MEXICO

Hotelito Desconocido
Playón de Mismaloya, S/N La cruz de Loreto
Costalegre, Mexico
telephone: +52.322.281 4010
email: reservaciones@hotelito.com
website: www.hotelito.com

Azúcar
Km 83.5 Carretera Federal Nautla-Poza
Rica Monte Gordo, Municipio de Tecolutla
Vera Cruz ZC 93588, Mexico
telephone: +52.323.210 678
facsimile: +52.323.210 804
email: gerencia@hotelazucar.com
website: www.hotelazucar.com

Hotel Eco Paraiso Xixim
Municipio de Celestún, Yucatán, Mexico
telephone: +52.988.916 2100
+52.988.916 2060
facsimile: +52.988.916 2111
email: info@ecoparaiso.com
website: www.ecoparaiso.com

WEST INDIES

Maca Bana
Point Salines, PO Box 496, St George's
GPO, Grenada, West Indies
telephone: +1.473.439 5355
facsimile: +1.473.439 6429
email: macabana@spiceisle.com
website: www.macabana.com

GREEN LIVING

SINGAPORE

Guz Wilkinson
3, Jalan Kelabu Asap, S278199
telephone: +65.6476.6110
facsimile: +65.6476.1229
email: guz@guzarchitects.com
website: www.guzarchitects.com

SPAIN

Nani Marquina
Esglesia 10, 3erD, 08024 Barcelona
telephone: +34.932.376.465
facsimile: +34.932.175.774
email: info@nanimarquina.com
website: www.nanimarquina.com

UK

Alex Michaelis & Tim Boyd
9B Ladbroke Grove, London, UK W11 3BD
telephone: +44.20.7221.1237
facsimile: +44.20.7221.0130
email: info@michaelisboyd.com
website: www.michaelisboyd.com

Greenhome
website: www.whatgreenhome.com

Green Moves
GreenMoves UK Ltd., The Old Farmhouse,
Allowenshay, Somerset, UK TA17 8TB.
telephone: +44.845.094 4663
website: www.greenmoves.com

Screw Head
website: www.screwhead.org

Stuart Haygarth
33 Dunloe Street, London, UK E2 8JR
telephone: +44.20.7503 4142
email: info@stuarthaygarth.com
website: www.stuarthaygarth.com

Town and Country Planning Association
17 Carlton House Terrace,
London, UK SW1Y 5AS
telephone: +44.20.7930.8903
facsimile: +44.20.7930.3280
website: www.tcpa.org.uk/

USA

Altenergy Store
telephone: +1.877.878 4060
website: www.altestore.com

El-furniture: Four 2 Five
Park Barrington Drive, Barrington, IL 60010
telephone: +1.847.382.9285
facsimile: +1.847.382.9311

El-furniture: Vernare
607, North Huntley Drive,
West Hollywood, CA 90069
telephone: +1.310.659.6400
facsimile: +1.310.659.6415

El-furniture: Modern at Design Atelier
1848 Merchandise Mart, Chicago, IL 60654
telephone: +1.312.822.0440
facsimile: +1.312.822.9489
website: www.el-furniture.com

Energystar.gov
1200 Pennsylvania Ave NW
Washington, DC 20460
telephone: +1.888.782.7937
website: www.energystar.gov

Emerging Green Builders
U.S. Green Building Council, 2101 L Street,
NW Suite 500, Washington, DC 20037
telephone: +1.202.828 5110
email: egb@usgbcny.org
website: www.egbny.org

Emerging Green Builders–Traci Rose Rider
email: traci.rider@gmail.com
website: www.traciroserider.com

Freecycle
website: www.freecycle.org

Kieran Timberlake
420 North 20th Street,
Philadelphia PA 19130–3828
telephone: +1.215.922.6600
facsimile: +1.215.922.4680
email: timberlake@kierantimberlake.com
website: www.kierantimberlake.com

Vivavi
Asheville, North Carolina, US
telephone: +1. 866.848.2840
facsimile: +1.866.801.0486
email: aron@vivavi.com
website: www.vivavi.com

William McDonough & Partners, Architecture and Design
700 East Jefferson Street,
Charlottesville, VA 22902
telephone: +1.434.979 1111
facsimile: +1.434.979 1112
email: clients@mcdonough.com
website: www.mcdonough.com

GREEN IS THE NEW BLACK

FRANCE

Yves Saint Laurent
7, avenue Georges V, 75008 Paris
telephone: +33.156.626 400
website: www.ysl.com

GERMANY

Jil Sander
headquarters: Via Beltrami, 5,
20121 Milan, Italy
telephone: +39.2.806 931
email: info@jilsander.com
website: www.jilsander.com

HONG KONG

Green2greener
Suite 2406, 24th Floor, 9 Queen's Road,
Central, Hong Kong
telephone: +852.2861.0360
email: ecochic@green2greener.com
website: www.green2greener.com

ITALY

Marni
Via Della Spiga 50, 20121 Milan, Italy
telephone: +39.2.7631 7327
facsimile: +39.2.7631 7335
email: info@marni.it
website: www.marni.com

Versace
Via Manzoni, 38, 20121 Milan, Italy
telephone: +39.2.760 931
facsimile: +39.2.7600 4122
website: www.versace.com

NETHERLANDS

World Fair Trade Organization
Prijssestraat 24 4101 CR Culemborg,
The Netherlands
telephone: +31.345.535 914
facsimile: +31.8.4747 4401
website: www.wfto.com

SPAIN

Zara
website: www.zara.com

UK

Anya Hindmarch
The Stable Block Plough Brewery 516
Wandsworth Road London UK SW8 3JX
telephone: +44.20.7501 0177
email: info@anyahindmarch.com
website: www.anyahindmarch.com

Edun
30-32 Sir John Rogersons Quay
Dublin 2, Ireland
telephone: +353.1.256 1289
facsimile: +353.1.256 1299
website: www.edunonline.com

Stella McCartney
30 Bruton Street, Mayfair,
London, UK W1J 6QR
telephone: +44.20.7518 3100
email: online.assistance@stellamccartney.com
website: www.stellamccartney.com

USA

Banana Republic
5900 North Meadows Drive
Grove City, OH 43123-8476
telephone: +1.888.277.8953
facsimile: +1.888.906.2465
email: custserv@bananarepublic.com
website: bananarepublic.gap.com

Calvin Klein
554 Madison Avenue, New York, NY 10021
telephone: +1.212.292 9000
website: www.calvinkleininc.com

Diane von Furstenberg
874 Washington Street, New York, NY 10014
email: cseshop@dvf.com
website: www.dvf.com

Donna Karan
819 Madison Avenue, New York NY 10021
telephone: +1.212.861.1001
website: www.donnakaran.com

Earth Pledge
telephone: +1.212.725.6611
email: info@earthpledge.org
website: www.earthpledge.org

Ecoist
telephone: +1.877.326 4787 (+1.877.ECOISTS)
website: www.ecoist.com

Kemplar
telephone: +1.800.893 9685 (US)
+44.207 9938 045 (UK)
email: info@kemplar.com
website: www.kemplar.com

Oscar de la Renta
website: www.oscardelarenta.com

Patagonia
8550 White Fir Street, P.O. Box 32050,
Reno, NV 89523-2050
telephone: +1.800.638 6464
facsimile: +1.800.543 5522
website: www.patagonia.com

Phillip Lim
115 Mercer Street, New York, NY 10012
telephone: +1.212.334 1160
facsimile: +1.212.840 0936
email: sales@31philliplim.com
website: www.31philliplim.com

Ralph Lauren
867 Madison Avenue, New York, NY 10021
telephone: +1.888.475 7674
email: CustomerAssistance@RalphLauren.com
website: www.ralphlauren.com

Rogan
330 Bowery New York, NY 10012
telephone: +1.646.827 7579
email: customercare@rogannyc.com
website: www.rogannyc.com

shopbop.com
101 E Badger Road, Madison WI 53713
telephone: +1.877.746 7267
facsimile: +1.608.270 3934
email: service@shopbop.com
website: www.shopbop.com

ECO BEAUTY: MORE THAN SKIN DEEP

AUSTRALIA

Mukti
37 Coral Street, Maleny Qld 4552
telephone: +61.7.5435 2111
facsimile: +61.7.5435 2311
website: www.muktibotanicals.com.au

directory

Fetish for Food
2 Church Lane, Prestwich,
Manchester UK M25 1AJ
telephone: +44.161.773 3366
email: enquiries@fetishforfood.com;
fetishforfood@hotmail.co.uk
website: www.fetishforfood.com

Greens
43 Lapwing Lane, West Didsbury,
Manchester, UK M20 2NT
telephone: +44.161.434 4259

Isinglass
46 Flixton Road Urmston,
Manchester UK M41 5AB
telephone: +44.161.749 8400
email: isinglass@ntlworld.com
website: www.isinglassrestaurant.co.uk

EUROPE — SHOPPING

UK: LONDON

Beyond Retro
Reflextion House
110-112 Cheshire Street, London, UK E2 6EJ,
telephone: +44.20.7613 3636
email: info@beyondretro.com
website: www.beyondretro.com

Eco
213 Chiswick High Road Chiswick,
London UK W4 2DW
telephone: +44.20.8995 7611
email: info@eco-age.com
website: www.eco-age.com

Enamore
207 Catherine Way, Batheaston,
Bath, UK BA1 7PA
telephone: +44.1225.851 004
              +44.7833.326 147
email: info@enamore.co.uk
website: www.enamore.co.uk

Equa
28 Camden Passage, London, UK N1,
telephone: +44.20.7359 0955
email: info@equaclothing.com
website: www.equaclothing.com/

Fair Share
102 Berwick Street London, UK W1F 0QP
telephone: +44.20.7287 8277
email: fairshare@tiscali.co.uk
website: www.fairshare-soho.org

Howies
42 Carnaby Street London, UK W1F 7DY,
telephone: +44.20.7287 2345
email: info@howies.co.uk
website: www.howies.co.uk

Karavan
167 Lordship Lane London UK SE22 8HX
telephone: +44.20.8299 2524
email: info@karavan.co.uk
website: www.karavaneco.co.uk

Luma
98 Church Road, London UK SW14 0DQ
telephone: +44.20.8748 2264
email: info@lumadirect.com
website: www.lumadirect.com

Nelsons Homeopathic Pharmacy
73 Duke Street, Mayfair
London UK W1K 5BY
telephone: +44.20.7629 3118
email: pharmacy@nelsonshp.com
website: www.nelsonshomeopathy.com

Our Eco Shop
303 Westbourne Grove, Notting Hill,
London, UK W11 2QA
email: mail@ourecoshop.co.uk
website: www.ourecoshop.co.uk

Palette London
21 Canonbury Lane, Islington,
London UK N1 2AS
telephone: +44.20.7288 7428
email: sales@palette-london.com
website: www.palette-london.com/

Red Door Gallery
10 Turnpin Lane Greenwich,
London, UK SE10 9JA
telephone: +44.20.8858 2131
email: kate@reddoorgallery.co.uk
website: www.reddoorgallery.co.uk

So Organic
7 Turnpin Lane Greenwich,
London, UK SE10 9JA
telephone: +88.2165.110 3557
telephone: +44.800.169 2579
website: www.soorganic.com

TRAID
2 Acre Lane, London UK SW2 5SG
telephone: +44.20.7326 4330
facsimile: +44.20.8903 9922
email: info@traid.org.uk
website: www.traid.org.uk

FRANCE: PARIS

Alter Mundi Beaurepaire
25 rue Beaurepaire, 75010 Paris
telephone: +33.1.4200 1573
email: paris-beaurepaire@altermundi.com
website: www.altermundi.com

Alter Mundi Paris
41 rue du Chemin vert 75011 Paris
telephone: +33.01.4021 0891
website: www.altermundi.com

Alter Mundi Rivoli
Address: 9 rue de Rivoli, 75001 Paris
telephone: +33.1.4459 8166
website: www.altermundi.com

Come on Eileen
16-18 des Taillandiers, 75011 Paris
telephone: +33.1.4338 1211

Como No
email: info@como-no.fr
website: www.como-no.fr

Ethos
12 Rue Marius Delcher,
94220 Charenton-le-Pont
telephone: +33.1.4378 8325
facsimile: +33.1 4378 8127
email: contact@ethosparis.com
website: www.ethosparis.com

g=9.8
21 Rue de la Gaité, 75014 Paris
telephone: +33.1.4631 2261
email: info@g98.fr
website: www.organiclingerie.fr

Monsieur Poulet
email: contact@monsieurpoulet.com.
website: www.monsieurpoulet.com

Nu jeans
8 rue Taylor, 75010 Paris
telephone: +33.1.8081 5030
email: info@nu-jeans.com
website: www.le-jeans-nu.com

FRANCE: NICE

Sobosibio
82 Avenue de Peygros, 06530 Peymeinade
telephone: +33.4.9340.2294

AFRICA + MIDDLE EAST — RESTAURANTS

AFRICA: KENYA

Campi ya Kanzi
PO Box 236 - 90128, Mtito Andei, Kenya
telephone: +254.45.622 516
facsimile: +254.45.622 516
Satellite: +88.2165.110 3557
email: lucasaf@africaonline.co.ke
website: www.maasai.com

Chowpaty Pure Vegetarian Restaurant
4th Parklands Ave, Parklands, Nairobi (at Diamond Plaza)
telephone: +254.20.374 8884
email: chowpaty@mitsuminet.com
website: www.geocities.com/chowpaty/

Slush Limited
Parklands Road, Corner Plaza, Westlands,
Nairobi (at Rank Xerox House)
telephone: +254.20.0375 1039

MOROCCO: MARRAKECH

Earth Café
No. 2 Derb Zawak, Riad Zitoun Kedim,
Medina
telephone: +212.661.289 402
email: earthcafemarrakech@yahoo.com
website: www.earthcafemarrakech.com

OMAN: ZIGHY BAY

Six Senses Hideaway Zighy Bay
Zighy Bay, Musandam Peninsula Sultanate of Oman
telephone: +968.26735 555
              +968.26735 888
facsimile: +968.26735 887
email: reservations-zighy@sixsenses.com
website: www.sixsenses.com/Six-Senses-Hideaway-Zighy-Bay/

SOUTH AFRICA: CAPE TOWN

Lola's
228 Long Street, cnr. Buiten
telephone:+27.021.423.0885

Organics Alive
42 Palmer Road, Muizenberg
telephone: +27.021.788.6012
email: ducabruzzi@webmail.co.za

Portbello Café
111 Long Street
telephone: +27.021.426.1418

SOUTH AFRICA: JOHANNESBURG

Earth 2
1 Olifandes Road, corner of 5th Avenue
telephone: +27.011.888.1748

Fruits and Roots
Hobart Corner Shopping Centre, corner of Hobart & Grosvenor Roads
telephone: +27.011.463.2928
email: info@fruitsandroots.co.za
website: www.fruitsandroots.co.za

UNITED ARAB EMIRATES: DUBAI

Organic Foods and Café
Sheikh Zayed Road, The Greens
telephone: +971.4.361 7974
facsimile: +971.4.361 9290
email: admin@organicfoodsandcafe.com
website: www.organicfoodsandcafe.com

Veg World Restaurant
Gould Souk, Deira
telephone: +971.4.225.4455

Bur Dubai Meena Bazar
telephone: +971.4.351.7070

ASIA + THE PACIFIC — SHOPPING

AUSTRALIA

Ambra
12 Lakeview Drive, Scoresby, VIC 3179
telephone: +61.3.9237 2200
facsimile: +61.3.9237 2299
website: www.ambra.net.au

Bassike
11–13 Macmilan Court, Avalon Parade,
Avalon NSW 2107
telephone: +61.2.9973 2942
facsimile: +61.2.8214.6686
website: www.bassike.com

Billabong
1 Billabong Place,
Burleigh Heads QLD 4220
telephone: +61.7.55.899 899
facsimile: +61.7.55.899 800
email: info@billabong.com.au
website: www.billabong.com

David Jones
65–77 Market Street
Sydney, NSW 2000
telephone: +61.2.9266 5544
facsimile: +61.2.9267 4770
website: www.davidjones.com.au

David met Nicole
382 Cleveland Street, Surry Hills,
Sydney, NSW 2010
telephone: +61.2.9698 7416
facsimile: +61.2.9698 7933
email: nicole@davidmetnicole.com
              david@davidmetnicole.com
website: www.davidmetnicole.com

Eco at Home
507 Willoughby Road, Willoughby,
Sydney, NSW 2068
telephone: +61.2.9958 0412
facsimile: +61.2.0058 2341
email: sales@ecoathome.com.au
website: www.ecoathome.com.au

Gorman
61 Church Street, Abbotsford, VIC 3067
telephone: +61.3.9429 0000
facsimile: +61.38420 0333
email: showroom@gorman.ws
website: www.gorman.ws

Incu
The Galeries Victoria, Shop RG 19–20, 23–24,
500 George Street, Sydney NSW 2000
telephone: +61.02.9283 7622
email: info@incuclothing.com
website: www.incuclothing.com/

McLean and Page
Shop 3c, 11–27 Wentworth Street,
Manly, NSW 2095
telephone: +61.02.9976 3277

Netapoter
telephone: +44.1473.323 032
email: customercare@net-a-porter.com
website: www.netaporter.com

The Bird Textiles Emporium store
380 Cleveland Street, Surry Hills, Sydney,
NSW 2010
telephone: +61.2.8399 0230
email: info@birdtextile.com
website: www.birdtextile.com

The Bird Textiles Showroom
13 Banksia Drive, Byron Bay, NSW 2481
telephone: +61.2.6680 8633
email: info@birdtextile.com
website: www.birdtextile.com

Todae
83 Glebe Point Road. Glebe NSW 2037
telephone: +61.1300.138 483
facsimile: +61.2.9660 7166
website: www.todae.com.au

Sam Elsom
telephone: +61.2.9011 7490
email: info@elsom.co.au
website:www.elsom.com.au

MALAYSIA: KUALA LUMPUR

Bijou Bazaar
telephone: +60.3.5630 0062/0064
facsimile: +60.3.5630 0060
email: bijoubazaar@gmail.com
website bijoubazaar.blogspot.com

Lafuma
16 Jalan Telawi, Bangsar Baru, 59100
telephone: +60.3.2287 1118
facsimile: +60.3.2287 1119
website: www.lafuma.com.my

SINGAPORE

Actually
29A Seah Street S189041
telephone: +65.6336 7298
website: www.actually.com.sg

222 ecochic

directory

Books Actually
No. 5, Ann Siang Road S069688
telephone: +65.6221 1170
email: kenny@booksactually.com
website: www.booksactually.com

Curiocity
38 Bencoolen Street, #A1-02 S189654
telephone: +65.6334 6022

Front Row
5 Ann Siang Road 069688
telephone: +65.6224 5501
facsimile: +65.6224 5502
email: info@frontrowsingapore.com
website: www.frontrowsingapore.com

La Libreria
University Cultural Centre. NUS Musuem,
Level 3, 50 Kent Ridge Crescent, S119279
telephone: +65.6516 8797
facsimile: +65.6775 0602
email: info@lalibreria.com.sg
website: www.lalibreria.com.sg

L'escalier
391 Orchard Road #04-20k
Ngee Ann City S238872
telephone: +65.6735 4228
email: info@lescalier.com.sg
website: www.lescalier.com.sg

Maki Squarepatch
33 Bali Lane (2nd storey) S189848
telephone: +65.6292 2248
email: info@makisquarepatch.com
website: www.makisquarepatch.com

Muji
2 Orchard Turn, #B4-16 Ion Orchard,
S238801
telephone: +65.6509 9321
website: www.muji.com/sg/stores

Oppt Shop
email: opptshop@gmail.com

Spin the Bottle
#03-06 The Heeren
260 Orchard Road, S238855

#01-02 The Cathay
2 Handy Road S229233
website: spinthebottlestore.blogspot.com

The Life Shop
12A Jalan Ampas, #07-02
Balestier Warehouse, S329516
telephone: +65.6732 2366
email: enquiry@thelifeshop.com
website: www.thelifeshop.com

The Tango Mango Bookshop
163 Tanglin Rd, #03-11A S247933
telephone: +65.6835 3895
facsimile: +65.6835 1630

Vik Lim
telephone: +65.9009 5561
email: kiv_vik@hotmail.com
website: www.viklim.com

THAILAND: BANGKOK

Benjarong
River City Shopping Complex 3rd Floor, room
No.325-326, 23 Trok Rongnamkaeng, Yotha
Road, Sampantawong, Bangkok 10100
telephone: +66.2.237 0077-8 ext 325
facsimile: +66.2.639 0716
email: rv@thaibenjarong.com
website: www.thaibenjarong.com

Chatuchak Weekend Market
Kamphaeng Phet 2 Road, Chatuchak,
Bangkok
telephone: +66.2.2724 6356

Chiiori
87 Thanon Sukhumvit, Bangkok 10110
telephone: +66.2.254 4976

Lotus Art de Vivre
41/21 Rama III Road, Chongnunsee,
Yannawa, Bangkok 10120
telephone: +66.2.294 1821-3
facsimile: +66.2.294 8076
email: pr@lotusartsdevivre.com
website: www.lotusartsdevivre.com

Lotus Art de Vivre
Four Seasons Hotel, 155 Rajadamri Road,
Bangkok 10330
telephone: +66.2.250 0732

Lotus Art de Vivre
The Oriental Hotel, 48 Soi 40
Charoenkrung Road, Bangkok 10500
telephone: +66.2.236 0400

ASIA + THE PACIFIC — SPAS

AUSTRALIA

Daintree EcoLodge & Spa
20 Daintree Rd, Daintree, Qld 4873
telephone: +61.7.4098 6100
email: info@daintree-ecolodge.com.au
website: www.daintree-ecolodge.com.au

CAMBODIA

Hotel de la Paix
Sivutha Boulevard, Siem Reap, Cambodia
telephone: +855.63.966 000
facsimile: +855.63.966 001
email: info@hoteldelapaixangkor.com
website: www.hoteldelapaixangkor.com

Shinta Mani
Junction of Oum Khum and 14th Street,
Siem Reap, Cambodia
telephone: +855.63.761 998
facsimile: +855.63.761 999
email: reservations@shintamani.com
website: www.shintamani.com

CHINA

Banyan Tree Spa Lijiang
PO Box 55, Lijiang 674100 Yunnan
The Philippines
telephone: +86.888.533 1111
email: lijiang@banyantree.com
website: www.banyantree.com/en/lijiang

Banyan Tree Spa Ringha
Hong Po Village, Jian Tang Town,
Shangri-La County, Diqing Tibetan
Autonomous Prefecture,
Yunnan Province, 674400
telephone: +86.887.828 8822
facsimile: +86.887.828 8911
email: ringha@banyantree.com
website: www.banyantree.com/ringha

Crosswaters Ecolodge & Spa
Mt. Nankun Ecotourism District, Longmen,
Guangdong 511276
telephone: +86.752.769 3666
facsimile:+86.752.769 3156
email: info@crosswaterseco.com
website: www.crosswaters.net.cn

INDONESIA

Jimbaran Puri Bali
Jalan Uluwatu, Jimbaran, Bali 80361
telephone: +62.361.701 605
facsimile: +62.361.701 320
email: info@jimbaranpuribali.com
website: www.jimbaranpuribali.com

Ubud Hanging Gardens
Desa Buahan, Desa Payangan,
Gianyar, Bali 80571
telephone: +62.361.982 700
facsimile: +62.361.982 800
email: reservations@ubudhanginggardens.com
website: www.ubudhanginggardens.com

JAPAN

Tobira Onsen Myojinkan
8967 Iriyamabe, Matsumoto City,
Nagano Prefecture 390-0222
telephone: +81.263.312 301
facsimile: +81.263.312 345
email: sizen@tobira-group.com
website:
www.tobira-group.com/emyojinkan/

NEW ZEALAND

Treetops Lodge & Wilderness Experience
351 Kearoa Road, RD1, Horohoro
Rotorua, New Zealand
telephone: +64.7.333 2066
facsimile: +64.7.333 2065
email: info@treetops.co.nz
website: www.treetops.co.nz

PHILIPPINES

El Nido Lagen Island Resort
Ten Knots Development Corporation
18th Floor 8747, Paseo de Roxas Street,
Salcedo Village, 1226 Makati City
telephone: +63.2.894 5644
+63.2.750 7600
facsimile: +63.2.810 3620
email: holiday@elnidoresorts.com
website: www.elnidoresorts.com

The Farm
119 Barangay Tipakan, Batangas,
The Philippines
telephone: +63.2.696 3795
facsimile: +63.2.696 3175
email: info@thefarm.com.ph
website: www.thefarm.com.ph

THAILAND

Anantara Phuket Resort & Spa
888 Moo 3 ,Tumbon Mai Khao,
Amphur Thalang, Phuket 83110
telephone: +66.76.336 100
facsimile: +66.76.336 177
email: phuket@anantara.com
website: www.anantara.com

Evason Phuket & Six Senses Spa
100 Vised Road, Moo 2, Tambol Rawai,
Muang District, Phuket 83130, Thailand
telephone: +66.76.381 010
facsimile: +66.76.381 018
email: reservations-phuket@sixsenses.com
website: www.sixsenses.com/Evason-Phuket

Six Senses Destination Spa Phuket
32 Moo 5, Tambol Paklok, Amphur Thalang,
Phuket 83110
telephone: +66.76.371 400
facsimile: +66.76.371 401
email: reservations-naka@sixsenses.com
website www.sixsenses.com/Six-Senses-Destination-Spa-Phuket/

Six Senses Hideaway Hua Hin
9/22 Moo 5 Paknampran Beach, Pranburi,
Prachuap Khirikhan 77220
telephone: +66.32.618 200
facsimile: +66.32.632 112
+66.32.632 131
email: reservations-huahin@sixsenses.com
website: www.sixsenses.com/Six-Senses-Hideaway-Hua-Hin/

Six Senses Soneva Kiri
Koh Kood, Trat Province 23000
telephone: +66.3961 9800
facsimile: +66.3961 9808
email: reservations-kiri@sixsenses.com
website: /www.sixsenses.com/Soneva-Kiri/

Six Senses Hideaway Samui—a Sala Property
9/10 Moo 5, Baan Plai Laem, Bophut, Koh
Samui, Suratthani 84320
telephone: +66.77.245 678
facsimile: +66.77.245 671
email: reservations-samui@sixsenses.com
website: www.sixsenses.com/Six-Senses-Hideaway-Samui/

THE INDIAN OCEAN

Anantara Dhigu Resort & Spa
PO Box 2014, Dhigufinolhu, South Male
Atoll, Male, Republic of Maldives
telephone: +960.664 4100
facsimile: +960.664 4101
email: dhigumaldives@anantara.com
website: www.anantara.com

Frégate Island Private
PO Box 330,Victoria, Mahé, the Seychelles
telephone: +248.282 282
email: reservations@fregate.com
website: www.fregate.com

Soneva Fushi by Six Senses
Kunfunadhoo Island, Baa Atoll,
Republic of Maldives
telephone: +960.660 0304
facsimile: +960.660 0374
email: reservations@sixsenses.com
website: www.sixsenses.com/soneva-fushi

Soneva Gili by Six Senses
Lankanfushi Island, North Male Atoll,
Republic of Maldives
telephone: +960.664 0304
facsimile: +960.664 0305
email: reservations-gili@sixsenses.com
website: www.sixsenses.com/Soneva-Gili

Ulpotha
Near Embogama, Kurunegala District,
Sri Lanka
telephone: +44.208.123 3603
email: info@ulpotha.com
website: www.ulpotha.com

VIETNAM

Evason Ana Mandara—Nha Trang
Beachside Tran Phu Boulevard, Nha Trang,
Khanh Hoa, Vietnam
telephone: +84.58.352 2222
facsimile: +84.58.352 5828
email: reservations-nhatrang@sixsenses.com
website: www.sixsenses.com/Evason-Ana-Mandara-Nha-Trang/

Hotel Majestic Saigon
01 Dong Khoi Street, District 1,
Ho Chi Minh City, Vietnam
telephone: +84.8.3829 5517 ext: 12/21/ 8805
email: majestic@majesticsaigon.com
website: www.majesticsaigon.com.vn/

Six Senses Hideaway Ninh Van Bay
Ninh Van bay, Ninh Hoa, Khanh Hoa,
Vietnam
telephone: +84.58.372 8222
+84.58.352 4268
facsimile: +84.58.372 8223
+84.58.352 4704 (Reservation)
email: reservations-ninhvan@sixsenses.com
website: www.sixsenses.com/Six-Senses-Hideaway-Ninh-Van-Bay/

THE AMERICAS — RESTAURANTS

ANTIGUA

Kalabashe
10 Vendor's Mall, St. John's
telephone: +268.562 6070
email: info@kalabashe.com
osei@Kalabashe.com
website: www.kalabashe.com

BRAZIL: RIO DE JANEIRO

Reino Vegetal
Rua Luiz de Camões, 98, Sobrado Centro
telephone: +55.21.2221 7416

Restaurante Vegetariano Beterraba
Rua da Alfândega, 25A, Centro
telephone: +55.21.2253 7460

directory

BRAZIL: SAO PAULO

Apfel
Rua Bela Cintra,1343, (Al. Santos and R. da Consolacao)
telephone: +55.11.3062 3727
website: www.apfel.com.br

BioAlternativa
Alameda Santos, 2214, atCerquira Cesar
telephone: +55.11.3898 2971

BioAlternativa II
Rua Maranhao 812,at Higienopolis
telephone: +55.11.3825 4759
website: www.bioalternativa.com.br

JAMAICA

Livity
30 Haining Road, Kingston 5
telephone: +876.906 5618

MEXICO: MEXICO CITY

El Natural Saks
Insurgentes Sur 1641
telephone: +52.598 7258

Vegetariano Madero
Madero 56 1er. Piso, Colonia Centro Historical,at Isabel la Catolica
telephone: +52.5521 6880

Yug
Varsovia 3B,Colonia Juarez, at Paseo de la Reforma
telephone: +52.533 3296

PUERTO RICO

Café Berlin
407 San Francisco Street, Old San Juan
telephone: +787.722 5205

Natural High Café
Freshmart Aguadilla, Plaza Victoria, Route #2, Km. 129.5, Rincon PR 00677
telephone: +787.882 2656
email: info@naturalhighcafe.com
website: www.naturalhighcafe.com

USA: LOS ANGELES

Abode Restaurant & Lounge
1541 Ocean Avenue, Santa Monica, CA 90401
telephone: +1.310.394 3463
website: www.aboderestaurant.com

Bulan Thai Vegetarian Kitchen
7168 Melrose Avenue, Los Angeles, CA 90046
telephone: +1.323.857 1882
website: www.bulanthai.com

Shojin
333 S. Alameda Street, Suite 310, (Little Tokyo Shopping Center 3F), Los Angeles, CA 90013
telephone: +1.213.617 0305
email: shojin-info@theshojin.com
website: www.theshojin.com

The Vegan Joint
10438 National Boulevard, in the Palms Area, Los Angeles, CA 90034
telephone: +1.310.559 1357
facsimile: +1.310.559 1360
email: theveganjoint@aol.com
website: www.theveganjoint.com

USA: CHICAGO

Alice and Friends' Vegetarian Café
5812 N. Broadway, Chicago, IL 60660
telephone: +1.773.275 8797
website: www.aliceandfriends.com/

Cousin's Incredible Vitality
3038 W. Irving Park Road, Chicago, IL 60618
telephone: +1.773.478 6868
email: info@cousinsiv.com
website: www.cousinsiv.com

Karyn's Cooked
738 N Wells Street, Chicago, IL 60654
telephone: +1.312.587 1050
email: karyninfo@karynraw.com
website: www.karynraw.com

Karyn's Fresh Corner
1901 North Halsted Street, Chicago, IL 60614
telephone: +1.312.255 1590
email: karyninfo@karynraw.com
website: www.karynraw.com

Veggie Bite
1300 N Milwaukee Ave, Chicago, IL 60622
telephone: +1.773.772 2483
website: www.veggiebite.net

USA: NEW YORK

24 Carrots Organic Juice Bar
244 West 72nd Street, Manhattan, NY 10023
telephone: +1.212.595 2550
facsimile: +1.212.595 2552

Angelica Kitchen
300E 12th Street, Manhattan, NY 10014
telephone: +1.212.228 2909
website: www.angelicakitchen.com

Blossom Vegan Restaurant
187, 9th Ave (between 21st & 22nd Street), Manhattan, NY 10011
telephone: +1.212.627 1144
email: blossomnyc@gmail.com
website: www.blossomnyc.com/

Bonobo's Vegetarian Restaurant
18 East 23rd Street, Manhattan, NY 10010
telephone: +1.212.505 1200
email: eatrawi@aol.com
website: www.bonobosrestaurant.com

Counter
105 First Ave (between 6th and 7th), New York, NY 10003
telephone: +1.212.982 5870
facsimile: +1.212.982 5630
email: counter@igc.org
website: www.counternyc.com

Franchia
12 Park Avenue (between 34th and 35th Street), New York, NY 10016
telephone: +1.212.213 1001
+212.213 2483
facsimile: +1.415.826 5125
email: info@franchia.com
website: www.franchia.com/

Gobo
401 Ave of the Americas, New York, NY 10014 (between Waverly Place & 8th Street)
telephone: +1.212.255 3242
facsimile: +1.212.255 0687
website: www.goborestaurant.com

1426 Third Ave, New York, NY 10028
telephone: +1.212.288 5099
facsimile: +1.212.288 3799
website: www.goborestaurant.com

HanGawi
12E 32nd Street (between 5th and Madison Ave), New York, NY 10016
telephone: +1.212.213 0077
+1.212.213 6068
facsimile: +1.212.689 0780
email: info@hangawirestaurant.com
website: www.hangawirestaurant.com/

Kate's Joint
58 Ave B, at 4th and 5th Street, Manhattan, NY 10009
telephone: +1.212.777 7059

Pure Food and Wine
54 Irving Place, New York, NY 10003
telephone: +1.212.477 1010
website: www.oneluckyduck.com/purefoodandwine/

Red Bamboo
140 West 4th Street, at Washington Square and 6th Avenue, New York, NY 10012
telephone: +1.212.260 1212
website: www.redbamboo-nyc.com

Sacred Chow
227 Sullivan Street, New York, NY 10012 (between West 3rd & Bleecker)
telephone: +1.212.337 0863
website: www.sacredchow.com

USA: SAN FRANCISCO

Alive! Vegetarian Cuisine
1972 Lombard Street, San Francisco, CA 94123
telephone: +1.415.923 1052
email: aliveveggie@sbcglobal.net
website: www.aliveveggie.com

Ananda Fuara
1298 Market Street at 9th Civic Center District, San Francisco, CA 94102
telephone: +1.415.621 1994
website: www.anandafuara.com

Café Gratitude
2400 Harrison Street (at 20th Street), San Francisco, CA 94110
telephone: +1.415.830 3014
facsimile: +1.415.695 1989
email: info@cafegratitude.com
website: www.cafegratitude.com

Herbivore
983 Valencia Street, San Francisco, CA 94110
telephone: +1.415.826 5657
facsimile: +1.415.826 5125
email: info@herbivorerestaurant.com
website: www.herbivorerestaurant.com

531 Divisadero, San Francisco, CA 94117
telephone: +1.415.885 7133
facsimile: +1.415.885 7135
email: info@herbivorerestaurant.com
website: www.herbivorerestaurant.com

Millennium
580 Geary Street, San Francisco, CA 94102
telephone: +1.415.345 3900
facsimile: +1.415.345 3941
email: sanfrancisco@hotelca.com
website: www.millenniumrestaurant.com

USA: SEATTLE

Mighty-O Donuts
2110 N 55th Street, WA 98103
telephone: +1.206.547 0335
website: http://www.mightyo.com/

Pizza Pi Vegan Pizzeria
5500 University Way NE, WA 98105
telephone: +1.206.343 1415
website: www.pizza-pi.net

THE AMERICAS — SHOPPING

CANADA

Grassroots - Annex Store
408 Bloor Street West,Toronto, ON M5S 1X5
telephone: +1.416.944 1993
email: commercial@grassrootsstore.com
website: www.grassrootsstore.com

Grassroots - Riverdale Store
372 Danforth Ave, Toronto, ON M4K 1N8
telephone: +1.416.466 2841
email: commercial@grassrootsstore.com
website: www.grassrootsstore.com

Toronto Hemp Company
665 Yonge Street (just south of Bloor Street) Toronto ON M4Y 1Z9
telephone: +1.416.920 1980
facsimile: +1.416.920 0764
email: dom@torontohemp.com
website: www.torontohemp.com

Truth Belts
588 Bloor Street West, Toronto, ON M6G 1K4
telephone: +1.647.350 3269
email: info@truthbelts.com
website: www.truthbelts.com

USA

Baggu
109 Ingraham #309, Brooklyn, NY 11237
telephone: +1.858.952 1032
email: info@baggubag.com
website: baggubag.com

Boris Bally
The Ryan Post Building, 789 Atwells Avenue @ Academy, Providence, RI 02909
email: boris@borisbally.com
website: www.borisbally.com

Brave Space
449 Troutman Street, Studio 2A, Brooklyn, NY 11237
telephone: +1.718.417 3180
email: info@bravespacedesign.com
website: www.bravespacedesign.com

Buffalo Exchange
1555 Haight Street, San Francisco, CA 94117
telephone: +1.415.431 7733
email: contact@bufex.com
website: www.buffaloexchange.com

Clary Sage Organics
2241 Fillmore Street, San Francisco, CA 94115
telephone: +1.415.673 7300
facsimile: +1.415.673 7444
email: info@clarysageorganics.com
website: www.clarysageorganics.com

Cosmo Modern
314 Wythe Avenue, Williamsburg, Brooklyn NY 11211
telephone: +1.718.302 4662
email: cosmomodern@mac.com
website: www.cosmomodern.com/

Eairth
Steven Alan Annexe, 103 Franklin Street, New York NY 10013
email: melissa@eairth.org
website: www.eairth.ph

Eco Citizen
1488 Vallejo Street, San Francisco, CA 94109
telephone: +1.415.614 0100
telephone: +1.415.415 0200
email: joslin@shopecocitizen.com
website: www.ecocitizenonline.com/

Kaight
83 Orchard Street, Lower East Side, Manhattan, NY 10002-4520
telephone: +1.212.680 5630
email: kaightnyc@yahoo.com
website: www.kaightshop.com/

Lizard Lounge
1323 NW Irving Street, Portland, OR 97209
telephone: +1.503.416 7476
email: info@lizardloungepdx.com
website: www.lizardloungepdx.com

Nau
710 NW 14th Street, Portland, OR 97209
telephone: +1.877.454 5628
email: customercare@nau.com
website: www.nau.com

Plush Pod
8406 Beverly Boulevard, Los Angeles, CA 90048
telephone: +1.323.951 0748
facsimile: +1.323.951 9210
email: contact@plushpod.com
website: www.plushpod.com

Ryann
210 East Broadway #404, New York, NY 10002
telephone: +1.212.533 3953
email: info@iloveryann.com
website: www.iloveryann.com

The Upper Rust
445E, 9th Street, New York, NY 10009
telephone: +1.212.533 3953

Urban Fox
telephone: +1.323.665 7454
email: info@urbanfoxeco.com
website: www.urbanfoxeco.com